The
General
Educator's Guide to
SPECIAL
EDUCATION
THIRD EDITION

D1500604

I dedicate this work to my husband Joel, daughter Lacee Jo, and son Jaden Joel.
It is your love, confidence, patience, and encouragement that allowed me the time
and energy needed to make this possible.

To my grandma, Dr. Thelma Anderson, I miss you so.

This accomplishment became reality because of you.
Because you believed in me, I believed in me!

The
General
Educator's Guide to
SPECIAL
EDUCATION
THIRD EDITION

JODY L.
Maanum

CORWIN

A SAGE Company

For information:

Corwin
A SAGE Company
2455 Teller Road
Thousand Oaks, California 91320
(800) 233-9936
Fax: (800) 417-2466
www.corwinpress.com

SAGE Ltd.
1 Oliver's Yard
55 City Road
London EC1Y 1SP
United Kingdom

SAGE Pvt. Ltd.
B 1/I 1 Mohan Cooperative
    Industrial Area
Mathura Road, New Delhi 110 044
India

SAGE Asia-Pacific Pte. Ltd.
33 Pekin Street #02-01
Far East Square
Singapore 048763

Printed in the United States of America.

Library of Congress Cataloging-in-Publication Data

Maanum, Jody L.
The general educator's guide to special education/Jody L. Maanum.—3rd ed.
    p. cm.
Includes bibliographical references and index.
ISBN 978-1-4129-7136-2 (cloth)
ISBN 978-1-4129-7137-9 (pbk.)

   1. Children with disabilities—Education—United States—Handbooks, manuals, etc. 2. Special education—Handbooks, manuals, etc. I. Title.

LC4019.M215 2009
371.9—dc22   2009006702

This book is printed on acid-free paper.

09   10   11   12   13   10   9   8   7   6   5   4   3   2   1

Acquisitions Editor:	David Chao
Editorial Assistant:	Brynn Saito
Production Editor:	Veronica Stapleton
Copy Editor:	Jeannette McCoy
Typesetter:	C&M Digitals (P) Ltd.
Proofreader:	Dennis W. Webb
Indexer:	Sheila Bodell
Cover Designer:	Scott Van Atta

Contents

Preface

Every year when a new school term begins, teachers nervously look over class lists in an attempt to make best practice and educationally sound decisions. What is commonly determined through the review of previous year's assessment results, anecdotal notes, and information found in the cumulative file is that every child arrives on the first day of school with unique and specific needs. It then becomes the teacher's obligation to synthesize the information and plan accordingly to best meet each student's needs.

One purpose of the No Child Left Behind Act of 2001 (NCLB) is to hold school districts, even more specifically, educators, accountable for adequate yearly progress of all students in their classroom. The Individuals with Disabilities Education Act (IDEA), requires that students with disabilities be provided a free and appropriate education in the least restrictive environment. Often the least restrictive environment is inclusion in the general education classroom. The combination of these two laws often places an overwhelming responsibility on the general education teacher—a responsibility for which many general classroom teachers feel unprepared.

General education and special education programs at the collegiate level are two separate courses of study. It is most common for college students to focus on one or the other area and not both. For example, students focusing in the area of general education often receive limited training in the laws, requirements, and best practices in area of special education. This creates a specific challenge considering that NCLB and IDEA require general educators to ensure appropriate progress of all students, including those with special needs.

Meeting the needs of all children within one classroom is a difficult challenge for veteran and rookie teachers alike. The purpose of this resource is to provide a user-friendly handbook for those who are responsible for and required to ensure that every child is making appropriate growth within the school setting. The information provided in this resource is not complex or complicated. It is simply arranged in a way that will provide easy to implement strategies, suggestions, and answers to questions that will help general education classroom teachers provide that best possible support to all students.

General educators are held accountable to teach and invoke progress in all students in their classrooms, a challenging task considering the variety of learning styles, ability levels, and diverse needs of each individual student. Educational research is continually being conducted to support and provide teachers with current, up-to-date, best practice teaching tools and methods to assist general educators in successfully meeting and exceeding this challenge. The third edition of this user-friendly resource provides new components, including complete descriptions of research-based intervention strategies to support student progress as well as an implementation guide, key points, and benefits of the Response to Intervention (RTI) model, to assist general educators in becoming as effective in the classroom as possible.

Acknowledgments

Corwin gratefully acknowledges the contributions of the following individuals:

Akina Luckett Canty
National Board Certified Teacher
Jefferson County Schools
Birmingham, Alabama

Martha A. Cocchiarella
Clinical Assistant Professor
Arizona State University at the Polytechnic Campus
School of Educational Innovation and Teacher Preparation
Mesa, Arizona

Christine Meyer
Doctoral Student
University of Michigan, School of Education
Ann Arbor, Michigan

Susan B. Neuman
Professor, University of Michigan
Ann Arbor, Michigan

Lynda L. West
Professor
The George Washington University
Washington, D.C.

About the Author

**Jody L. Maanum** received her bachelor of arts degree in Elementary Education from Concordia College in Moorhead, Minnesota, and obtained a master of science degree in Special Education from the University of Minnesota, Moorhead. She has taught in both the general and special education settings for 13 years, working diligently to implement best practice techniques and differentiated strategies to meet the individual needs of all students. Maanum is currently the literacy coach and Response to Intervention Training Specialist for the Midwest Special Education Cooperative in West-Central Minnesota. She has been instrumental in promoting early literacy achievement in all children and fully implementing the RTI model in the nine school districts within the cooperative in which she works.

1

Federal Special Education Disability Categories

IDEA (2004)

Individuals with Disabilities Education Act (IDEA), is a federal law that regulates all special education services in the United States. IDEA provides federal funding to state and local education agencies to guarantee appropriate special education and related services for those students who meet the criteria for eligibility. The federal guidelines for special education, defined in the 2004 reauthorization of IDEA, recognizes 13 different disability categories through which students may be deemed eligible to receive special education and related services. Individual states may break some of these disabilities into separate categories; however, determination of qualification in any of these categories requires that a complete, appropriate evaluation be conducted, utilizing a variety of assessment tools and strategies. IDEA states that functional, developmental, and academic information about the child must be gathered to assist in making eligibility determinations.

■ THE 13 QUALIFYING CATEGORIES

1. Autism
2. Deaf-Blindness
3. Deafness
4. Emotional Disturbance
5. Hearing Impairment
6. Mental Retardation
7. Multiple Disabilities
8. Orthopedic Impairment
9. Other Health Impairment
10. Specific Learning Disability
11. Speech or Language Impairment
12. Traumatic Brain Injury
13. Visual Impairment (Including Blindness)

On the following pages, you will find specific definitions of the 13 alphabetically organized disability categories, along with specific examples of possible medical conditions that may fall under each category, useful educational approaches to utilize while working with children who qualify for services in these categories, and teacher resources to guide you in developing further understanding of each category.

■ AUTISM

Autism, also referred to as Autism Spectrum Disorder (ASD) and/or Pervasive Developmental Disorder (PDD), is a developmental disability that affects a child's ability to communicate, understand language, play, and interact with others. Autism is a behavioral syndrome, which means that its definition is based on the pattern of behaviors that a child exhibits. To help better understand the autism spectrum, it should be noted that there are five disorders listed under ASD or PDD in the DSM-IV manual by the American Psychiatric Association (1994). These disorders include Autistic Disorder, Asperger's Disorder, Pervasive Developmental Disorder, Not Otherwise Specified, Rett's Disorder, and Childhood Disintegrative Disorder. All disorders in this category exhibit abnormalities in socialization skills, use of language for communication, and behavior, but each group differs in the severity of the deficits.

Autism is not an illness or a disease and is not contagious. It is a neurological and developmental disability that is presumed to be present from birth and is always apparent before the age of three. Although autism affects the functioning of the brain, the specific cause is unknown. It is widely assumed that there are multiple causes, each of which may manifest in different forms. Children who have any diagnosis which fall in the autism spectrum may qualify to be eligible to receive special education and support services.

GENERAL AUTISM

Symptoms of Autism

As described by Nielsen (2009), autism has many varied symptoms and characteristics. Although not all people with autism manifest every characteristic, the following areas and specific behaviors are typical.

Social Interactions and Relationships

- Significant difficulty developing nonverbal communication skills
  o Eye-to-eye gazing
  o Facial expressions
  o Body posture
- Failure to establish friendships with children the same age
- Lack of interest in sharing enjoyment, interests, or achievement with other people
- Appearing to be unaware of others
- Lack of empathy
- Difficulty relating to people

Verbal and Nonverbal Communication

- Delay in or lack of learning to talk
- Problem taking steps to start and/or continue a conversation
- Nonspeech vocalizations
  o Grunting
  o Humming
- Stereotyped and repetitive use of language
  o Echolalia
  o Repeated what one has heard again and again
- Difficulty understanding listener's perspective
  o Does not understand humor
  o Takes conversation literally (communicates word for word)
  o Fails to catch implied meaning

Activities and Play

- An unusual focus on pieces (e.g., focus on the wheels on the toy car rather than on the entire car)
- Using toys and objects in an unconventional manner
- Preoccupation with certain topics
  o Fascination with train schedules
  o Weather patterns
  o Numbers
- A need for sameness and routines.
  o Insists that environment and routine remain unchanged
  o Insists on driving the same route to school everyday
- Stereotyped behaviors
  o Body rocking
  o Hand flapping

o Self-stimulatory behavior
o Self-injurious behavior (head banging)
o Preoccupation with hands

Treatment Options for Autism

According to the Autism Speaks Web site (2008), there is no single treatment protocol for all children with autism; however, most individuals respond best to highly structured behavioral programs. Brief statements of the most commonly used behavior programs include the following aspects.

Applied Behavior Analysis (ABA)

The use of positive reinforcement and other principles are used to build communication, play, social, academic, self-care, work, and community living skills and to reduce problem behaviors in learners with autism of all ages. The final goal of ABA intervention is to enable the child to function independently and successfully in a variety of settings.

Verbal Behavior Intervention

The verbal behavior approach focuses on teaching specific components of expressing language (mands, tact, intraverbals, and others). This approach begins with mand training, which teaches a child to request desired items, activities, and information—teaching the child that "words" are valuable and lead them to getting their wants and needs met.

Floortime

Developed by child psychiatrist Stanley Greenspan, Floortime is a treatment method and a philosophy for interacting with autistic children. The goal and purpose for this strategy is to move the child through the six basic developmental milestones in emotional and intellectual growth. Those six include (1) self-regulation and interest in the world, (2) intimacy, (3) two-way communication, (4) complex communication, (5) emotional ideas, and (6) emotional thinking. The intervention is called *Floortime* because those working with the child get down on the floor to engage with the child at his or her level.

Gluten Free, Casein Free Diet (GFCF)

This is a very popular dietary intervention that consists of the removal of gluten (a protein found in barley, rye, oats, and wheat) and casein (a protein found in dairy products). This theory is based on the hypothesis that these proteins are absorbed differently in children with autism spectrum disorder. There is no scientifically based research indicating the effectiveness of this intervention; however, families report that dietary elimination of gluten and casein has helped to regulate bowel habits, sleep, activity, habitual behaviors, and enhance overall progress in their child.

Occupational Therapy

The focus of utilizing occupational therapy as treatment for children with autism is to maintain, improve, or introduce skills that allow an individual to participate as independently as possible in meaningful life activities. Coping skills, fine motor skills, play skills, self-help skills, and socialization are all targeted areas that can be addressed in this setting.

Picture Exchange Communication System (PECS)

PECS is a type of augmentative and alternative communication technique where individuals with little or no verbal ability learn to communicate using picture cards. Children use the pictures to "vocalize" a desire, observation, or feeling. Many children with autism learn visually, and therefore, this type of communication technique has been shown to be effective at improving independent communication skills. A formalized training program is offered to ensure the best utilization of the program (Bondy & Frost, 2002).

Note: More information regarding PECS, the Pyramid Approach to Education, or Pyramid Educational Consultants Inc. is available on www.pecs.com.

Relationship Development Intervention (RDI)

This intervention is based on the work of psychologist Steven Gutstein and focuses on improving the long-term quality of life for all individuals on the spectrum. It is a parent-based treatment that focuses on the core problems of gaining friendships, feeling empathy, expressing love, and being able to share experiences with others (Gutstein & Sheely, 2002).

Note: Further information regarding RDI is available on www.rdiconnect.com.

The SCERTS Model

The SCERTS model is a comprehensive, team-based, multidisciplinary model for enhancing abilities in social communication and emotional regulation and implementing transactional supports for children with autism. This model is mostly concerned with helping persons with autism to achieve "authentic progress," which is defined as the ability to learn and apply functional skills in a variety of settings and with a variety of partners (Prizant, Wetherby, Rubin, Rydell, & Laurent, 2006).

Note: For further information, see www.scerts.com.

Sensory Integration Therapy

This intervention involves the process through which the brain organizes and interprets external stimuli such as movement, touch, smell, sight, and sound. It is often common for children with autism to exhibit symptoms of Sensory Integration Dysfunction (SID), making it difficult to process information brought in through the senses. Children can have mild, moderate, or severe SID deficits, manifesting in either increased or decreased sensitivity to sound, touch, and movement. The goal of sensory integration therapy is to facilitate the development of the nervous system's ability to process sensory input in a more typical way. When successful, this has been known to improve attention, concentration, listening, comprehension, balance, coordination, and impulsivity control in some children.

Note: For additional information, see www.sensorynation.com.

Speech Therapy

The communication difficulties of children with autism vary depending on the intellectual and social development of the individual. Some children are unable to speak, whereas others have well-developed vocabularies and can speak at length on topics that interest them. Although some children have little difficulty with pronouncing words, most children with autism have difficulty effectively using language.

Children with autism frequently exhibit difficulties in the pragmatic use of language such as knowing what to say, how and when to say it, and how to use language to socially interact in an acceptable way with others. Many children with autism will repeat verbatim what they have heard (echolalia) or repeat irrelevant scripts they have memorized. Others will speak in a high pitched voice or use robotic sounding speech.

Educational Strategies and Approaches for Teaching Students With Autism

- Directions should be given one at a time.
- Avoid giving repetition of the directions.
- Break instructions down into smaller chunks.
- Confer with other support teachers.
- Provide positive behavior management opportunities.
- Provide clear expectations and rules.
- Use concrete, tangible visual aids (e.g., pictures and charts).
- Encourage the use of talent areas and provide additional learning opportunities in these areas.
- Practice functional real life skills (e.g., use real money rather than play money when learning to count money).
- Use real places when learning about acceptable public behavior.
- Use field trips to provide concrete learning experiences.

Web Sites

Autism Research Institute: www.autism.com

Autism Society of America: www.autism-society.org

Resource Books

Title: *1001 Great Ideas for Teaching and Raising Children With Autism Spectrum Disorder*

Authors: Veronica Zysk and Ellen Notbohm

Publisher: Future Horizons, 2004

Story Profile: This resource offers pages and pages of immediately ready solutions that have worked for thousands of children with autism spectrum disorder struggling with social, sensory, behavioral, and self-care issues, plus many more.

Title: *Autism Spectrum Disorders*

Author: Richard Simpson

Publisher: Paul Brookes Publishing Company, 2005

Story Profile: Autism Spectrum Disorders (ASD) was developed to respond directly to the difficulty school professionals and families face in selecting and applying appropriate interventions and treatments for the children in their care.

Title: *Demystifying Autism Spectrum Disorders—A Guide to Diagnosis for Parents and Professionals*

Author: Carolyn Thorwarth Burey

Publisher: Woodbine House, 2004

Story Profile: This guide for parents, educators, and caregivers describes the five types of autism that fall under the ASD umbrella, spells out the distinctions among them, demystifies the technical jargon, and provides an overview of treatment.

Title: *Ten Things Every Child With Autism Wishes You Knew*

Author: Ellen Notbohm

Publisher: Future Horizons, 2005

Story Profile: Framed with both humor and compassion, this book defines, from a child's perspective, the top ten characteristics that illuminate the minds and hearts of children with autism.

Title: *"You're Going to Love This Kid!" Teaching Students With Autism in the Inclusive Classroom*

Author: Paula Kluth

Publisher: Paul Brookes Publishing Company, 2004

Story Profile: This is a strategy-filled guidebook for including students with autism in both primary and secondary school classrooms. The publication demonstrates how educators can adapt their own classrooms to support student participation, school routines, social activities, and more.

(Continued)

(Continued)

Children's Resources

Title: *Andy and His Yellow Frisbee*

Author: Mary Thompson

Publisher: Woodbine House, 1996

Story Profile: This book tells the story of a new girl at school who tried to befriend Andy, an autistic boy who spends every recess by himself.

Title: *The Autism Acceptance Book: Being a Friend to Someone With Autism*

Author: Ellen Sabin

Publisher: Watering Can Press, 2006

Story Profile: An interactive, educational, and character building book that introduces children to the challenges of living with autism. It uses informative narrative and engaging activities that invite children to "walk inside someone else's shoes" as they learn to treat others in the same ways they would like to be treated themselves.

Title: *Mori's Story: A Book About a Boy With Autism*

Author: Zachary Gartenber

Illustrator: Jerry Gay

Publisher: The Lerner Publishing Group, 1998

Story Profile: A young boy discusses his home life and schooling with his autistic brother, Mori. He discusses how his family learned that Mori was autistic, the kinds of treatment Mori receives, and how it affects all of their lives.

Title: *My Brother Sammy*

Author: Becky Edwards

Publisher: Millbrook Press, 1999

Story Profile: This book's narrator longs for a brother who can talk to him, build towers with him, and join his friends at play. His autistic brother, Sammy, mimics his speech, knocks down his building blocks, and lies alone on the grass staring at the leaves on trees. As the older boy tries doing and seeing things Sammy's way, a special relationship develops between them.

Title: *Since We're Friends: An Autism Picture Book*

Author: Celeste Shally

Illustrator: David Harrington

Publisher: Awaken Specialty Press, 2007

Story Profile: Children with autism struggle to make friends and find it very difficult to interact appropriately in social situations. In this book, one child makes a significant impact in the life of a child with autism by offering compassion, understanding, and friendship.

ASPERGER SYNDROME (ASPERGER DISORDER)

Asperger syndrome (AS) refers to the mildest and highest functioning on the spectrum and is characterized by higher cognitive abilities ranging from average to superior intelligence. There are many similar characteristics that can be seen between

Asperger syndrome and autism, but the characteristics differ in the degree of severity and overall ability of the child. Nielsen (2009) explains that children with Asperger syndrome have a higher verbal IQ than performance IQ, which is opposite for children with autism who have a higher performance IQ than verbal IQ. Children with Asperger syndrome can also be found to have more normal language ability than children with autism, and the onset of Asperger is generally later than the onset of autism. Asperger, just like autism, is characterized by deficits in social and communication skills; however, the deficits are to a lesser severity with Asperger syndrome, and the long-term outlook for these children is more positive as well.

Symptoms of Asperger Syndrome

Nielsen (2009) also describes the work of Christopher Gillberg, a Swedish physician who expanded the list of characteristics to better diagnose a child with Asperger syndrome. According to Gillberg's list, all of the following six criteria must be met before a child is diagnosed with Asperger syndrome.

- Severe impairment in reciprocal social interaction
  o Inability to interact with peers
  o Lack of desire to interact with peers
  o Lack of appreciation of social cues
  o Socially and emotionally inappropriate behavior

- All-absorbing narrow interest
  o Exclusion of other activities
  o Repetitive adherence
  o More rote than meaning

- Imposition of routines and interests
  o On self, in aspects of life
  o On others

- Speech and language problems
  o Delayed development
  o Superficially perfect expressive language
  o Formal, pedantic language
  o Odd prosody, peculiar voice characteristics
  o Impairment of comprehension, including misinterpretations of literal/ implied meanings

- Nonverbal communication problems
  o Limited use of gestures
  o Clumsy, gauche body language
  o Limited facial expression
  o Inappropriate expression
  o Peculiar, stiff gaze

- Motor clumsiness
  o Poor performance on neurodevelopmental examination

Treatment of Asperger Syndrome

There is no cure for Asperger syndrome; however, children with Asperger's will benefit from psychosocial and psychopharmacological interventions. The medications used are to help reduce the symptoms that accompany Asperger. The Autism Society has provided the following intervention opportunities.

Psychosocial Interventions

- Individual therapy to help the individual process the feelings aroused by being socially handicapped
- Parent education and training
- Behavioral modification
- Social skills training
- Educational interventions

Psychopharmacological (Medications)

- Stimulants—to assist hyperactivity, inattention, and impulsivity
- Mood stabilizers—to assist irritability and aggression
- Selective Serotonin Reuptake Inhibitor (SSRIs)—to assist preoccupations, rituals, compulsions, and anxiety

Educational Strategies for Asperger Syndrome

Assist the Student in Developing Communication Skills

- Have patience.
- Listen to all attempts made by the student.
- Allow extended time for processing after a questions has been asked to the student; refrain from rephrasing the question or interrupting.
- Accept the child's language pattern and word choice; refrain from correcting the child's speech.
- Continually model appropriate and correct format of speech.
- In conversation, listen for message behind the words and *not* how the message was conveyed. Ignore peculiarities in the volume of speech, intonation, and inflection of the child's voice.
- Encourage continued communication through positive and accepting responses.
- Be concise, concrete, and specific with the language that you use.
- Avoid using vague terms such as *maybe, later,* or *perhaps.*
- Specifically state questions (e.g., "Why did you get out of your chair?" rather than, "Why did you do that?").
- Specifically state requests (e.g., "Please sit with all four legs of your chair on the floor," rather than, "Please don't do that.").

Provide a Well-Structured, Consistent Environment

- Have a seating plan in place.
- Post the class schedule either in the classroom, or if the student with AS is different than the rest of the class, post the schedule on the student's desk or notebook planner.
- Post classroom rules either in the classroom, or if the student with AS is different than the rest of the class, post the rules on the student's desk or notebook planner.
- Inform the student if a change is coming in the seating plan or class schedule.
- Provide prior notification for any change in the normal school day, such as special events, vacation dates, lyceums, or days when a substitute teacher may be in the classroom.

Promote Self-Confidence

- Encourage students to assist other students in academic areas.
- Highlight students' areas of strengths in cooperative learning situations; in return, foster respect among the peer group.

Other Accommodations Inside the Classroom

- Present assignments visually and verbally.
- Provide copies of teacher notes.
- Tape record the lecture.
- Provide headphones or earplugs in the classroom to reduce noises.
- Allow homework to be typed rather than handwritten.
- Allow students to tape record answers to written examinations.

Web Sites

ASPEN Society of America, Inc. Asperger Syndrome Education Network: www.asperger.org

Asperger's Disorder Homepage: www.aspergers.com

Collection or resources pertaining to Asperger syndrome: www.udel.edu/bkirby/asperger

Resources

Title: *School Success for Kids With Asperger Syndrome: A Practical Guide for Parents and Teachers*

Authors: Stephan Silverman and Rich Weinfeld

Publisher: Prufrock Press, 2007

Story Profile: Kids with Asperger syndrome have average to above-average intelligence; however, they often have obsessive interests, are socially awkward, and do not understand the subtleties of language and conversation. With concentrated effort on the part of parents and educators, these children can begin to overcome the difficulties of this disorder and find success in school and life.

Title: *Freaks, Geeks, and Asperger Syndrome: A User's Guide to Adolescence*

Author: Luke Jackson

Publisher: Jessica Kingsley, 2002

Story Profile: Luke Jackson is 13 years old and has Asperger syndrome. Over the years, Luke has learned to laugh at such names that he has been called such as "freak" or "geek." Adolescence and the teenage years are a minefield of emotions, transitions, and decisions, and when that is coupled with Asperger syndrome, the results can be explosive. Luke wrote this enlightening, honest, and witty book in an attempt to address difficult topics such as bullying, friendships, when and how to tell others about AS, school problems, dating, relationships, and morality.

Title: *Asperger Syndrome and the Elementary School Experience: Practical Solutions for Academic and Social Difficulties*

Author: Susan Thompson Moore

Publisher: Autism Asperger Publishing Company, 2002

Story Profile: A great resource and guide for a classroom teacher that fully incorporates all needed information to assist kids with Asperger syndrome to be successful in the general education classroom.

(Continued)

(Continued)

Children's Resources

Title: *Can I Tell You About Asperger Syndrome? A Guide for Family and Friends*

Author: Jude Welton

Illustrator: Jane Telford

Publisher: Jessica Kingsley Publishers, 2002

Story Profile: In this book, Adam helps children understand the difficulties faced by a child with AS; he tells them what AS is, what it feels like to have AS, and how readers can help children with AS by understanding their differences and appreciating their many talents. This book serves as an excellent starting point for family and classroom discussions.

Title: *Different Like Me: My Book of Autism Heroes*

Author: Jennifer Elder

Illustrator: Marc, Thomas

Publisher: Jessica Kingsly Publishing, 2005

Story Profile: This book, told from the perspective of a young boy named Quinn, describes the achievement and characteristics of the lives of autism heroes, both famous and historical, who found it difficult to fit into society. From Albert Einstein, Dian Fossey, and Wassily Kandinsky to Lewis Carroll, Benjamin Banneker, and Julia Bowman Robinson, among others. All excelled in different fields but are united by the fact that they often found it difficult to fit in—just like Quinn.

Title: *I Am Utterly Unique: Celebrating the Strengths of Children With Asperger Syndrome and High-Functioning Autism*

Authors: Elaine Larson and Vivian Strand

Publisher: Autism Asperger Publishing Company, 2006

Story Profile: The ABCs of Asperger syndrome and autism. Using the alphabet, the authors find 26 unique traits shared by many children who have Asperger syndrome or high-functioning autism.

Pervasive Developmental Disorder, Not Otherwise Specified (PDD-NOS)

According to the National Dissemination Center for Children with Disabilities (NICHCY) fact sheet 20, (2003), PDD-NOS has been referred to as a "milder" form of autism where some but not all features of autism are identified. PDD-NOS is often called simply "PDD"; however, the term PDD refers to the umbrella under which the various diagnoses fall—PDD-NOS being one diagnosis that falls under the PDD umbrella. There are no set patterns or symptoms and signs in children with PDD-NOS, and there is a very wide range of diversity seen in children with PDD-NOS. The diagnosis of PDD-NOS should be used when a child exhibits a severe and pervasive impairment in the development of social interaction or verbal and nonverbal communication skills, but when not all criteria are met for a specific PDD.

Treatment for PDD-NOS

Treatment for a diagnosis of PDD-NOS is the same as the treatments used to treat the other PDD. Each child will demonstrate individual and unique needs, and therefore, treatment will be determined accordingly.

Web Site

Disability information on Pervasive Developmental Disorders: www.nichy.org/pubs/factshe/fs20txt.htm

Resource

Title: *Pervasive Developmental Disorders: Diagnosis, Options, and Answers*

Author: Mitzi Waltz

Publisher: Future Horizons, 2003

Story Profile: Written for professionals, parents, or newly diagnosed adults who struggle with PDD, this book is considered the definitive resource on this neurological condition.

RETT SYNDROME

Rett syndrome is an extremely rare medical condition that has only been reported in females. It has been added to the ASD category because in addition to the medical symptoms, children with Rett syndrome tend to display social, communication, and play difficulties associated with ASD.

Symptoms of Rett Syndrome

The physical development of children with Rett's syndrome is very distinct. Children have normal prenatal and perinatal development with typical early motor growth and head circumference. Between five and 30 months of age, mental and physical breakdowns begin to appear, and children begin to exhibit some of the following characteristics:

- Loss of purposeful hand movement, such as grasping with fingers, reaching for things, or touching things on purpose
- Loss of speech
- Balance and coordination problems, including losing the ability to walk
- Stereotypic hand movements, such as hand wringing
- Breathing problems, hyperventilation, breath holding, or sleep apnea
- Anxiety and social-behavioral problems
- Intellectual disability/mental retardation

Treatment of Rett Syndrome

There is no cure for Rett syndrome; however, treatments are available for some of the problems associated with the syndrome. These treatments generally aim to slow the loss of abilities, improve or preserve movement, and encourage communication and social contact. The team approach is the most beneficial form of care for children with Rett syndrome. Along with the family, members of this team may include the following professionals.

Physical Therapists

- Help patients improve or maintain mobility and balance
- Reduce misshapen back and limbs

Occupational Therapists

- Help patients improve or maintain use of their hands
- Reduce stereotypic hand movements

Speech and Language Therapists

- Assist patients in the use of nonverbal ways of communication
- Improve social interaction

Medical Doctors

- Provide medication for some symptoms such as constipation, irregular heartbeat rhythm, or seizure, or to reduce breathing problems

---

Web Sites

International Rett Syndrome Foundation: www.rettsyndrome.org

We Move—Rett Syndrome: www.wemove.org/rett

Resources

Title: *Understanding Rett Syndrome: A Practical Guide for Parents, Teachers, and Therapists*

Author: Barbro Lindberg

Publisher: Hogrefe and Huber Publishing, 2006

Story Profile: This brand new edition of this book describes the difficulties and challenges of girls and women with Rett syndrome. The book proposes solutions that can help them in everyday life and is primarily intended for people who work with people with Rett syndrome on a frequent basis.

Title: *Your Daughter Has Been Diagnosed With Rett Syndrome*

Author: Kim Isaac Greenblatt

Publisher: Kim Greenblatt, 2006

Story Profile: A personal account by the author on what it is like to receive the information that your daughter has been given a diagnosis of Rett syndrome. The book provides different ways of dealing with the diagnosis, provides coping mechanisms, and encourages readers to celebrate life!

CHILDHOOD DISINTEGRATIVE DISORDER (CDD)

CDD is a condition in which young children develop normally until age three or four but then demonstrate a severe loss of social, communication, and other skills. Doctors sometimes confuse this rare disorder with late-onset autism because both conditions involve normal development followed by significant loss of language, social, play, and motor skills. However, autism typically occurs at an earlier age. There's also a more dramatic loss of skills in children with CDD and a greater likelihood of mental retardation. In addition, CDD is far less common than autism.

Symptoms of Childhood Disintegrative Disorder

NICHCY fact sheet 20 (2003) suggests that specific symptoms of CDD typically include the following.

- Normal development for at least the first two years of life
  - o Normal development of verbal and nonverbal communication
  - o Social relationships
  - o Motor skills
  - o Self-care skills

- Significant loss of previously acquired or learned skills
  - o Ability to say words or sentences
  - o Ability to understand verbal and nonverbal communication
  - o Social skills and self-care skills
  - o Bowel and bladder control
  - o Play skills
  - o Motor skills (ability to voluntarily move the body in a purposeful way)

- Lack of normal function or impairment
  - o Social interaction—this may include impairment in
    nonverbal behaviors,
    failure to develop peer relationships,
    lack of social or emotional reciprocity
  - o Communication—this may include delay or lack of spoken language, inability to initiate or sustain a conversation, stereotyped and repetitive use of language, lack of varied imaginative or make-believe play

- Repetitive and stereotyped patterns of behavior, interests, and activities
  - o Hand flapping
  - o Rocking
  - o Spinning (motor stereotypes and mannerisms)
  - o Development of specific routines and rituals
  - o Difficulty with transitions or changes in routine
  - o Maintaining a fixed posture or body position (catatonia)
  - o Preoccupation with certain objects or activities

Treatment of Childhood Disintegrative Syndrome

There is no cure for CDD. Treatment for this disorder is much the same as treatment of autism. Specific treatment options may include the following medications.

- The medication will not directly treat the disorder.
- Antipsychotic medications may help control severe behavior problems such as aggression and repetitive movements.
- Anticonvulsant drugs may help control epileptic seizures.

Behavior Therapy

- This therapy technique may be utilized by psychologists, speech therapists, physical therapists, occupational therapists, parents, teachers, and caregivers.
- Behavior therapy programs may be designed to specifically meet the needs of each child.

Behavior therapy programs can be designed to help children learn or relearn language, social, and self-care skills. These programs use a system of reward to reinforce desirable behaviors and discourage problem behavior. Consistency among all members working with the child is very important in behavior therapy.

The outcome for children with childhood disintegrative disorder is usually very poor and even worse than for children with autism. The loss of language, cognitive, social, and self-care skills tends to be severe and permanently disabling. As a result, children with the disorder often need residential care in a group home or long-term care facility.

Web Sites

Childhood Disintegrative Disorder: www.mayoclinic.com/health/childhood-disintegrative-disorder/DS00801

Definition, description, causes and symptoms, and treatments: www.minddisorders.com/Br-Del/Childhood-disintegrative-disorder.html

Resources

Title: *Identifying, Assessing, and Treating Autism at School*

Authors: Stephen E. Brock, Shane R. Jimerson, and Robin L. Hansen

Publisher: Springer, 2006

Story Profile: An invaluable resource for school psychologists, educational professionals, and parents. It provides an excellent overview of the assessment and treatment of autism and related disorders and outlines the interventions that can be provided for students with autism in school.

Educational Strategies and Approaches for Teaching Students With PDD-NOS, Rett Syndrome, and Childhood Disintegrative Disorder

- Directions should be given one at a time.
- Avoid giving repetition of the directions.
- Break instructions down into smaller chunks.
- Confer with other support teachers.
- Provide positive behavior management opportunities.
- Provide clear expectations and rules.
- Use concrete, tangible visual aids (e.g., pictures and charts).
- Encourage the use of talent areas and provide additional learning opportunities in these areas.
- Practice functional real life skills (e.g., use real money rather than play money when learning to count money).
- Use real places when learning about acceptable public behavior.
- Use field trips to provide concrete learning experiences.

Other Areas That Need Specific Consideration in the Classroom

Physical structure is the way the classroom is set up and organized. A child with autism needs clear physical and visual boundaries in the classroom environment. Minimizing visual and auditory distractions is also important to help the child focus on learning concepts and not irrelevant details. The child also needs to know the basic teaching areas of the room. There should be specific, designated areas that the child uses daily for a snack, playtime, and transition times as well as individual and independent work times. These areas should be consistent so there are no "surprises" in the child's routine. If a child with autism is accustomed to having a snack on the carpeted area at the front of the room every day and suddenly is expected to eat a snack at his desk, this will likely cause agitation. Children with autism require consistency in all aspects of their day.

Daily schedules are essential. Visual schedules help the child to see what activities will occur and the order of events for the day. The child will work best if a concrete reference of the daily schedule is in view. This will help the child to better accept change and become a bit more flexible, as long as the child knows in advance of a schedule change. A fire drill, for example, may be a devastating addition to the day, since the child is unaware that it will occur. In the eyes of an autistic child, if an event is not written on the schedule, then the event should not occur. Helping the child to become aware of upcoming event changes will ensure easier transition times when those events occur.

Visual structure helps children with autism to capitalize on their visual aptitude and strengths and minimize their deficits in auditory processing. Visually highlighting important information will help to clarify the relevant concepts of which the child should be aware. This may include color-coding areas and labeling things to visually draw the child's attention. Providing visual instructions for the child is also helpful when presenting the child with an assignment or task.

■ DEAF-BLINDNESS

Deaf-blindness is a medically verified hearing impairment coexisting with a medically verified visual impairment. Together, these two impairments must cause severe communication difficulties and other developmental and education problems that cannot be accommodated in special education programs solely for children with exclusive blindness or deafness.

■ DEAFNESS

Deafness is a hearing impairment so severe that the child cannot understand what is being said even with a hearing aid. The causes of a child being or becoming deaf are described in terms of exogenous or endogenous. Exogenous causes stem from factors outside the body such as disease, toxicity, or injury. Endogenous hearing impairments are genetic.

Educational Considerations for a Deaf Child

Today, more than 60% of deaf children in the United States attend local school programs, and many are included in the regular classroom at least part of the day. Deafness does not affect a person's intellectual capacity or ability to learn; however, children who are deaf generally require some form of special education services in order to receive adequate instruction. The most difficult challenge in educating deaf students is teaching spoken language to children who cannot hear. Many deaf students are not able to communicate effectively with classmates and therefore benefit by having a sign language interpreter to assist with the communication barrier. It is important for teachers and audiologist to work together to teach the child to use his or her residual hearing to the maximum extent possible, even if the preferred means of communication is manual. For more in-depth information concerning hearing impairments, see that section following "Emotional Disturbance" as IDEA separates deafness and hearing impairments and organizes them alphabetically.

Web Sites

American Speech-Language-Hearing Association: www.asha.org

Raising Deaf Kids: www.raisingdeafkids.org

Resource Books

Title: *Helping Deaf and Hard of Hearing Students to Use Spoken Language: A Guide for Educators and Families*

Authors: Susan Easterbrooks and Ellen L. Estes

Publisher: Corwin, 2007

Story Profile: As a result of IDEA 2004 and NCLB, students with hearing loss are frequently being educated alongside their peers in the general education classroom. This book provides teachers and service professionals with the knowledge and skills in spoken language development to meet the needs of students who are deaf or hard of hearing. It is an essential resource that addresses creative and scientific ways of interacting with children and provides effective approaches, techniques, and strategies for working with children to develop spoken communication.

Title: *Raising and Educating a Deaf Child: A Comprehensive Guide to the Choices, Controversies, and Decisions Faced by Parents and Educators*

Author: Marc Marschark

Publisher: Oxford University Press, 2007

Story Profile: The book focuses on the choices and decisions faced by parents and educators and analyzes many important influences on a child's successful rearing.

Children's Resources

Title: *I'm Deaf and It's Okay*

Authors: Lorraine Aseltine, Evelyn Mueller, and Nancy Tait

Publisher: Albert Whitman & Company, 1986

Story Profile: A story about an elementary-aged boy who expresses his feelings about deafness. He describes his experiences with fear, jealously, anger, and frustration until he meets a teenage boy who is also deaf and helps him to see that he can lead a normal life.

Title: *I Have a Sister—My Sister is Deaf*

Author: Jeanne Whitehouse Peterson

Illustrator: Deborah Kogan Ray

Publisher: Harper Trophy

Story Profile: An excellent book for explaining the world of the totally deaf to very young children.

■ EMOTIONAL DISTURBANCE

Serious emotional disturbance, also referred to in the law as emotional disturbance, refers to an established pattern exhibiting one of more of the following characteristics.

- An inability to learn that cannot be explained by intellectual, sensory, or health factors
- An inability to build or maintain satisfactory interpersonal relationships with peers and teachers
- Inappropriate types of behavior or feelings under normal circumstances
- A general, pervasive mood of unhappiness or depression
- A tendency to develop physical symptoms or fears associated with personal or school problems

Symptoms of Emotional Disturbance

According to Nielsen (2009), some basic characteristics and behaviors are commonly seen in children who have been diagnosed with emotional disturbance. Such characteristics include the following:

- Hyperactivity
- Short attention span
- Impulsiveness
- Inconsistencies of behavior
- Low frustration tolerance
- Aggression (acting out, fighting)
- Self-injurious behavior
- Withdrawal from interaction with others
- Inappropriate social skills
- Immaturity (inappropriate crying, temper tantrums)
- Poor coping skills
- Learning problems
- Unfocused
- Unexplainable mood shifts

Children with the most serious emotional disturbances exhibit distorted thinking, excessive anxiety, bizarre motor acts, and abnormal mood swings. This may include children with schizophrenic disorders, affective disorders, anxiety disorders, and other sustained disorders of conduct or adjustment when an established pattern adversely affects educational performance and results in an inability to build or maintain satisfactory interpersonal relations necessary to the learning process. It should be noted that the established pattern of behavior must occur to a marked degree and over a long period of time.

Educational Strategies for Serious Emotional Disturbance

It is important to remember and understand that all children will misbehave at some time, but students who meet the Serious Emotional Disturbance criteria have a continuous pattern of misbehavior that consistently disrupts the classroom environment. Unfortunately, the teacher is required to devote much time and attention to the student and behaviors in an attempt to restore and maintain order to the learning environment. Challenging behaviors can be overwhelming and cause frustration. Nielsen (2009) provides a detailed list of strategies for teachers to use when educating students with serious emotional disturbances.

Structure the Classroom

- Define clear and explicit limits and consequences for unacceptable behaviors.
- Ensure that the system also provides opportunity for positive reinforcement for acceptable behavior.
- Ensure that the student is aware of and understands the system in place.
- Post a written copy of Rules/Consequences/Rewards in the classroom for easy reference.
- The teacher is always in charge, never the student.
- Ensure consistent follow through of consequences and rewards when appropriate.

Develop a Good Rapport With Students

- Take every advantage possible throughout the day to reinforce feelings of self-worth.
- Make eye contact and smile at the child.
- Provide praise for good work.
- Exhibit close proximity.

Focus Attention on Desired Behavior and Not on Unacceptable Behavior

- Provide praise, even for approximation of the desired behavior.
- Provide consistent, positive reinforcement for acceptable behavior.
- Reward positive behavior by using a token system.
- Begin with tangible, extrinsic rewards and eventually replace them with intrinsic rewards.
- Ensure that the student is aware of and understands the token system in place.
- Withhold the reward, if necessary, as a consequence for inappropriate behavior.

Prepare a Behavior Plan to Address Physically Aggressive Behavior

- Write a plan that will include removal from the classroom if student behavior becomes aggressive and threatens the safety of others.
- Make arrangements with a support person to assist you (e.g., teacher next door, principal, special education teacher).
- Utilize the Nonviolent Crisis Intervention movement and restraint techniques to ensure the care, welfare, safety, and security of yourself, the student, and others around you.

Be Alert to Any Indication That the Student May Be Experiencing Difficulty

- Provide a predetermined time-out area or place where the student can go.
- Allow the student to go to that area in order to regain composure or sidetrack an incident.

- The student is not required to ask permission to go to the time-out place.
- Divert attention away from the source of difficulty as much as possible.
- Send the child for a walk, to run an errand, get a drink, or any other reason to leave the classroom to provide time for the child to regain composure.

Go Slowly, Prioritize Behaviors, Be Patient, and Praise Baby Steps When Attempting to Change Behavior

- Accept the need for possible change in your behavior pattern.
- List behaviors to be changed and prioritize by importance.
- Determine one behavior to focus on at a time.
- When appropriate and possible, ignore nonpriority, undesirable behaviors, as annoying behavior that receives attention tends to be repeated.
- Praise and reward appropriate, priority behaviors to continue improvement of the behavior.

Web Sites

Center on Positive Behavioral Interventions and Supports: www.pbis.org

National Alliance on Mental Illness (NAMI): www.nami.org

National Mental Health Information Center: www.mentalhealth.org

Resource Books

Title: *The Effective Teachers' Guide to Emotional and Behavioral Difficulties: Practical Strategies*

Author: Michael Farrell

Publisher: Routledge, 2005

Story Profile: A guide for teachers that provides an overview of the basic theories surrounding behavior. The book also provides a variety of strategies to be used in the classroom to increase acceptable behavior and decrease unacceptable behavior. Ideas are also provided to assist in monitoring the effectiveness of the strategies on the specific behaviors.

Children who have been diagnosed with the medical disorders listed below may be deemed eligible to receive special services under the Serious Emotional Disturbance category.

Title: *The Explosive Child: A New Approach for Understanding and Parenting Easily Frustrated, Chronically Inflexible Children*

Author: Ross W. Greene

Publisher: Harper Paperbacks, 2005

Story Profile: A book for those who are trying to parent, guide, and lead a difficult child. This book provides a description of a more contemporary approach to understanding and helping the inflexible and easily frustrated child at home and school.

SCHIZOPHRENIA

Schizophrenia is a psychosis or impairment of thinking in which the interpretation of reality and of daily events is severely abnormal. Childhood Schizophrenia affects about 1 in 40,000 children and in general, the earlier the diagnosis, the more severe the disorder tends to be. The symptoms of Childhood-Onset Schizophrenia can overlap quite a bit with common symptoms to bipolar disorder, autism, or Asperger syndrome.

Signs and Symptoms of Schizophrenia

- Delusions (talking with people who do not exist)
- Incoherence
- Lack of or inappropriate display of emotions
- Inability to concentrate
- Disorganized thinking or behavior
- Inability to read social cues
- Excessive fatigue
- Emotional withdrawal
- Extreme moodiness
- Odd behavior

Schizophrenia usually appears during adolescence or early adulthood. The cause is unknown; however, many believe that it is an inherited disorder.

Medical Treatment of Schizophrenia

The National Institute of Mental Health (2008) states that the treatment of schizophrenia includes pharmacotherapy (medications) using antipsychotic medications such as Risperdal, Risperidone, and Haldol (three of many prescribed medications) combined with psychosocial interventions: cognitive therapy, rehabilitation day programs, peer support groups, or nutritional supplements. The psychosocial interventions include supportive therapy with family, educational interventions, and vocational rehabilitation when appropriate.

Educational Strategies for Schizophrenia

It is essential to remember that schizophrenia is an illness just like diabetes. Children who experience schizophrenia need to realize that something is wrong in their body, and they have no control over what is happening. Even if the symptoms are well controlled by medication, extra support from the school system may be necessary, or a completely different educational program may be appropriate.

- Understand that the child may miss a lot of school due to medication issues or the illness itself.
- Relieve pressure and stress if possible.
- Expect the child's attention, energy, and abilities to rise and fall
  o Provide sympathy, encouragement, and understanding rather than forcing the child to behave and shape up on an "off day."
- Base the student's grades on what *has been* done rather than what *has not been* done, as these children are very sensitive to criticism.
- Medication*s may* make the child less tolerant of heat and sunshine.
- Noise and activity of the normal school day may become overwhelming.
- Provide and allow use of a refuge when the student feels it's necessary.
- If a psychotic episode or breakdown occurs at school, remain calm, speak softly, and be available to the child—do not try to talk the child out of the episode, belittle the child, or point out that he or she is being ridiculous.
- Allow partial school day attendance.

Web Sites

Schizophrenia Education Center: Facts, Symptoms, Treatment, More: www.healthcentral.com

Schizophrenia Home Page: www.schizophrenia.com

Schizophrenia in Children: www.puberty101.com/aacap_schizo.shtml

Resource Books

Title: *I Am Not Sick, I Don't Need Help!*

Authors: Xavier Amador and Anna-Lica

Publisher: Vida Press, 2000

Story Profile: This book explains in simplistic language how a family can work with a family member who is struggling with a mental illness. The authors translate the research on mental illness into a highly readable and very practical book.

Title: *Me, Myself, and Them: A Firsthand Account of One Young Person's Experience With Schizophrenia*

Authors: Kurt Snyder, Raquel W. Gur, and Linda Wasmer Andrews

Publisher: Oxford University Press, USA, 2007

Story Profile: Written by a man with schizophrenia, this book provides a realistic peek at what schizophrenia looks like. Not only does it tell a story, it also provides an explanation for how to recognize warning signs, where to find help, and what treatments have proved to be effective. This book offers practical advice on topics of particular interest to young people such as suggestions on managing the illness at home, school, and work and in relationships with family and friends.

Title: *Mental Health and Growing Up: Fact Sheets for Parents, Teachers, and Young People*

Author: Ann York

Publisher: American Psychiatric Publishing, 2004

Story Profile: The book is filled with short, informative leaflets that offer parents, teachers, and young people practical and up-to-date information on what you can do if you are worried about your child, student, or friend.

Children's Resources

Title: *Helicopter Man*

Author: Elizabeth Fensham

Publisher: Bloomsbury USA Children's Books, 2005

Story Profile: Peter and his dad are homeless and live on the run, trying to stay one step ahead of the helicopters. Pete's dad is convinced that the helicopters are a secret organization that is after him. As Pete gets older, he questions his father's reality and eventually realizes he must come to terms with his father's mental illness of schizophrenia.

Title: *Sometimes My Mommy Gets Angry*

Author: Bebe Morre Campbell

Publisher: Putnam Juvenile, 2003

Story Profile: Told from Annie's perspective, the story tells of the confusion and responsibility of living with a parent with a mental illness. The author introduces coping strategies and helps the readers to understand that they are not to blame for their parents' difficulties.

AFFECTIVE DISORDERS

MANIC-DEPRESSIVE ILLNESS (BIPOLAR DISORDER)—AN AFFECTIVE DISORDER

Bipolar is an alternating pattern of emotional highs and high-spirited behavior (manic) and emotional lows (depression). The manic episodes and depressive episodes may alternate rapidly every few days. The mood swings experienced with this illness are unlike the mood swings that most people experience. Extreme and unpredictable mood swings from highly excited euphoria to the darkest depths of despair and depression are likely to be experienced by those affected by bipolar disorder. The elation and depression occurs without relation to the circumstances. It is common to experience two or more complete cycles (e.g., a manic episode with a major depression episode with no period of remission) within a year (Juvenile Bipolar Research Foundation, n.d.).

Symptoms of Bipolar Disorder

Manic Phase

- Inflated self-esteem
- Increased performance of goal-directed activities
- Alcohol or drug abuse
- Irritability or anger
- Irresponsible spending
- Engaging in dangerous acts
- Hyperactivity
- Fight of ideas, racing thoughts
- No need or little need for sleep
- Rapid speech that others can't understand

Depressive Phase

- Low self-esteem or self-loathing
- Fatigue, lethargy, or feeling slowed down
- Increased need for sleep or the ability to sleep as many as 18 hours without feeling refreshed
- Social withdrawal
- Loss of emotional control—cries easily or for no reason
- Headaches, backaches, or digestive problems
- Unable to concentrate, make decisions, or remember details
- Suicidal thoughts
- Inability to feel pleasure or happiness

Medical Treatment of Bipolar Disorder

Treatment of bipolar disorder is most effective through the use of medications along with psychosocial therapy. The medication treats the illness directly, and the psychotherapy provides the skills needed to manage it and avoid new episodes. The primary goal of drug treatment is to stabilize the extreme mood swings of mania and depression. Antidepressants, such as Prozac, Paxil, and Zoloft, are used to treat symptoms of depression, and lithium has been the primary form of treatment to regulate and prevent manic episodes. Seroquel is used by some to treat the symptoms of both the manic and depressive episodes. Antiseizure and antipsychotic medications are also used to combat side effects depending on individual symptoms.

Educational Strategies for Bipolar Disorder

- Be flexible and willing to adapt assignments, curriculum, and presentation style as needed.
- Be patient and ignore minor negative behaviors.
- Provide encouragement to promote positive behaviors.
- Provide positive behavioral choices.
- Remain calm and be a good model of desired behavior.
- Obtain good conflict management skills to resolve conflicts in a nonconfrontational, noncombative, safe, and positive manner.
- Be able to laugh at oneself and situations (not at the child)—teachers who can laugh at their own mistakes and bring fun and humor into the classroom reduce the level of stress that students feel.
- Be receptive to change and to working collaboratively with the child's parents, doctors, and other professionals to best meet the needs of the child.
- Reduce stress by providing the following.
  - Consistent scheduling that includes planned and unplanned breaks
  - Seating with few distractions
  - Shortened assignments and homework focusing on quality not quantity
  - Prior notice of transitions or changes in routine, minimizing surprises
  - Scheduling considerations so the student's most challenging tasks are scheduled at a time when the child is best able to perform

---

Web Sites

The Bipolar Child: www.bipolarchild.com

Juvenile Bipolar Research Foundation: www.bpchildresearch.org

Resource Books

Title: *Bipolar Disorder in Childhood and Early Adolescence*

Editor: Barbara Geller and Melissa P. DelBello

Publisher: Guildford Press, 2003

Story Profile: This book provides an overview of the theory, research, and knowledge in childhood-onset bipolar illness. It addresses such topics as epidemiology diagnosis and assessment and the life course of the disorder. It describes ways in which the bipolar illness presents itself differently in children than in adults.

Title: *The Childhood Bipolar Disorder Answer Book*

Authors: Tracy Anglada and Sheryl Hakala

Publisher: Sourcebooks, 2008

Story Profile: This book provides practical answers to the top 275 questions parents ask about the bipolar disorder and how it relates to their child. The book has been written to provide answers to these questions based on the most up-to-date information in the medical field. This book combines personal experience and medial expertise to result in a medically accurate picture with firsthand knowledge of what parents really want and need to know.

(Continued)

(Continued)

Title: *The Life of a Bipolar Child: What Every Parent and Professional Needs to Know*

Author: Trudy Carlson

Publisher: Benline Press, 2001

Story Profile: Mood swings? Behavioral problems? Attention Deficit Hyperactivity in children? This book describes effective methods of helping youth to cope with their problems.

Children's Resources

Title: *Brandon and the Bipolar Bear: A Story for Children With Bipolar Disorder*

Author: Tracy Anglada

Publisher: Trafford Publishing, 2004

Story Profile: This book provides an opportunity to help children with bipolar disorder understand the illness in using child-friendly, truthful language. The book explains the disorder itself as well as treatment options using illustrations that allow the child to see him or herself in the story.

Title: *My Bipolar Roller Coaster Feelings Book*

Author: Bryna Herbert

Publisher: Trafford Publishing, 2005

Story Profile: This children's story is written from the perspective of Robert, a boy with bipolar disorder. Robert helps us understand his strong emotions and the strategies his parents and doctor have taught him for coping with them. The purpose of this book is to help the child with bipolar disorder better understand his or her feelings, learn coping strategies, and feel less alone in this world.

Title: *Turbo Max: A Story for Siblings and Friends of Children With Bipolar Disorder*

Author: Tracy D. Anglada

Illustrator: Deirdre Baxendale

Publisher: BPChildren, 2008

Story Profile: This book describes the summer events of a young boy who is struggling to understand his sister's illness of bipolar disorder. The story describes a journey from confusion to understanding, embarrassment to advocacy, and from anger and guilt to acceptance.

CHILDHOOD DEPRESSION

A major depressive disorder is not simply sadness or grief but is a genuine psychiatric illness that affects both the mind and body. Because children are not as articulate as adults in expressing their emotions, it is unlikely that they will be able to say, "I'm depressed." The National Alliance on Mental Illness (2008) indicates that it is important to know what signs to look for in order to help these children cope. The warning signs fall into four different categories: emotional signs, cognitive signs (those involving thinking), physical complaints, and behavioral changes. Not every child who is depressed will experience every symptom listed.

Symptoms of Childhood Depression

Emotional Symptoms

- Sadness—feelings of hopelessness—may cry easily
- Loss of pleasure or interest—those who have enjoyed playing sports may suddenly decide not to try out for the team; they may complain of feeling bored and choose not to participate in activities which they've always enjoyed in the past
- Anxiety—the child may become anxious, tense, and panicky—the source of the anxiety may provide a clue to what's causing the depression
- Turmoil—the child may feel worried and irritable

Cognitive Symptoms

- Difficulty organizing thought—this may be evidenced by problems in school or an inability to complete tasks
- Negative view—may become pessimistic perceiving themselves, their life, and their world in a very negative light
- Worthlessness and guilt—may obsess over their perceived faults and failures, feel tremendous guilt, and declare themselves worthless.
- Helplessness and hopelessness—often believe that there is nothing they can do to relieve their feelings of depression
- Feelings of isolation—may become very sensitive to slights from peers
- Suicidal thoughts—express thoughts and wishes of being dead

Physical Symptoms

- Change in appetite or weight—appetite will decrease or increase—children with a normally healthy appetite may suddenly lose interest in eating, or children may respond the opposite way and will begin eating too much to self-medicate feelings
- Sleep disturbances—may have difficulty falling asleep and staying asleep once they do—they may wake too early or oversleep; they may have trouble staying awake during the day at school
- Sluggishness—may talk, react, and walk slower, or they may be less active and playful than usual
- Agitation—exhibit fidgeting or not being able to sit still

Behavioral Symptoms

These signs will be the most obvious and easiest to detect.

- Avoidance and withdrawal—may avoid everyday or enjoyable activities—they may withdraw from friends and family, and the bedroom can become a favorite place to escape
- Clinging and demanding—may become more dependent on some relationships and behave with an exaggerated sense of insecurity
- Activities in excess—may appear to be out of control in regard to certain activities (e.g., playing video games for long hours or overeating)
- Restlessness—may exhibit fidgeting, acting up in class, or reckless behavior
- Self-harm—may cause themselves physical pain (self-injury) or take excessive risks

Medical Treatment of Depression

Treatment for depression involves a multifaceted approach. The first line of treatment is pharmacotherapy (medication) intervention. Effective antidepressant medications such as Wellbutrin, Serzone, Desyrel, Effexor, and Remeron have been shown to help a significant number of people experience complete remission or at least significant improvement in their symptoms. Psychotherapy (counseling) is another important component of the treatment of depression. This is thought to be the most effective form of treatment, especially when it is coupled with medication.

Educational Strategies for Depression

Given the statistics on the incidence of depression in children and adolescents, it is likely that all teachers will encounter students with depression at some time in their teaching careers. Students will remain in school throughout the assessment process, and after a formal diagnosis of depression, most students remain in school. It is therefore imperative that teachers are provided with strategies that will best support the child. The British Columbia Ministry of Education (2001) provides the following strategy suggestions.

Create an Inviting Classroom

All students must feel safe to take healthy risks. Students with depression may avoid school if they feel threatened or insecure there. Teachers *must* believe that they can make a difference in the lives of students. The emotional tone of the classroom is powerful.

- Demonstrate unconditional acceptance of students.
- Be a good listener.
- Avoid singling out the student with depression.
- Keep a positive tone—humor is great; sarcasm is hurtful.
- Keep suggestions for improvement constructive, specific, and brief.
- Avoid overgeneralizing—using words like "always" and "never."
- Be specific when providing feedback regarding academic or behavior improvement.
- Develop routines that are conducive to learning.

Teach and Require the Use of Organizational Strategies

Students with depression may need help keeping materials and assignments organized. Use the following strategies to help students be better organized.

- Provide reminders to students to use assignment books to record assignment and test requirements. For example, say, "Write this in your assignment book," each time an assignment is given. Memory is not reliable when a person is depressed.
- Provide opportunities and assistance with keeping desks, binders, backpacks, and lockers organized.
- Encourage students to use positive self-talk and problem solving when confronted by difficult work.
- Help students organize assignments, especially longer projects. Set a project timeline and check back frequently with the students to provide verbal reminders or deadlines and ask if the students need assistance to meet the deadline.

Provide Positive Interaction Experiences

While teachers are not responsible for providing specific therapy, appropriate interaction with students and portraying understanding of the disorder are essential for a supportive environment in which the student can learn.

- Maintain a pleasant, interested tone and be prepared to listen; do not press students for details on family problems.
- Find out what motivates students, such as working with pets or younger students, and how they learn best.
- Be aware of any special needs or learning problems.
- Initiate conversation when students arrive, leave, or during breaks, as students with depression are not likely to do so.
- Stop by student's desk during seatwork or sit in on small groups.
- Make accommodations for assignments and exams using the following:
  - Allow student to go to a quiet space.
  - Extend the amount of time given.
  - Allow more time to formulate answers and respond.
  - Check regularly to ensure class assignments are done.
  - Use a variety of assessment methods so students can demonstrate knowledge using their stronger skills.

Web Sites

Childhood Depression: Guidelines for Parents and Teachers: www.accg.net/Childhood Depression.htm

Resources for Parents and Teacher to Help Understand and Treat Depression: www.pbskids.org/itsmylife/parents/resources/depression.html

Resource Books

Title: *Beating Depression: Teens Find Light at the End of the Tunnel*

Authors: Faye Zucker and Joan E. Huebl

Publisher: Franklin Watts, 2007

Story Profile: A new and up-to-date resource for parents and children who are trying to find answers behind their feelings of despair and hopelessness. The book defines depression and gives guidance to what it looks and feels like. It also provides a scientifically based explanation as to what is happening inside the body causing depression as well as newly researched treatments that are being discovered everyday.

Title: *Help Me, I'm Sad*

Authors: David G. Fassler and Lynne S. Sumas

Publisher: Penguin USA, 1998

Story Profile: A reassuring guide for parents of adolescents whose lives are darkened by depression. This book helps to recognize, treat, and prevent childhood and adolescent depression.

Title: *My Depression: A Picture Book*

Author: Elizabeth Swados

Publisher: Hyperion, 2005

(Continued)

(Continued)

Story Profile: Elizabeth Swados candidly presents this zingy cartoon memoir in which she chronicles her struggles with severe depression. In expressively scribbled drawings and scrawled, to the point commentary, Swados charts the course her depression takes and itemizes the symptoms, which range from insulting her friend to failing to get out of bed. This seemingly simple talk conveys a wealth of helpful information and dispels the gloom a bit by making readers laugh.

Children's Resource

Title: *When Devon Met Oz: Helping Children Cope With Depression*

Authors: Mary Martin, Don Martin, and Erin Martin

Publisher: New Horizon Press, 2008

Story Profile: A friendship between a boxer dog named Oz and a boy named Devon develops at the park. Oz begins to realize that Devon is both sad and angry and follows Devon home so that he can make Devon's family aware that the boy needs help. Devon is sad, sleeps a lot, does not eat, worries about schoolwork, thinks he's bad at sports, and feels like the other kids don't like him. This sympathetic book includes reassuring advice and important tips from both children and parents on finding help.

SEASONAL AFFECTIVE DISORDER (SAD)

SAD is a depression caused by a specific season of the year, most often winter. Symptoms most often start in September or October and end in April or May. Specific symptoms of SAD may include the following.

- Feeling sad, grumpy, moody, or anxious
- Crying spells
- Loss of interest in usual activities
- Low energy level
- Increase in appetite
- Craving of carbohydrates, such as breads and pasta
- Weight gain
- Increase in sleep, feeling drowsy during the daytime

The depression experienced by people who have SAD is much more significant than the gloomy dullness felt by many people during the winter months. This disorder is one that is not taken seriously by many people.

Treatment of Seasonal Affective Disorder

SAD most often is treated by a doctor-prescribed light therapy. There are two types of light therapy.

Bright Light Treatment

- Patient sits in front of a "light box" for approximately a half hour, usually in the morning

Dawn Simulation

- A dim light goes on in the morning while patient sleeps, and it gets brighter over time, like a sunrise.

Light therapy works well for most people suffering from SAD. It is easy to use and relief from symptoms is felt within a week or so. It is important to continue with the therapy throughout the season, even if symptoms have disappeared, because symptoms could return quickly if light therapy is stopped.

SAD can also be treated with antidepressant medications such as Celexa, Prozac, Zoloft, Wellbutrin, Norpramin, or Effexor.

Educational Strategies for Seasonal Affective Disorder

- Communicate with parents and medical professionals to ensure the best educational programming during the critical stages of the disorder
- Be patient and understanding while waiting for the treatment to be effective
- Provide organization assistance

Web Sites

Light Therapy for Seasonal Affective Disorder (SAD), Winter Depression: www.bi-light.com

Seasonal Affective Disorder: www.Kidshealth.org/parent/emotions/feelings/sad.html

Resource Books

Title: *Banishing the Blues of Seasonal Affective Disorder*

Author: Bruce C. Barr

Publisher: Indoor Sun Shoppe, 2000

Story Profile: This publication is a very clear and easy-to-read book about SAD. It provides information regarding the diagnosis for this condition as well as treatment plans available. Partial treatment focuses on using bright light therapy for the successful treatment of SAD.

Title: *Winter Blues, Revised Edition: Everything You Need to Know to Beat Seasonal Affective Disorder*

Author: Norman E. Rosenthal

Publisher: The Guildford Press, 2005

Story Profile: Information is provided on the dimensions of SAD. The book includes a self-test to help evaluate your own level of SAD, as well as information regarding treatment of and coping with SAD.

ANXIETY DISORDERS

GENERALIZED ANXIETY DISORDER

The National Institute of Mental Health (2008) indicates that Generalized Anxiety Disorder (GAD) is a relatively common anxiety problem, affecting 3% to 4% of the population. People who struggle with this disorder tend to turn their daily life into a state of worry, anxiety, and fear by thinking and dwelling excessively on the "what ifs." GAD does not usually cause people to avoid situations, nor do they experience a "panic attack." It's more a matter of *thinking and dwelling and worrying and thinking and dwelling and worrying* to the point where they are unable to shut their mind off to irritation and overexaggerated thoughts of everyday events.

Symptoms of Generalized Anxiety Disorder

- Excessive, ongoing worry and tension
- An unrealistic view of problems
- Restlessness or a feeling of being "edgy"
- Irritability
- Muscle tension
- Headaches
- Sweating
- Difficulty concentrating
- Nausea
- Need to go to the bathroom frequently
- Tiredness
- Tardiness and/or absences
- Lack of interaction with peers
- Trouble falling or staying asleep
- Trembling
- Being easily startled
- Lack of energy or "zest" for life
- No desire to do much

Many times there is no "trigger" or "cause" for these feelings, and the person realizes these feelings are irrational. Nevertheless, the feelings are very real.

Treatment of Generalized Anxiety Disorder (GAD)

GAD treatments include psychological interventions (counseling), biological interventions (medicines), and accommodations at home and school that reduce sources of stress for the child. Frequent, ongoing interventions provided by the child's doctor, therapist, school staff, and family optimize the care and quality of life for the child.

Psychotherapy (Counseling)

Cognitive Behavior Therapy (CBT) is usually recommended for children and adolescents with Generalized Anxiety Disorder (GAD). The overall goals of the approach are to help children identify problematic beliefs and thought patterns, which are often irrational or unrealistic, and replace them with more rational and realistic views.

Pharmacotherapy (Medication)

Some children may also benefit from treatment with antidepressant or anti-anxiety medication to help them feel calmer while they are working through their psychotherapy. Medication alone is not considered the treatment of choice given the high likelihood for relapse for individuals who receive medication without psychotherapy. Medication such as Xanax, Librium, Valium, Ativan, Buspar, Paxil, and Effexor may be used to treat anxiety, as the medications work to decrease physical symptoms such as muscle tension and restlessness.

Educational Strategies for Generalized Anxiety Disorder

- Work closely with parents to develop expectations and strategies.
- Frequently communicate with parents and provide feedback from what you observe in the classroom.
- Encourage and provide support for students to meet expectations and completion of activities and assignments.
- Allow extra time to finish assignments and activities.
- Develop and follow a regular predictable classroom routine.
- Decrease homework load, when appropriate.
- Assist students in keeping an assignment book by helping them record assignment requirements and due dates.
- Allow students to take a "break" (e.g., get a drink, go to the bathroom) if they appear to become overwhelmed.

Web Sites

ADAA–Anxiety Disorders Association of America: www.adaa.org

Childhood Anxiety Network: www.childhoodanxietynetwork.org

Resource Books

Title: *Freeing Your Child From Anxiety: Powerful, Practical Solutions to Overcome Your Child's Fears, Worries, and Phobias*

Author: Tamar E. Chansky

Publisher: Broadway, 2004

Story Profile: This book is a great resource for anyone who is working with a child who suffers from anxiety. It provides practical and useful examples on what to do and what not to do to help a child with anxiety. It provides samples on language to use and how to handle different difficult day-to-day situations.

Title: *What to Do When You're Scared and Worried: A Guide for Kids*

Author: James J. Crist

Publisher: Free Spirit Publishing, 2004

Story Profile: This book provides advice, reassurance, and ideas to children who are experiencing frequent worrying and fears. The book explains where fears and worries come from and how the mind and body work together to make fears worse or better. He also describes various kinds of fears and offers 10 Fear Chasers and Worry Erasers kids can try to feel safer, stronger, and calmer. This book also includes a special "Note to Grown-ups" and a list of resources.

Title: *What to Do When You Worry Too Much: A Kid's Guide to Overcoming Anxiety*

Authors: Dawn Huebner and Bonnie Matthews

Publisher: Magination Press, 2005

Story Profile: An easy-to-understand book that shows children who worry a new way of life. They will learn solutions that really work through the cognitive-behavioral techniques. This self-help book is the complete resource for educating, motivation, and empowering kids to overcome their worries.

(Continued)

(Continued)

Children's Resource

Title: *David and the Worry Beast: Helping Children Cope With Anxiety*

Author: Anne Marie Guanci

Illustrator: Caroline Attia

Publisher: New Horizon Press, 2007

Story Profile: Learning to deal with anxiety is an important step in a child's healthy emotional growth. Conquering fears, and not avoiding them, is the lesson imparted in this story. David could not stop thinking about the basket he had missed at the end of the big game. He was worried that he might do it again. He was worried that his teammates would be angry with him. He was worried that his parents would not be proud of him. He was also worried about an upcoming math test. He worried a lot, wondered if he should "quit the team," and asked himself, "should I be sick tomorrow and miss the math test?" Luckily, David finally confided in his parents and school nurse, both of whom gave him support and techniques for controlling the "worry beast" within him.

OBSESSIVE COMPULSIVE DISORDER (OCD)

According to the National Institute of Mental Health (2008), OCD is an anxiety disorder in which people suffer intensely from recurrent, unwanted thoughts (obsessions), and/or repetitive behaviors (compulsions) that they feel they cannot control.

Symptoms of OCD

What Are Obsessions?

A kid who has OCD might have obsessions about illness or injury or cleanliness, but the thoughts and worries just do not quit. The brain keeps repeating them instead of moving on to something else. Obsessive thoughts also come with anxiety. With OCD, someone may have obsessions about the following.

- Germs or dirt
- Illness or injury (involving the person or someone else)
- Coming across unlucky numbers or words
- Things being even or straight
- Things being perfect or just right in a certain way
- Making mistakes or not being sure
- Doing or thinking something bad

What Are Compulsions?

Compulsions are behaviors or actions that someone with OCD does to try to shut down the worry thoughts. Another name for compulsions are rituals. By doing compulsions or performing rituals, people with OCD think they will keep the bad things they worry about from happening. Kids with OCD don't want to perform the rituals; however, they feel scared that if they don't do the rituals, something bad will happen to them or others. Some of the common COD compulsions include the following,

- Continuous hand washing or showering (much more frequent than usual or having a hard time stopping)
- Counting (such as having to count 25 white cars before going into school)
- Touching (touching every fence post between home and the bus stop)
- Checking things over and over (such as doors, lock, or stoves)
- Doing things a certain number of times (such as having to try on five dresses before leaving the room)
- Arranging things in a very particular or neat way
- Asking the same question over and over
- Tying and retying shoes over and over until they feel just right

Other illnesses that may be related to OCD are trichotillomania (the repeated urge to pull out scalp hair, eyelashes, eyebrows, or other body hair), body dysmorphic disorder (excessive preoccupation with imaginary or exaggerated defects in appearance), and hypochondriasis (the fear of having, despite medical evaluation and reassurance, a serious disease).

Treatment of Obsessive Compulsive Disorder

OCD treatments include psychological interventions (counseling), biological interventions (medicines), and accommodations at home and school that reduce sources of stress for the child. Frequent, ongoing interventions provided by the child's doctor, therapist, school staff, and family optimize the care and quality of life for the child.

Psychotherapy (Counseling)

Cognitive Behavior Therapy (CBT) is usually recommended for children and adolescents with OCD. Children are assisted in becoming aware of problem behaviors or thoughts in particular situations, and alternative behaviors are given to try in place of those situations. The focus is on replacing the compulsive and/or obsessive behaviors with more positive thinking patterns as alternatives to the negative thoughts.

Pharmacotherapy (Medication)

In addition to psychotherapy, the use of medication may also be appropriate and necessary. Antidepressants such as Anafranil, Luvox, Prozac, Celexa, Laxapro, Paxil, and Zoloft are all commonly prescribed medications for treating OCD. Most often, medications are noted to reduce rather than completely eliminate the symptoms.

Educational Strategies for Obsessive Compulsive Disorder

It is important for the teachers to be active members of the planning and programming team for a child with OCD. Team meetings will assist in developing appropriate school programming for the child. Effective accommodations, modifications, and strategies will include the following.

- Check in with the child each to day to determine if the child will find success in certain classes that day.
- Allow more time to complete homework, projects, and assignments.

- Accommodate late arrival due to symptoms at home.
- Have a plan in place, created with the support of the child's medical doctor and therapist, to assist the child in breaking out of an obsession or compulsion.
- Offer strategies, provided to you by the medical doctor and child's therapist, to assist the child in resisting uncomfortable thoughts.
- Allow the child to tape record homework if the child cannot touch writing materials.
- Give the child a choice of projects if the child has difficulty beginning a task.
- Suggest that the child change the sequence of homework problems or projects (e.g., if the child has fears related to odd or even numbers).
- Adjust the homework load to prevent the child from becoming overwhelmed. Academic stressors will aggravate symptoms.
- Help the child to identify less intrusive rituals (such as tapping one desk rather than tapping every desk).
- Assist with peer interactions to help minimize concerns for the child and peers.
- Understand that transitions may be difficult. When a child with OCD refuses to follow directions of transition to the next task, the reason may be anxiety related rather than opposition.
- Allow and encourage the child to help develop interventions. This will foster the child's ability to problem solve and will allow for ownership in the intervention to be taken.

Web Sites

Does Your Child Have OCD?: www.kidshealth.org/parent/emotions/behavior/OCD.html

Obsessive Compulsive Disorder: Symptoms, Tools, and More: www.ocdcenter.org

Resource Books

Title: *Confronting the Bully of OCD: Winning Back Our Freedom One Day at a Time*

Author: Linda Maran

Publisher: Fifteenth Street Publishing, 2004

Story Profile: A clearly written book and practical guide for all people suffering from OCD. It offers a great combination of a personal and professional story of OCD.

Title: *Rewind, Replay, Repeat: A Memoir of Obsessive-Compulsive Disorder*

Author: Jeff Bell

Publisher: Hazelden, 2007

Story Profile: A memoir written by Jeff Bell, a husband, father, and highly successful radio news anchor, who was living with obsessive-compulsive disorder. This story recounts the depth to which this disorder reduced him to driving his car in continuous circles, scouring his hands in scalding water, and endlessly rewinding, replaying, and repeating in his head even the most mundane daily experiences. It is an attempt to explain what OCD feels like and how healing is possible.

Children's Resources

Title: *Mr. Worry: A Story About OCD*

Author: Holly L. Niner

Illustrator: Greg Swearingen

Publisher: Albert Whitman & Company, 2004

Story Profile: A story about a young boy named Kevin who is trying to overcome the terrors of OCD in his daily life. Kevin receives support from all the people in his life as they try to help him manage his problem, which he names Mr. Worry. The use of simple language and straightforward information clarifies the situation, and readers are soon cheering for his success.

Title: *Up and Down the Worry Hill: A Children's Book About Obsessive-Compulsive Disorder and Its Treatment*

Authors: Aureen P. Wagner and Paul A. Jutton

Publisher: Lighthouse Press, 2004

Story Profile: Over one million children and adolescents in the United States suffer from OCD, a baffling illness that can be debilitating for the child in school, with friends, and family.

Title: *What to Do When Your Brain Gets Stuck: A Kid's Guide to Overcoming OCD*

Author: Dawn Huebner

Illustrator: Bonnie Matthews

Publisher: Magination Press, 2007

Story Profile: A guide for children and their parents through cognitive-behavioral techniques used to treat OCD. This self-help book turns kids into super-sleuths who can recognize OCD's tricks. Examples, activities, and step-by-step instructions help children master the skills needed to break free from the sticky thoughts and urges of OCD and live happier lives.

PANIC DISORDER

People with panic disorder suffer unexpected and repeated episodes of intense, overwhelming terror for no apparent reason (panic attacks). A panic attack is a brief period of intense fear or discomfort accompanied by distinct symptoms. An attack usually comes to a gradual end on its own and rarely lasts beyond 10 minutes.

Symptoms of Panic Disorder

- Heart palpitations
- Chest discomfort
- Sweating
- Trembling
- Nausea
- Numbness or tingling
- Hot/cold flashes
- Feeling short of breath
- Feeling dizzy
- Feeling disconnected from oneself
- Fear of losing control
- Fear of dying

Treatment of Panic Disorder

Panic disorder treatments include psychological interventions (counseling), biological interventions (medicines), and accommodations at home and school that reduce sources of stress for the child. Frequent, ongoing interventions provided by the child's doctor, therapist, school staff, and family optimize the care and quality of life for the child.

Psychotherapy (Counseling)

CBT is usually recommended for children and adolescents with panic disorder. Children are guided and trained to think of new, more positive alternatives, including techniques for anticipating and preventing the emergence of full-blown panic attacks.

Pharmacotherapy (Medication)

In addition to psychotherapy, the use of medication may also be appropriate and necessary. Antidepressants such as Luvox, Prozac, Celexa, Laxapro, Paxil, and Zoloft are all commonly prescribed medications for treating panic disorder. Most often, medications are noted to reduce rather than eliminate the symptoms.

Educational Strategies for Panic Disorder

It is important for the teachers to be an active member of the planning and programming team for a child with panic disorder. Team meetings will assist in developing appropriate school programming for the child. Effective accommodations, modification, and strategies will include the following.

- Check in with the child each day to determine if the child will find success in certain classes that day.
- Allow the student to "cue" teachers or staff if a panic attack is occurring so that the student can go to a less stressful (or embarrassing environment).
- Reward the student, when appropriate, for efforts to remain in class and control the panic attacks.
- Allow more time to complete homework, projects, and assignments.
- Accommodate late arrival due to symptoms at home.
- Offer strategies, provided to you by the medical doctor and child's therapist, to assist the child in resisting uncomfortable thoughts.
- Adjust the homework load to prevent the child from becoming overwhelmed. Academic stressors will aggravate symptoms.
- Develop relaxation techniques to help reduce anxiety at school. Using techniques developed at home can be beneficial.
- Identify a safe place within the school building where the child may go to reduce anxiety during stressful periods.
- Anticipate issues such as school avoidance if there are unresolved social and/or academic problems.
- Understand that transitions may be difficult. When a child with panic disorder refuses to follow directions of transition to the next task, the reason may be anxiety related rather than opposition.
- Allow and encourage the child to help develop interventions. This will foster the child's ability to problem solve and will allow for ownership in the intervention to be taken.

Web Sites

Anxiety/Panic Attack Resource Site: www.anxietypanic.com

Panic Disorder in Children and Adolescents: www.childanxiety.net/Panic.htm

Resource Books

Title: *10 Simple Solutions to Panic: How to Overcome Panic Attacks, Calm Physical Symptoms, and Reclaim Your Life*

Authors: Martin M. Antony and Randi E. McCabe

Publisher: New Harbinger Publications, 2004

Story Profile: This book provides easy-to-follow guidelines that will help sufferers of panic attacks better understand their condition and gain control over it. Readers will learn how to monitor episodes of panic and find out how to replace anxious, racing inner thoughts with calm, realistic thinking. Breathing exercises and stress reduction techniques are examples given to overcome the panic.

Title: *Panic Attacks Workbook: A Guided Program for Beating the Panic Trick*

Author: David Carbonell

Publisher: Ulysses Press, 2004

Story Profile: This book will help people understand the true nature of their panic attacks. It demonstrates the vicious cycle of habitual responses that lead to a debilitation attack, teaches how to halt this self-destructive process, and guides people along a proven path that promotes recovery. Such cognitive-behavioral methods such as diaphragmatic breathing, progressive exposure, desensitization, relaxation, keeping a panic diary, and much more are described.

PHOBIA

According to information provided by the Childhood Anxiety Network (2001), a phobia is a persistent, irrational fear of something, either an object or a situation. This phobia produces a compelling desire to avoid the feared object of situation. People who have a phobia are unable to control their emotions and may try to avoid the object creating the phobia. Some students experience school phobias and will try to avoid school at all costs.

Examples of Specific Phobias

Situational Type (Fear of Specific Situations)

- Riding public transportation
- Riding in a car
- Driving
- Airplanes
- Tunnels
- Bridges
- School

Natural Environment Type (Fear of Natural Environment Things)

- Storms
- Heights
- Water

- Animal Type
- Animals
- Insects

Blood-Injection-Injury Type (Fear of Seeing Blood or Invasive Medical Procedures)

- Injections
- Blood tests
- Injury

Other Type (Fear Cued From Other Stimuli)

- Falling down
- Loud sounds

Physical Symptoms of Phobia

- Dizziness
- Shaking
- Heart palpitations
- Obsessive thoughts (difficulty thinking about anything other than the fear)
- Desire to flee (an intense instinct to leave the situation)
- Anticipatory anxiety (persistent worrying about upcoming events that involve the phobic object or situation)

Treatment of Phobia

Phobia treatments include psychological interventions (counseling), biological interventions (medicines), and accommodations at home and school that reduce sources of stress for the child. Frequent, ongoing interventions provided by the child's doctor, therapist, school staff, and family optimize the care and quality of life for the child.

Psychotherapy (Counseling)

CBT is usually recommended for children and adolescents with phobia disorder. Children are guided to help become aware of and describe negative thoughts, feelings, or reactions surrounding the phobic encounters. They are then trained to think of new, more positive alternatives when having to interact in situations that increase the phobia.

Pharmacotherapy (Medication)

In addition to psychotherapy, the use of medication may also be appropriate and necessary. Antidepressants such as Luvox, Prozac, Celexa, Lexapro, Paxil, and Zoloft are all commonly prescribed medications for treating phobia disorder. Most often, medications are noted to reduce rather than eliminate the symptoms.

Educational Strategies for Phobias

The most common phobia interfering with a child's ability to make progress and learn in the school setting is school or social phobia. The strategies provided below are interventions that can be attempted to assist children who suffer from social phobia to succeed in the classroom.

It is important for the teachers to be active members of the planning and programming team for a child with phobia disorder. Team meetings will assist in developing appropriate school programming for the child. Effective accommodations, modifications, and strategies will include the following.

- Check in on arrival to reduce the child's initial anxiety and facilitate transition into school.
- Identify a safe place where the child may go to reduce anxiety during stressful periods.
- Develop and encourage the use of relaxation techniques to help reduce anxiety at school.
- Accommodate late arrival due to difficulty separating.
- Adjust the homework load to prevent the child from becoming overwhelmed. Academic stressors will aggravate symptoms.
- Modify stressful social situations (e.g., develop a small lunch group for the child or speak to the child individually rather than in a large group).
- If the child or adolescent is avoiding school, address the cause and initiate an immediate plan for returning to school. This may require implementing a gradual reintroduction plan by allowing the student to attend for less than a full day at first.
- Understand that transitions may be difficult. When a child with social phobia refuses to follow directions of transition to the next task, the reason may be anxiety related rather than opposition.
- Reward a child's efforts. Every good effort deserves to be praised.
- Provide assistance with peer interactions. An adult's help may be very beneficial for both the child and peers.

Web Sites

Childhood Specific Phobia Disorder: www.childhoodanxietynetwork.org/htdocs/htm/sp.htm

Self-Help for Specific Phobia: www.anxietybc.comresources/specific.php

Resource Books

Title: *Anxiety, Phobias, and Panic*

Author: Reneau Z. Peurifoy

Publisher: Grand Central Publishing, 2005

Story Profile: This book helps readers to understand and overcome all types of anxiety-related disorders. Anxiety is an unpleasant, although mostly unavoidable aspect of life, and for many, it can be serious and debilitating. Information in this book provides readers with information on how their condition developed and how to overcome their problems. Specific areas include the causes of anxiety, building stress tolerance, identifying and correcting harmful modes of thinking, relaxation techniques, and tools for managing anxiety.

Title: *Freeing Your Child From Anxiety: Powerful, Practical Solutions to Overcome Your Child's Fears, Worries, and Phobias*

Author: Tamar E. Chansky

Publisher: Broadway, 2004

Story Profile: This book is a great resource for anyone who is working with a child who suffers from anxiety. It provides practical and useful examples on what to do and what not to do to help a child with anxiety. It provides samples on language to use and how to handle different, difficult day-to-day situations.

Post Traumatic Stress Disorder (PTSD)

PTSD is an anxiety disorder that can develop after exposure to a terrifying event or ordeal in which grave physical harm occurred or was threatened. As described by the National Center for PTSD (2007), traumatic events that may trigger PTSD include violent personal assaults, natural or human-caused disasters, accidents, or military combat.

Symptoms of PTSD

There are three groups of symptoms that are required to be evident in order for the diagnosis of PTSD to be assigned.

Recurrent Re-Experiencing of the Trauma

- Troublesome memories
- Flashbacks that are usually caused by reminders of the traumatic events
- Recurring nightmares about the trauma
- Reliving of the trauma

Avoidance to the Point of Having a Phobia About Specific Things

- People
- Places
- Experiences that remind the sufferer of the trauma

Chronic Physical Signs of Hyperarousal

- Sleep problems
- Trouble concentrating
- Irritability
- Anger
- Poor concentration
- Blackouts
- Difficulty remembering things
- Increased tendency and reaction to be startled

Treatment for Post Traumatic Stress Disorder

PTSD treatments include psychological interventions (counseling), biological interventions (medicines), and accommodations at home and school that reduce sources of stress for the child. Frequent, ongoing interventions provided by the child's doctor, therapist, school staff, and family optimize the care and quality of life for the child.

Psychotherapy (Counseling)

CBT is usually recommended for children and adolescents with PTSD.

Pharmacotherapy (Medication)

Some children may also benefit from treatment with antidepressant or anti-anxiety medication to help them feel calmer while they are working through their psychotherapy. Medication alone is not considered the treatment of choice, given the likelihood of relapse for individuals who receive medication without psychotherapy. Antidepressants such as Prozac, Catapres, Tenex, Paxil, and Zoloft are all commonly prescribed medications for treating PTSD. Most often, medications are noted to reduce rather than eliminate the symptoms.

Educational Strategies for PTSD

The strategies provided below are interventions that can be attempted to assist children who suffer from PTSD to succeed in the classroom. It is important for the teachers to be active members of the planning and programming team for a child with PTSD. Team meetings will assist in developing appropriate school programming for the child. Effective accommodations, modifications, and strategies may include the following.

- Check in on arrival to reduce the child's initial anxiety and facilitate transition into school.
- Identify a safe place where the child may go to reduce anxiety during stressful periods.
- Develop and encourage the use of relaxation techniques to help reduce anxiety at school.
- Accommodate late arrival due to earlier encountered difficulties.
- Adjust the homework load to prevent the child from becoming overwhelmed. Academic stressors will aggravate symptoms.
- Modify stressful social situations (e.g., develop a small lunch group for the child or speak to the child individually rather than in a large group).
- Understand that transitions may be difficult. When a child with PTSD refuses to follow directions of transition to the next task, the reason may be anxiety related rather than opposition.
- Reward a child's efforts. Every good effort deserves to be praised.
- Provide assistance with peer interactions. An adult's help may be very beneficial for both the child and peers.

Web Sites

National Center for PTSD: www.ncptsd.va.gov

Post Traumatic Stress Disorder (PTSD) WebMD: www.webmd.com/anxiety-pani/guide/post-traumatic-stress-disorder

Resource Book

Title: *Supporting Children With Post Traumatic Stress Disorder: A Practical Guide for Teachers and Professionals*

Author: David Kinchin

Publisher: David Fulton Publish, 2001

Story Profile: It is estimated that at any one time, around 135,000 schoolchildren are suffering from PTSD. They may be survivors of abuse or bullying. Some may have been involved in a road accident, accident at home, or any other traumatic event. This book provides teachers, support staff, and other educational professionals with the information they need to really understand the implications of PTSD and effectively support and educate a traumatized child. This also helps teachers to understand how PTSD might affect the education of children at school.

(Continued)

(Continued)

Children's Resource

Title: *The Handbook for Helping Kids With Anxiety and Stress*

Authors: Tip Frank and Kim Frank

Publisher: Youthlight, 2003

Story Profile: This book provides a collection of practical, easy-to-follow tips and activities to help kids with various types of fears, anxieties, and phobias. The first section includes insights, hints, and suggestions for helping professionals and parents who are working to help kids learn to cope with their anxiety and stress. The second section is for kids themselves. It includes stories, activities, and suggestions that can help kids face their fears.

SEPARATION ANXIETY DISORDER

Separation anxiety disorder is described as excessive worry and fear about being apart from family members or individuals to whom a child is most attached. Children with separation anxiety disorder fear being lost from their family or fear something bad will happen to a family member if they are separated from them. According to Separation Anxiety Solution (2008), symptoms of anxiety or fear about being separated from family members must last for a period of at least four weeks to be considered a separation anxiety disorder.

Symptoms of Separation Anxiety Disorder

Specific symptoms associated with separation anxiety disorder that may be seen in the school setting include the following.

- Difficulty transitioning from home to school
  - Late arrival times
  - Long and tearful morning drop-offs
  - Tantrums at school
- Refusal or reluctance to attend school
  - Child may insist on staying home
- Avoidance of activities
- Low self-esteem
  - In social and situations and academic activities
- Difficulty concentrating
  - Persistent worry
  - Difficulty following directions
  - Difficulty completing assignment
  - Difficulty paying attention
- Behavioral or cognitive effects from medication

Treatment for Separation Anxiety Disorder

Anxiety disorders can be effectively treated. The treatment should always be based on a comprehensive evaluation of the child and family. Treatment recommendations may include the following.

Psychotherapy (Counseling)

CBT is the most common type of therapy used, where the focus is to help the child or adolescent learn skills to manage the anxiety and to help the child master the situations that contribute to the anxiety.

Pharmacotherapy (Medication)

Some children may also benefit from treatment with antidepressant or anti-anxiety medication to help them feel calmer while they are working through their psychotherapy. Medication alone is not considered the treatment of choice given the high likelihood of relapse for individuals who receive medication without psychotherapy. Antidepressants such as Celexa, Lexapro, Luvox, Paxil, Prozac, and Zoloft are commonly prescribed to treat the symptoms of separation anxiety disorder.

Educational Accommodations and Modifications for Separation Anxiety Disorder

- Check in on arrival to reduce the child's initial anxiety and facilitate transition into school.
- Identify a safe place where the child may go to reduce anxiety during stressful periods.
- Develop and encourage the use of relaxation techniques to help reduce anxiety at school.
- Accommodate late arrival due to earlier encountered difficulties.
- Adjust the homework load to prevent the child from becoming overwhelmed. Academic stressors will aggravate symptoms.
- Provide time for the child to convey messages to family. Brief contact with family may substantially reduce anxiety and may help children recognize that their connection to their parent is intact.
- Ask the parent to send short notes for the child to read as a reward for staying in school. These can also be placed in the child's lunchbox or locker.
- If the child or adolescent is avoiding school, address the cause and initiate an immediate plan for him or her to return. This may require a gradual reintroduction to school, and the child may readjust more quickly if allowed to attend for partial days at first.
- Understand that transitions may be difficult. When a child with separation anxiety disorder refuses to follow directions for transition to the next task, the reason may be anxiety related rather than opposition.
- Reward a child's efforts. Every good effort deserves to be praised.
- Provide assistance with peer interactions. An adult's help may be very beneficial for both the child and peers.
- Encourage the child to help develop interventions. Asking the child for ideas in the task will lead to more successful strategies and will foster the child's ability to problem solve.

Web Sites

Separation Anxiety: www.kidshealth.org/parent/emotions/feelings/separation_anxiety.htm

The Separation Anxiety Solution: www.separation-anxiety-solution.com

Resource Book

Title: *Helping Your Child Overcome Separation Anxiety or School Refusal: A Step-by-Step Guide for Parents*

Authors: Andrew R. Eisen, Linda B. Engler, and Joshua Sparrow

Publisher: New Harbinger Publications, 2006

Story Profile: Written by a child anxiety expert, this parenting book focuses specifically on separation anxiety disorder, providing parents with the skills they need to cope with distressing challenges such as tantrums, nightmares, inconsolable crying, and screaming that occur during times of separation.

Children's Resources

Title: *I Don't Want to Go to School: Helping Children Cope With Separation Anxiety*

Author: Nancy Pando

Illustrator: Kathy Voerg

Publisher: New Horizon Press, 2005

Story Profile: Separation anxiety is common in young children and can make going to school a trial. This book teachers children coping skills and reminds them that they can love, even miss, their parents and still enjoy school. In addition, it provides specific tips for both children and parents.

Title: *Will You Come Back for Me?*

Author: Ann Tompert

Illustrator: Robin Kramer

Publisher: Albert Whitman & Company, 1992

Story Profile: Four-year-old Suki is worried about being left in day care for the first time until her mother reassures her that she loves her and will always return for her.

BEHAVIORAL DISORDERS

CONDUCT DISORDERS

The American Academy of Child and Adolescent Psychiatry (2004a), describes conduct disorders as a childhood behavior disorder that is characterized by a consistent pattern of having difficulty following rules and behaving in a socially acceptable way. Others often view them as being "bad" or delinquent rather than mentally ill.

Symptoms of Conduct Disorders

Children with conduct disorders may exhibit some of the following behaviors.

Aggressive With People

- Bullies, threatens, or intimidates others
- Often initiates physical fight
- Uses a weapon that could cause serious physical harm (e.g., bat, brick, broken bottle, knife, or gun)
- Physically cruel to people and/or animals
- Steals from a victim while confronting them (e.g., assault)
- Forces someone into sexual activity

Destruction of Property

- Deliberately engages in fire setting with the intention to cause damage
- Deliberately destroys other's property

Deceitfulness, Lying, or Stealing

- Has broken into someone else's building, house, or car
- Lies to obtain goods or favors or to avoid obligations
- Steals items without confronting a victim (e.g., shoplifting)

Serious Violations of Rules

- Often stays out at night despite parental objections
- Runs away from home
- Often truant from school

Children with conduct disorder consistently break rules, often act in aggressive or threatening ways, may destroy property, and show little regard for others. These behaviors must occur over an extended period of time. A diagnosis of conduct disorder is not considered unless the child has displayed such behavior for a year or more.

Treatment of Conduct Disorders (CD)

Treatment of children with conduct disorders can be challenging, as it is necessary to utilize treatment approaches that address both the child and the environment. Behavioral therapy and psychotherapy can help a child with CD to control anger and develop new coping skills. Family group therapy is often essential, and parents need to be counseled on how to set appropriate limits with their child and be consistent and realistic when disciplining. If an abusive home life is at the root of the conduct problem, every effort should be made to move the child to a more supportive environment. Treatment is often very time consuming and lengthy, as establishing new attitudes and behavior patterns take time. Treatment recommendations may include the following.

Family Therapy

Intense family therapy is essential in order for parents to understand the seriousness of their child's behavior, as well as the probability of a poor, long-term prognosis if there is no significant parental intervention.

Behavioral Therapy and Psychotherapy (Counseling)

CBT is the most common type of therapy used, where the focus is to help the child or adolescent learn skills to manage the disorder and to help the child master the situations that contribute to the disorder.

Pharmacotherapy (Medication)

While there are no formally approved medications for conduct disorder, some medication have been seen to help specific symptoms. Some children may benefit from treatment with antidepressant or anti-anxiety medication to help them feel calmer while they are working through their psychotherapy. Such medications that have been used to promote positive growth when working with conduct disorders include stimulants such as Dexedrine and Ritalin, antidepressants such as Wellbutrin and Prozac, and anticonvulsants such as Dilantin, Tegretol, and Depakene.

Educational Accommodations and Modifications for Conduct Disorders

- Establish clear and consistent rules. Rules should be few, fair, clear, displayed, taught, and consistently enforced. Be clear about what is nonnegotiable.
- Ensure curriculum is at the appropriate level. Frustration sets in easily if expectations appear too hard, boredom if expectations are too easy.
- Provide age appropriate materials to teach basic skills.
- Use technology when possible. Computers with active programs tend to work well.
- Provide possible learning opportunities outside of the school setting; the school setting can be intimidating and stress producing.
- Avoid power struggles and arguments at all costs. Youth with CD like to argue; be sure to remain calm and detached.
- Provide respect. Monitor impressions, keep them neutral, and communicate in a positive regard for students. Give students the benefit of the doubt whenever possible.
- Avoid escalating prompts such as shouting, touching, nagging, or cornering a student.
- Give students options. Stay away from direct demands or statement such as "you must" or "you need to."
- Reward a child's efforts. Every good effort deserves to be praised.
- Specifically teach social skills such as anger management, conflict resolution skills, and appropriate assertiveness.

Web Sites

Mental Health America: Conduct Disorder: www.mentalhealthamerica.net/go/conduct-disorder

Support for Parent of Difficult-to-Parent Children: www.conductdisorders.com

Resource Books

Title: *Conduct Disorders: The Latest Assessment and Treatment Strategies*
Author: Mark J. Eddy
Publisher: Jones and Bartlett Publishers, 2006

Story Profile: The conduct disorders are considered some of the most costly child mental health problems in the United States and account for nearly one half of referrals for children's mental health treatment. Specific information regarding the identification and treatment of CD is provided in this resource.

Title: *Creative Interventions for Troubled Children and Youth*

Author: Liana Lowenstein

Publisher: Champion Press, 1999

Story Profile: This resource is filled with creative interventions that help youth to navigate the troubled waters of childhood. Covering topics that range from emotional literacy to self-esteem building, the techniques presented are both practical and playful. The flexible format of the book allows room for interventions to be used for individual, family, or group sessions.

Title: *Helping Children With Aggression and Conduct Problems: Best Practices for Intervention*

Authors: Michael L. Bloomquist and Steven V. Schnell

Publisher: The Guilford Press, 2002

Story Profile: This book is an excellent resource for those professionals working in mental health, social welfare, and school settings that provides an up-to-date overview of the research base and clinical procedures for intervening with childhood aggression and conduct problems.

Children's Resources

Title: *How to Take the GRRR Out of Anger*

Authors: Elizabeth Verdick and Marjorie Lisovskis

Publisher: Free Spirit Publishing, 2002

Story Profile: This book speaks directly to kids and offers strategies that they can start using immediately on how to manage their anger. Blending tips and ideas with jokes and funny cartoons, it guides kids to understand that anger is normal and can be expressed in many ways.

Title: *What to Do When Your Temper Flares: A Kid's Guide to Overcoming Problems With Anger*

Author: Dawn Huebner

Illustrator: Bonnie Matthews

Publisher: Magination Press, 2007

Story Profile: This book provides engaging examples, lively illustrations, and step-by-step instruction to teach children a set of "anger dousing" methods aimed at cooling angry thoughts and controlling angry actions, resulting in calmer, more effective kids.

OPPOSITIONAL DEFIANCE DISORDER (ODD)

All children are oppositional from time to time, particularly when tired, hungry, stressed, or upset, and such behavior is a very normal part of development for two to three year olds and early adolescents. However, openly uncooperative and hostile behavior becomes a serious concern when it is so frequent and consistent that it stands out when compared with other children of the same age and developmental level and when it affects the child's social, family, and academic life. According to the American Academy of Child and Adolescent Psychiatry (2004b), children with ODD exhibit an ongoing pattern of uncooperative, defiant, and hostile behavior toward authority figures that seriously interferes with the child's day-to-day functioning. Behaviors frequently displayed may include the following.

- Frequent temper tantrums
- Excessive arguing with adults
- Active defiance and refusal to comply with adult requests and rules
- Deliberate attempts to annoy or upset people
- Blaming others for mistakes of misbehavior
- Often being touchy or easily annoyed by others
- Frequent anger and resentment
- Mean and hateful talking when upset
- Seeking revenge

These symptoms are usually seen in multiple settings but may be more noticeable at home or at school.

Treatment for ODD

A comprehensive evaluation should be conducted to look for other disorders that may be present. It may be difficult to improve the symptoms of ODD without treating any other disorders that may exist. Treatment of ODD may include the following.

- Parent training programs to help manage the child's behavior
- Individual psychotherapy (counseling) to develop effective anger management skills
- Family psychotherapy to improve communication
- CBT to assist problem solving and decrease negativity
- Social skills training to increase flexibility and improve frustration tolerance with peers

Educational Accommodation/Modification for ODD

- Always build on the positives; provide positive reinforcement when flexibility or cooperation is shown.
- Pick your battles; decide which behaviors you are going to ignore. It is difficult to include all behaviors in a behavior management plan. Thus, target only a few important behaviors rather than trying to fix everything.
- Provide consistency, structure, and clear consequences for the student's behavior.
- Establish clear classroom rules. Be clear about what is nonnegotiable.
- Post the daily schedule so the student will know what to expect.
- Establish rapport with the child. If the child perceives you as reasonable and fair, you'll be able to work more effectively with him or her.
- Avoid making comments or bringing up situations that may be a source of argument for them.
- Never raise your voice or argue with this student. Regardless of the situation do not get into a "yes you will" contest. Silence is a better response.
- Do not take defiance personally. Remember, you are the outlet and not the cause for the defiance, unless you are shouting, arguing, or attempting to handle the student with sarcasm.
- Avoid all power struggles with this student. They will get you nowhere. Thus, try to avoid verbal exchanges. State your position clearly and concisely and choose your battles wisely.

- Make sure academic work is at the appropriate level. When work is too hard, students become frustrated. When it is too easy, they become bored.
- Systematically teach social skills. Include anger management, conflict resolution, and how to be assertive in an appropriate manner.
- Select materials that encourage student interaction. Students with ODD need to learn to talk to their peers and to adults in an appropriate manner.
- Minimize downtime and plan transitions carefully. Students with ODD do best when kept busy.
- Allow the ODD students to redo assignments to improve their score or final grade.
- Structure activities so the student with ODD is not always left out or the last person picked.

Web Sites

Solutions to Oppositional Defiant Disorder: www.guidance-facilitators.com

Troubled Teens With Oppositional Defiance Disorder: www.4troubledteens.com

Resource Books

Title: *131 Creative Strategies for Reaching Children With Anger Problems*

Author: Tom Carr

Publisher: Educational Media Corporation, 2004

Story Profile: This practical guide is full of insight, techniques, and activities for managing and helping chronically angry children and ODD children. It provides teachers, counselors, parents, and other professionals with numerous helpful strategies for dealing with challenges they face when attempting to reach and help these children.

Title: *Defying the Defiance: 151 Insights, Strategies, Lessons, and Activities for Helping Students With ODD*

Authors: Kim Frank, Mike Paget, and Jerry Wilde

Publisher: YouthLight, 2005

Story Profile: This book will help the classroom teacher find effective ways to avoid disruption and increase cooperation from the most resistant students. As you begin to understand the underlying causes and dynamics of opposition, you will be able to develop additional strategies that will lead to increased classroom success and satisfaction for both the defiant student and the teacher.

Children's Resources

Title: *Don't Rant and Rave on Wednesdays! The Children's Anger-Control Book*

Author: Adolph Moser

Illustrator: David Melton

Publisher: Landmark Editions, 1994

Story Profile: This wonderful book for children explains anger as the feeling we have when we are really annoyed or really mad. Anger, children learn here, affects their thinking, excites emotions, and makes muscles tense. The book also explains that to become productive and happy, kids should avoid being angry.

(Continued)

(Continued)

Title: *A Volcano in My Tummy: Helping Children to Handle Anger*

Author: Elaine Whitehouse and Warwick Pudney

Publisher: New Society Publishers, 1996

Story Publisher: This book presents a clear and effective approach to helping children understand and deal constructively with children's anger. This book presents easy to understand, yet rarely taught skills for anger management and includes how to teach communication of emotions. Well-organized activities are offered that will help to overcome the fear of children's anger.

■ HEARING IMPAIRMENT

Children receiving services for a hearing impairment generally exhibit difficulty with hearing, whether permanent or fluctuating, that adversely affects educational performance. Sound is measured by its loudness (measured in units called decibels, dB) and its frequency or pitch (measured in units called hertz, Hz). Impairments in hearing can occur in either or both areas and may exist in only one ear or in both ears. Hearing loss is generally described as slight, mild, moderate, severe, or profound depending upon how well a person can hear the intensities or frequencies most greatly associated with speech. Deafness is a hearing impairment so severe that the child cannot understand what is being said even with a hearing aid.

Educational Approaches for Hearing Impairments

The American Society for Deaf Children (2006) explains that hearing loss or deafness does not affect a person's intellectual capacity or ability to learn. Children who are hard of hearing will find it much more difficult than children who have normal hearing to learn vocabulary, grammar, word order, idiomatic expressions, and other aspects of verbal communication. Services that may be beneficial for children in the educational setting may include the following.

- Regular speech, language, and auditory training from a specialist
- Amplification systems
- Services of an interpreter for those students who use sign language
- Seating within 10 feet of the teacher to facilitate lip reading and better interpret visual cues
- When speaking to the student, face the student and speak in a normal conversational voice—do not overexaggerate mouth movements
- Write assignments on the board and then face the student before explaining the assignment
- Use captioned films/videos
- Assistance of a note taker so the student can fully attend to instruction
- Consider the lighting in the room—it should not fall directly on the face of the student, as it will make it difficult for the student to observe the teacher and will make it harder for the student to lip-read or interpret the teacher's visual clues
- Instruction for the teacher and peers in alternate communication methods such as sign language

Educational Approaches for Deafness

As mentioned under the "Deafness" section, more than 60% of children who are deaf in the Unites States attend local school programs, and many are included in the regular classroom at least part of the day. Deafness does not affect a person's intellectual capacity or ability to learn; however, children who are deaf generally require some form of special education services in order to receive adequate instruction. The most difficult problem in educating deaf students is teaching spoken language to children who cannot hear. Many deaf students are not able to communicate effectively with classmates and therefore benefit by having a sign language interpreter to assist with the communication barrier. It is important for teachers and audiologists to work together to teach the child to use his or her residual hearing to the maximum extent possible, even if the preferred means of communication is manual.

Web Sites

Alexander Graham Bell Association for the Deaf and Hard of Hearing: www.agbell.org

American Society for Deaf Children: www.deafchildren.org

American Speech-Language-Hearing Association: www.asha.org

Resource Book

Title: *Helping Deaf and Hard of Hearing Students to Use Spoken Language: A Guide for Educators and Families*

Authors: Susan Easterbrooks and Ellen L. Estes

Publisher: Corwin, 2007

Story Profile: As a result of IDEA 2004 and NCLB, students with hearing loss are frequently being educated alongside their peers in the general education classroom. This book provides teachers and service professionals with the knowledge and skills in spoken language development to meet the needs of students who are deaf or hard of hearing. It is an essential resource that addresses creative and scientific ways of interacting with children and provides effective approaches, techniques, and strategies for working with children to develop spoken communication.

Children's Resources

Title: *Moses Goes to School*

Author: Isaac Millmans

Publisher: Farrar, Straus, and Giroux (BYR), 2000

Story Profile: Moses goes to a special school where he and all of his classmates are deaf or hard of hearing. Everyone in the school communicates in American Sign Language (ASL), using visual signs and facial expressions. The story follows Moses through his first day of school, telling the story in pictures and written English and in ASL, introducing readers to the signs of the key words and ideas.

Title: *Some Kids Are Deaf (Understanding Differences)*

Author: Lola M. Schaefer

Publisher: Capstone Press, 2008

Story Profile: Simple text and photographs describe the condition of deafness and some of the everyday activities of children who are deaf.

(Continued)

(Continued)

Title: *Tell Me How the Wind Sounds*

Author: Leslie D. Guccione

Publisher: Scholastic Paperbacks, 1989

Story Profile: Amanda is 15 when she meets Jake on Clard's Island. She is angered at every encounter with him until he tells her he is deaf.

Title: *When I Grow Up*

Author: Candri Hodges

Publisher: Jason and Nordic Publishers, 1994

Story Profile: Jimmy is a deaf youth who takes a field trip and encounters various careers of deaf individuals.

■ MENTAL RETARDATION

This category refers to a condition resulting in significantly below-average intellectual functioning and concurrent deficits in adaptive behavior that adversely affect educational performance and require special education and related services. This category does not include conditions primarily due to sensory or physical impairments, traumatic brain injury, autism, severe multiple impairments, cultural influences, or inconsistent educational programming.

Adaptive Functioning Skills for Mental Retardation

- Daily living skills such as getting dressed, using the bathroom, and feeding oneself
- Communication skills such as understanding what is said and being able to answer
- Social skills with peers, family members, spouses, adults, and others

For programming purposes, once a student has met the eligibility criteria to receive special education and related services in the category of mental retardation, the student may be placed into either the mild-moderate range or the severe-profound range. A student's intellectual functioning, as indicated by an intelligence quotient (IQ) below 70, is necessary in order for the student to be considered in the mild-moderate range. A student must also demonstrate a delay in adaptive functioning, which is related to the student's personal independence and social responsibility.

Mild to Moderate Mental Retardation

Students with mild to moderate developmental cognitive disabilities make up 80% to 85% of the children identified in this category. For the majority of students with mild impairments, the cause is unknown. Although there is no direct evidence that social and familiar interactions cause mental impairments, it is generally believed that these influences may have some effect on the mild cases of mental impairments.

Educational Approaches for Mild to Moderate Mental Retardation

The trend of educating students with mild-moderate mental retardation is changing. Traditionally, the students in the mild-moderate range were educated in self-contained classrooms apart from their age peers. Today, increasing numbers of students are spending more of their school day in the general education classroom with supplemental instruction provided by a resource teacher or a special education assistant. Simply placing a student into general education does not mean that the student will be immediately successful. Systematically planning for the student's integration into the classroom through team activities, group investigation projects, and directly training all students in specific skills for interaction with one another are just some of the methods that will help increase the chance of success in the general education setting. Peer tutoring has also proven to be very effective.

Many students in the mild-moderate range are educated in the regular classrooms with extra support provided as needed. These students are generally able to master standard academic skills and often tend to plateau at approximately a sixth-grade level. Students with moderate mental impairments are also frequently taught communication, self-help, daily living, and vocational skills in addition to limited academics.

Severe to Profound Mental Retardation

Students who are placed into the severe-profound range exhibit significantly subaverage general intellectual functioning resulting in or associated with concurrent deficits in adaptive behavior that may require special education instruction and related services. A student's intellectual functioning as indicated by an IQ must be below 50 for the student to be placed into the severe-profound range. A student must also demonstrate a delay in his or her ability to be independent and socially responsible, which is considered a student's adaptive functioning.

Educational Approaches for Moderate to Severe Mental Impairments

The self-contained special education classroom is the most common educational placement for students with a severe-profound developmental cognitive disability, although the trend is changing, and more students are placed in the general education setting for a portion of their school day.

Developing functional curriculum goals for these students is the primary intent for most educators. Curriculum choices include developing goals around the domains that represent the person as he or she lives, works, plays, and moves through the community. Personal maintenance and development, homemaking, community life, vocation, and leisure and travel are the five domains on which many curriculums for mentally impaired students are based.

One effective technique to use with students with severe-profound mental retardation is task analysis. This is a method in which large skills are broken down and sequenced as a series of small subtasks. The small, easier subtasks enable the student to learn more easily and experience success more frequently. The subtasks are sequenced in the natural order in which they are performed. The curriculum stresses function, communication, and self-help skills. If students are provided with practice and repeated opportunities to respond as well as positive reinforcement for appropriate behavior, they are much more likely to be successful.

Causes of Mental Retardation

The ARC of the United States (2001) suggests that there are many known causes for mental retardation; however, specific reasons are determined in only 25% of the cases. Causes of mental retardation generally can be broken down into the following categories. Listed below are the possible categories of cause, and when appropriate, explanations of medical diagnosis have been provided.

- Unexplained
- Trauma (before or after birth)
- Infections
- Chromosomal abnormalities
- Genetic/metabolic abnormalities
- Toxic
- Nutritional
- Environmental

Unexplained

This category is the largest when discussing known causes of mental retardation.

Trauma

This category is characterized by but not limited to bleeding on the brain before or after birth; lack of oxygen to the brain before, during, or after birth; and/or severe head injury.

INFECTIONS

CONGENITAL RUBELLA (GERMAN MEASLES)

Congenital rubella is the destructive action by the rubella (German measles) virus on the fetus during the critical development stages. The effects of the rubella virus are most damaging during the first trimester of pregnancy. The incidence rate of congenital rubella has decreased significantly since the introduction of the rubella vaccine.

MENINGITIS

Meningitis is the inflammation of the lining around the brain and spinal cord. The cause is most often by microorganisms such as viruses or bacteria that spread into the blood and then into the cerebrospinal fluid. Viral meningitis is very unpleasant, however, almost never life threatening, and a quick, complete recovery can be made. Bacterial meningitis is more serious and is caused by a range of different bacteria. Those with less-competent immune systems are more at risk for all types of meningitis. The long-term outlook for children who develop meningitis varies depending on the child's age, the microorganism causing the infection, complications, and the treatment the child receives. Some complications of bacterial meningitis can be very serious and include negative neurological effects.

ENCEPHALITIS (SWELLING OF THE BRAIN)

Encephalitis is most often caused by a viral infection. Exposure to viruses can occur through insect bites (most likely mosquitoes or ticks), food or drink contamination, chickenpox, measles, mumps, rubella, rabies, or West Nile Virus. When the virus enters the blood stream, it may localize in the brain causing the swelling of the brain tissue. The swelling brain tissue may cause destruction of nerve cells and brain damage. This is uncommon and affects approximately 1,500 people each year.

CONGENITAL CYTOMEGALOVIRUS (CMV)

CMV is a common virus that most adults and children encounter; however, they do not experience symptoms or problems. It is estimated, however, that approximately 1% of newborns are infected with CMV passed to them from their mothers while in utero. CMV infections result in serious disabilities in more than 4,000 babies each year.

Web Sites

An excellent site that answers kids questions using vocabulary and language that kids can understand: Kidshealth.org/kid/health_problems/birth_defect/mental_retardation.html

Congenital Rubella Syndrome: Health Care Challenges: www.dblink.org/lib/topics/crsguide.htm

Disability Info: Mental Retardation Fact Sheet (FS8) From NICHCY (National Information Center for Children and Youth with Disabilities): www.nichcy.org/pubs/factshe/fs8txt.htm

Health and Disease Information: www.hmc.psu.edu/childrens/healthinfo/m/mentalretardation.htm

Resource Book

Title: *Behavior Modification in Mental Retardation: The Education and Rehabilitation of the Mentally Retarded Adolescent and Adult*

Author: William Gradner

Publisher: Aldine Transaction, 2006

Story Profile: Information provided is related to the application of behavior modification principles and techniques to the training of mentally handicapped adolescents and adults. Topic areas covered include self-care skills (eating, dressing, toileting, motor skills), social skills (language, classroom behavior, increasing desirable behaviors, reducing undesirable behavior), and ethics.

CHROMOSOME ABNORMALITIES

DOWN SYNDROME

Down syndrome is caused by the presence of an extra chromosome 21. It is common and occurs in approximately one in 900 births. Children with Down syndrome show some distinctive physical characteristics such as upwardly slanting eyes; small ears, nose, feet, and hands; a flattened facial profile; short stature; a large tongue; and a gap between the first and second toes. Other results of this syndrome may be visual and auditory problems, thyroid disease, cardiac conditions, premature senility, loose ligaments, and decreased muscle tone. Due to low muscle tone, many people with Down syndrome have a tendency to keep their mouths open. This problem of muscle tone coupled with a large tongue makes speech articulation more difficult. Mental retardation accompanies this syndrome, but the level of intellectual ability varies. Most people with Down syndrome function in the mild or moderate range of retardation. Many individuals with Down syndrome also have the same changes in the brain as those who have Alzheimer's disease. This does not mean that every person with Down syndrome will indicate signs of Alzheimer's disease; however, it is noted hat there is a 25% chance that individuals with Down syndrome who are over the age of 35 will develop Alzheimer's-type dementia. Cardiac problems are the major cause for concern of people with Down syndrome.

Educational Approaches for Children With Down Syndrome

Down syndrome is recognizable at birth, which allows for early intervention from a variety of professionals. Early intervention gives parents new information so they can help their child get a head start on learning. Typical professionals who can be involved in early intervention, screening, and follow-up are physicians, speech and language professionals, audiologists, educational specialists, and physical and occupational therapists. The National Down Syndrome Society (2008) indicates that a strength that is commonly noted about people with Down syndrome is that they often have a pleasant disposition and behavior problems are uncommon.

Once a child is three years old, he or she is guaranteed educational services under the Individuals with Disabilities Education Act (IDEA). Under IDEA (2004), school districts must provide "a free appropriate education in the least restrictive environment." Some kids with Down syndrome have needs that are best met in a specialized program, while many other students are mainstreamed for special classes and activities in the regular general education class. Whatever the programming needs for a student with Down syndrome, it is important that the classroom teacher communicate with the parents, special education teachers, and all other members of the student's educational support system.

Studies have shown that inclusive practices are extremely beneficial for both the child with Down syndrome as well as the other children in the class. It is essential that the nondisabled children in the class are well informed of the characteristics of the child with Down syndrome in order to heighten awareness and understanding.

Web Sites

Down Syndrome Research Foundation: www.dsrf.org

KidsHealth (information written by health experts for kids): www.kidshealth.org/kid/health_problems/birth_defect/down_syndrome.html

National Down Syndrome Society—increase public awareness, assist families, and sponsor scientific research: www.ndss.org

Resource Books

Title: *Early Communication Skills for Children With Down Syndrome—A Guide for Parents and Professionals*

Author: Libby Kumin

Publisher: Woodbine House, 2006

Story Profile: This publication includes the latest research on DS and communication. The book focuses on speech and language development from birth through three-word phrases, usually beginning at age four or five. It fully covers speech and language assessment, what to expect in the early years, and the range of augmentative and alternative communication options and discusses the impact of literacy on articulation.

Title: *Road Map to Holland: How I Found My Way Through My Son's First Two Years With Down Syndrome*

Author: Jennifer G. Groneberg

Publisher: NAL Trade, 2008

Story Profile: This book is a mother's honest and touching recount of learning her son has Down syndrome and the challenges she is faced with during the first two years of his life.

Title: *Teaching Children With Down Syndrome About Their Bodies, Boundaries, and Sexuality*

Author: Terri Couwenhoven

Publisher: Woodbine House, 2007

Story Profile: This book provides information and practical ideas for teaching children with Down syndrome about their bodies, puberty, and sexuality. The book covers relevant issues and concerns for children of all ages.

Title: *Teaching Math to People With Down Syndrome and Other Hands-On Learners: Basic Survival Skills*

Author: DeAnna Horstmeier

Publisher: Woodbine House, 2004

Story Profile: Educators and parents can use this guide to teach meaningful math to students with and without disabilities. A key feature of this method is the early introduction of the calculator, which allows students to progress without memorizing math facts. This book may be used to help students learn critical math survival skills needed to live independently.

Title: *Teaching Reading to Children With Down Syndrome*

Author: P. Oelwein

Publisher: Woodbine House, 1995

Story Profile: This nationally known reading program ensures success by presenting lessons that are both imaginative and functional and can be tailored to meet the needs of each student. The book includes 100 pages of reproducible materials to supplement the program. This program will not only help students with DS but many struggling readers.

Children's Resources

Title: *Be Good to Eddie Lee*

Author: Libby Kumin

Publisher: Putnam Publishing, 2006

(Continued)

(Continued)

Story Profile: Eddie Lee is a boy with Down syndrome. Christy discovers special things about Eddie Lee when Eddie Lee follows Christy into the woods.

Title: *My Friend Isabelle*

Author: Eliza Woloson

Illustrator: Bryan Gough

Publisher: Woodbine House, 2003

Story Profile: Isabelle and Charlie are friends. They both like to draw, dance, read, play at the park, and cry if their feelings are hurt. They are also different from each other. Isabelle has Down syndrome, and Charlie does not. This book opens the door for young children to talk about differences and the world around them.

Title: *Our Brother Has Down's Syndrome: An Introduction for Children*

Authors: Shelley Cairo and Jasmine Cairo

Publisher: Firefly Books, LTD, 1991

Story Profile: Two sisters tell about their experience with having a little brother who has Down syndrome.

Title: *Russ and the Almost Perfect Day*

Author: Janet E. Rickert

Illustrator: Pete McGahan

Publisher: Woodbine House, 2001

Story Profile: Russ, a student with Down syndrome, is having a perfect day until he realizes that the five-dollar bill he has found probably belongs to a classmate.

Title: *Russ and the Firehouse*

Author: Janet E. Rickert

Illustrator: Pete McGahan

Publisher: Woodbine House, 2000

Story Profile: Russ, a five-year-old with Down syndrome, visits his uncle's firehouse and gets to help with the daily chores.

Title: *We'll Paint the Octopus Red*

Author: Stephanie Stuve-Bodeen

Illustrator: Pam DeVito

Publisher: Woodbine House, 1998

Story Profile: Emma and her father discuss what they will do when the new baby arrives, but they adjust their expectations when he is born with Down syndrome.

Title: *Where's Chimpy?*

Authors: Bernice Rabe and Diane Schmidt

Publisher: Albert Whitman, 1988

Story Profile: Text and photographs in this book show Misty, a little girl with Down syndrome, and her father reviewing her day's activities in their search for her stuffed monkey.

FRAGILE X SYNDROME

The Fragile X Research Foundation (2008) indicates that Fragile X syndrome accounts for the most common inherited form of mental retardation. This syndrome is linked to an irregularity in the X chromosome and usually results in mental retardation in males and learning disorders in females. Physical characteristics of this syndrome include a prominent jaw and large head, ears, and testes in males. Behavioral concerns may be autistic-like behaviors such as withdrawal, heightened interest in sensations, stereotypical hand movements, behavior problems (hand biting), and hyperactivity.

Fragile X syndrome is often difficult to diagnose in a child. The physical characteristics may be minimal or not noticeable until they become more pronounced following puberty. There is a slow regression in abilities over time.

Educational Approaches for Children With Fragile X Syndrome

Early intervention is recommended so that physical therapy, speech and language therapy, and occupational therapy can be started. Positive behavioral strategies and medications may be used to improve problems of self-injury and hyperactivity.

Web Sites

The Fragile X Research Foundation: www.fraxa.org

The National Fragile X Foundation: www.nfxf.org

What Is Fragile X?: www.fragilex.org/html/what.htm

Resource Books

Title: *Educating Children With Fragile X Syndrome: A Multi-Professional View*

Author: Denise Dew-Hughes

Publisher: Taylor & Francis, 2003

Story Profile: Pupils with Fragile X syndrome are currently being educated in many different types of mainstream and special school settings. This book provides invaluable information, support, and guidance on educating a child with Fragile X. It also provides background information on the origins of this syndrome, and the implications for such a child's teaching and learning.

Title: *Fragile X Syndrome: A Guide for Teachers*

Author: Suzanne Saunders

Publisher: David Fulton Publishers, 2004

Story Profile: Fragile X syndrome is thought to be the most common inherited cause of learning difficulties. Many people, however, have never heard of it, and those who have, have little knowledge or understanding of the condition. This book brings up-to-date research, information, and advice from teachers who are discovering firsthand the best ways of educating children with Fragile X.

PRADER-WILLI SYNDROME

Prader-Willi syndrome is caused by the deletion of a gene on chromosome 15. It is present from birth and is characterized by obesity, decreased muscle tone, decreased mental capacity, and hypogonadism (sex glands produce little or no hormones). At birth, infants are often small and very floppy. The growing child will exhibit slow mental development with the IQ most likely not to exceed 80. Children with Prader-Willi are generally very happy, smile frequently, and are pleasant to be around. Children will develop increasing obesity, often times, morbid obesity, with an intense craving for food resulting in uncontrollable weight gain.

Educational Approaches for Children With Prader-Willi Syndrome

Specific educational planning will need to be made to ensure programming will parallel the student's level of functioning. Weight control will also need to be in place to ensure a more comfortable and healthy lifestyle.

Web Site

Prader-Willi Syndrome Association: www.pwsausa.org

Resource Book

Title: *Dinah's Story: The Struggles and Triumphs of Parenting a Child With Prader-Willi Syndrome*

Author: Loretta Stafford

Publisher: Xulon Press, 2002

Story Profile: This book is an exploration of the impact of having a child with Prader-Willi syndrome on a family. It is unique from the other writings of professionals in that it is full of insight concerning how it is to live daily with a child with Prader-Willi syndrome.

GENETIC/ METABOLIC ABNORMALITIES

GALACTOSEMIA

Galactosemia is a genetic disease that is caused by the lack of a liver enzyme required to digest galactose, which is a breakdown product of lactose commonly found in milk products. Because galactose cannot be broken down, it builds up in the cells and becomes toxic (Save Babies Through Screening Foundations, 2006). If not detected immediately, it results in liver disease, cataracts, mental retardation, and even death. Treatment for galactosemia is the elimination of galactose and lactose from the diet throughout life. There is no chemical or drug substitute for the missing enzyme. If diagnosis is made early and milk products are strictly avoided, the prognosis is a relatively normal life. Despite strict avoidance of galactose, mild intellectual impairment may still develop.

Educational Approaches for Children With Galactosemia

All children with galactosemia need to be educated to strictly avoid not only milk and milk products but also foods that contain dry milk products. Parents and school staff (teachers, cooks, and principals) will need to develop a plan to ensure strict adherence to the special diet. Each child will be affected differently by this disorder, and therefore, specific educational planning will have to be made according to individual needs.

Web Sites

Galactosemia: An Overview: depts.washington.edu/transmet/gal.html

Information about galactosemia and a resource for families living with galactosemia: www .galactosemia.org

---

PHENYLKETONURIA (PKU)

Schuett (2008) states that PKU occurs when a person inherits a genetic mutation that disrupts the function of a metabolic enzyme. With PKU, a person can accumulate dangerously high phenylalanine levels in the brain that could cause poisoning of the neurons, resulting in mental retardation and epilepsy if the condition is not treated.

Educational Approaches for Children With Phenylketonuria (PKU)

Children with PKU must adhere to a low-protein diet. Even after 12 years of age, relaxation of the diet can change a person's behavior; therefore, experts recommend people stick to a low-protein diet for life. Parents and school staff (teachers, cooks, and principals) will need to develop a plan to ensure strict adherence to the special diet. Each child will be affected differently by this disorder, and therefore, specific educational planning will have to be made according to individual needs.

Web Site

Information on PKU: www.pku.com

Resource Book

Title: *Janice VanCleave's Food and Nutrition for Every Kid: Easy Activities That Make Learning Science Fun* (Science for Every Kid Series)

Author: Janice VanCleave

Publisher: Jossey-Bass, 1999

Story Profile: This resource book invites students to learn about food groups, vitamins, minerals, and how to read nutrition labels. The activities introduced in the book require adult supervision but are great science experiments for school or home use. A brief description of PKU is provided to assist children in understanding the effects of PKU.

HUNTER SYNDROME

This condition is an X-linked syndrome that is genetically transmitted and effects only males but is carried by females. It is rare, as it occurs in approximately one in 50,000 births. Infants born with Hunter syndrome show no immediate outward signs. Normal or excessive growth within the first two years follows. The effects of Hunter syndrome become quite apparent after the second year of life. At this time, there is observable mental deterioration that can result in aggressive and hyperactive behaviors. Typical physical characteristics will include small stature; short neck; joint contracture; large head (hydrocephalus); broad, low nose; full cheeks; thick lips; and wide spaced teeth. Impaired hearing usually begins later in childhood.

There are two types of Hunter syndrome: Type A and Type B. Type A is also called juvenile type and is the most severe. This type has rapid progression, severe mental retardation, and death before 15 years of age due to liver and cardiac problems. Type B progresses much more slowly. There is slight or no noticeable mental impairment, and those with Type B may live to be 50 or 60 years old.

Educational Approaches for Children With Hunter Syndrome

The interventions necessary for a child with Hunter syndrome will depend on the type and severity of the symptoms. Early intervention is most helpful to address each individual's needs. Speech and language consultants can provide recommendations to enhance communication. Audiologists can assess and provide hearing devices for those with auditory problems. Surgery can be used to correct hernias, and shunting can be implemented to decrease pressure on the brain. Behavior management consultants or psychologists can provide guidance in decreasing aggressive behaviors, increasing productive expression of wants and needs, and managing hyperactivity.

Web Sites

Comprehensive Overview of the Disorder: www.mayoclinic.com/health/hunter-syndrome/DS00790

Description of the definition, symptoms, causes, and prevention of the disease: www.RightHealth.com/Endrocrinology

---

SANFILIPPO SYNDROME

This is a rare, genetic disorder that occurs when the enzymes needed to break down the heparin sulfate sugar chain are missing or defective. It is commonly characterized by mental deterioration, mild physical defects, and behavioral problems. Infants born with Sanfilippo syndrome show no immediate outward signs; however, as the child grows and more cells become damaged, the symptoms become more obvious and worsen. Such characteristics of the syndrome may include an enlarged head, coarse facial features and hair, excessive hair growth, joint stiffness, hyperactivity, aggressive and destructive behavior, poor attention span, and severe intellectual impairment.

Educational Approaches for Children With Sanfilippo Syndrome

The interventions necessary for a child with Sanfilippo syndrome will depend on the type and severity of the symptoms. Early intervention is most helpful to address each individual's needs. Speech and language consultants can provide recommendations to enhance communication. Audiologists can assess and provide hearing devices for those with auditory problems. Behavior management consultants or psychologists can provide guidance in decreasing aggressive behaviors, increasing productive expression of wants and needs, and managing hyperactivity.

Web Site

Description of the disorder and lists characteristics of children with the disorder: www .specialchild.com/archives/dz-034.html

---

RETT SYNDROME

According to the International Rett Syndrome Foundation (2008), Rett syndrome is a disorder of the nervous system that leads to reverse development, especially in the areas of expressive language and hand use. Rett syndrome occurs almost exclusively in girls and may be misdiagnosed as autism or cerebral palsy. An infant with Rett syndrome usually has normal development for the first six to 18 months before symptoms begin to appear. Such symptoms may include hypotonia (floppy arms and legs); slowing head growth, beginning at approximately five to six months of age; severe language development problems; loss of purposeful hand movements; shaky, unsteady, or stiff gait; toe walking; loss of social engagement; intellectual disabilities; and learning difficulties.

Educational Approaches for Children With Rett Syndrome

The interventions necessary for a child with Rett syndrome will depend on the type and severity of the symptoms. Early intervention is most helpful to address each individual's needs. Speech and language consultants can provide recommendations to enhance communication.

Web Sites

How Rett syndrome is similar to and differs from autism: www.autismspeaks.org/navigating/ rett_syndrome.php

Rett Syndrome Fact Sheet: www.ninds.nih.gov/disorders/rett/detail_rett.htm

Resource Book

Title: *Understanding Rett Syndrome: A Practical Guide for Parents, Teacher, and Therapists*

Author: Barbro Lindberg

Publisher: Hogrefe & Huber Publishing, 2006

Story Profile: This book provides information that describes the difficulties and challenges of Rett syndrome. It offers solutions that can help those affected in everyday life and is primarily intended for use by people close to those with Rett syndrome.

TOXIC

FETAL ALCOHOL SYNDROME (FAS)/FETAL ALCOHOL EFFECTS (FAE)/PRENATAL DRUG EXPOSURE (PDE)

FAE/PDE refers to the fetal developmental defects that result from a woman's alcohol consumption or narcotic use during pregnancy. In situations in which the defects are not severe enough to meet all the criteria for an FAS diagnosis, the term fetal alcohol effects (FAE) is used. FAS/FAE or PDE are the leading causes of mental retardation and the second most common birth defect. The Department of Health and Human Services Center for Disease Control and Prevention (2008) states that FAS occurs in one in 600 to 700 births, and stresses that it is 100% preventable. FAS and PDE are conditions characterized by physical and behavioral disabilities that occur because of exposure to alcohol or drugs prior to birth. The mother's use of alcohol or drugs during pregnancy is a criterion for diagnosis of these conditions. Other indicators of this syndrome are small size; distinctive facial features such as a small head; distinctive eye shape, size, and position; flat nasal bridge; lack of crease between the nose and lip, thin upper lip; and a small jaw. Other physical problems such as joint and limb malformations, heart problems, kidney disorders, and cleft lip/palate may be seen. Mental impairment is also a feature of this syndrome and can include mental retardation, learning disorders, behavior problems, and gross motor limitations.

Problems stemming from these disorders can be seen in infancy. Babies with FAS or PDE are usually born small and underdeveloped. Behavioral concerns may consist of hyperactivity, a short attention span, and decreased physical abilities; all are commonly noted in preschool and school-aged children.

Educational Approaches for Children With FAS or PDE

The National Organization on Fetal Alcohol Syndrome (2002) suggests that early intervention does increase the child's chances for later success. Early intervention provides a variety of assessments in the areas of physical and mental ability. Physicians, physical and occupational therapists, speech and language therapists, and people who specialize in child development can assess the child's strengths and abilities along with areas where additional supports are needed. The best time for intervention to begin is shortly after birth. The many disorders exhibited by students with FAS, FAE, and PDE require teachers to make various educational modifications. Support and understanding from family, community members, teachers, and peers is imperative in order for a child with FAS, FAE, or PDE to reach his or her potential. Statistics indicate that there will be an increasing number of babies born with FAS, FAE, or PDE, and therefore, it is critically important to educate teachers, students, and parents about the dangers of alcohol and drugs.

Nutritional/Environmental Factors

Ignored or neglected infants who are not provided the mental and physical stimulation required for normal development may suffer irreversible learning impairments. Children who live in poverty and suffer from malnutrition, unhealthy living conditions, and improper or inadequate medical care are at a higher risk. Exposure to lead can also cause mental retardation. Many children have developed lead poisoning by eating the flaking lead-based paint often found in older buildings.

Web Sites

Definition, Description, Causes, and Symptoms: www.faqs.org/health/Sick-V3/Mental-Retardation.html

The National Organization on Fetal Alcohol Syndrome Homepage: www.nofas.org

Teacher resources and tips for educators who are educating children with FAS/FAE: www.teach-nology.com/teachers/special_ed/disabilities/fas/

Resource Books

Title: *Educating Drug-Exposed Children: The Aftermath of the Crack-Baby Crisis*

Author: Janet Y. Thomas

Publisher: Routledge, 2004

Story Profile: This research-based resource provides readers with the ability to better understand how children have been affected by their mother's drug addiction and how this exposure increases a child's vulnerability to early school failure. Ideas and suggestions are provided to support and assist educators in effectively serving the needs of these children.

Title: *FAS—A Cry for Help*

Author: Sandra Lemmon-Orton

Publisher: First Books Library, 2002

Story Profile: A "from the heart" biography written by a grandmother raising two grand-daughters plagued with FAS. This book provides insight to the daily challenges and difficulties faced with living with a disease that is 100% preventable.

Title: *Prenatal Exposure to Drugs/Alcohol: Characteristics and Educational Implications of Fetal Alcohol Syndrome and Cocaine/Polydrug Effects*

Author: Jeanette M. Soby

Publisher: Charles C. Thomas Publisher, 2006

Story Profile: This resource provides support for educators to better assist children who have been affected by prenatal drug/alcohol exposure. The book is divided into three sections, which provide information regarding the characteristics of children exposed, background on the cognitive processes involved in learning, and instructional strategies for learning and everyday life experiences that children with disabilities find challenging. A great resource for parents, educators, social workers, and other service or care providers.

■ MULTIPLE DISABILITIES

The category called "Multiple Disabilities" involves severe learning and developmental problem resulting from two or more disability conditions determined by assessment. A student is eligible to receive services for the severely multiply impaired if the student meets the entrance criteria for two or more of the following disabilities.

1. Autism

2. Emotional Disturbance

3. Hearing Impairment

4. Mental Retardation

5. Orthopedic Impairment

6. Visual Impairment

■ ORTHOPEDIC IMPAIRMENT (PHYSICAL IMPAIRMENT)

The category of orthopedic impairment involves a severe impairment that may adversely affect a child's physical and academic functioning and result in the need for special education and related services. The category includes impairments caused by congenital abnormality (deformity or limb deficiency), impairments caused by disease (e.g., muscular dystrophy), and impairments from other causes (e.g., cerebral palsy, amputations, or burns).

CONGENITAL ABNORMALITIES

LIMB DEFICIENCY

A limb deficiency is the absence or partial loss of an arm or leg. A congenital limb deficiency or absence of a limb at birth is rare. Acquired limb deficiencies (amputations) are more common and are often the result of surgery or an accident.

Educational Considerations for Limb Deficiencies

Some students may use a prosthesis or artificial limb to assist with a variety of tasks and to create a more normal appearance. Some students, however, prefer not to use the prosthesis. Most children become quite proficient at using their remaining limbs. Some children who are missing both arms, for example, may need to learn different tasks and skills, such as learning to write with their feet. Unless children have other impairments in addition to the absence of limbs, they should be able to function in a regular classroom with only minor modifications.

ARTHROGRYPOSIS

Arthrogryposis is a disorder characterized by multiple joint contractures through the body present at birth. A newborn with arthrogryposis lacks the normal range of motion in one or more joints. Decreased fetal movement in the womb is the usual causes for this. The fetus needs to move his or her limbs to develop muscle and joints. If the joints do not move, extra connective tissue develops around the joint and fixes it in pace.

Treatment of Arthrogryposis

There is no cure; however, vigorous physical therapy can help stretch out the contracted joints and develop the weak muscles. Splints can also help stretch joints, especially at night. Orthopedic surgery may also be necessary to relieve or correct joint problems.

Educational Considerations for Arthrogryposis

- Gross and fine motor skills therapy at the student's pace and ability
- Appropriate seating in the classroom to facilitate fine motor skills
- Assist with self-help tasks such as feeding and toileting when needed
- Utilize assistive technology devices when appropriate
- Provide adaptive physical education to assist in the development of leisure and play skills

---

Web Sites

Arthrogryposis: www.rarediseases.about.com/cs/arthrogryposis/a/121403.htm

Support Group for Arthogryposis Multiplex Congenita: www.amcsupport.org

---

SPINA BIFIDA

The National Dissemination Center for Children with Disabilities Spina Bifida Fact Sheet (2004) indicates that spina bifida is a term used to describe a neural tube defect that occurs anywhere along the spine. The most common form of spina bifida is myelomeningocele, in which there is an opening in both the backbone and the skin around it, so that the spinal cord protrudes through the back. The damaged spinal cord results in a loss of sensation and movement in some parts of the body. Usually, spina bifida results in problems with mobility and bowel and bladder control. The severe form of spina bifida almost always affects the function of the limbs and organs in the lower part of the body. The child's ability to walk depends on what part of the spine is affected and how severe the spina bifida is.

Symptoms of Spina Bifida

Spinal cord damage caused by severe spina bifida may cause problems such as

- inability to control urine or bowel movements;
- constipation;
- little or no feeling in the legs and feet;
- inability to move or feel the legs, and less often, the arms;
- curvature of the spine (scoliosis);
- hunchback;
- allergy to latex;
- absence seizure, such as staring into space momentarily, or motor involvement ranging from tremors to spasms of the large muscles.

Educational Considerations for Spina Bifida

A multidisciplinary team of individuals will be responsible for determining the treatment and interventions for a child with spina bifida in order to enable the person to be as comfortable and independent as possible. Specific areas of support may come from the following.

- Physical therapists
- Occupational therapists

- Neurologists
- Neurosurgeons
- Orthopedists
- Pediatricians
- Nutritionists
- Psychologists
- Mechanical aids (e.g., wheelchairs, walkers, braces)
- Assistive technology

Web Sites

Information on Spina Bifida: www.fortunecity.com/millenium/plumpton/268/sb.htm

Spina Bifida Fact Sheet: www.nichcy.org/pubs/factshe/fs12txt.htm

Spina Bifida Home Page: www.sbadv.org

Resource Books

Title: *Children With Spina Bifida: A Parents' Guide*

Author: Marlene Lutkenhoff

Publisher: Woodbine House, 2007

Story Profile: The purpose of this text is to provide parents of children with spina bifida with easy to understand, nonfrightening, and supportive information about raising a child with spina bifida.

Title: *Living With Spina Bifida: A Guide for Families and Professionals*

Author: Adrian Sandler

Publisher: The University of North Carolina Press, 2003

Story Profile: The author presents an approach that encourages families to focus more on the child and less on the disability while providing abundant information about spina bifida. Parents of children with spina bifida add their personal insights in several chapters as well.

Children's Resource

Title: *Patrick and Emma Lou*

Author: Nan Holcomb

Illustrator: Dot Yoder

Publisher: Jason and Nordic Publishers, 1992

Story Profile: Despite his excitement over walking with a new walker, three-year-old Patrick finds it isn't easy and becomes discouraged until his new friend, six-year-old Emma Lou, who has spina bifida, helps him discover something important about himself.

IMPAIRMENTS CAUSED BY DISEASE

MUSCULAR DYSTROPHY (MD)

The Kidshealth Association (2005) indicates that MD is a group of hereditary muscle diseases that cause progressive weakness in the muscles that help the body move. People with MD have incorrect or missing information in their genes, which prevents them from making the proteins they need for healthy muscles.

MD weakens muscles over time, and so those who have the disease gradually lose the ability to do the things most people take for granted, like walking or sitting up. Someone with MD might show signs as a baby; others may develop MD as an adult. There are several forms of MD that may affect children, and each form weakens a different muscle group in various ways.

Treatment for Muscular Dystrophy

While there currently is no cure, doctors and scientists are working hard to find one. Children and teens with MD can do things to help their muscles. Exercises and physical therapy can help to avoid stiffening of the muscles near the joints. Specialized fitted braces are used to ensure flexible joints and tendons. Surgery is sometimes used to reduce pain and increase movement from contractures. Respiratory aids, such as a ventilator, will help some whose breathing muscles are affected. Some medications may be useful for specific forms of MD.

Educational Considerations for Children With Muscular Dystrophy

Most children with muscular dystrophy can do the same level of schoolwork as their classmates, and many are, in fact, intellectually gifted. But in-class and homework assignments present special challenges for any child who can't lift or hold a book or even a pencil. Specific modifications and accommodations can be added to a child's plan to ensure the most appropriate level of educational challenge.

- Decreased homework assignments
- Quality not quantity of work
- Use of a variety of assistive technology
- Extended time on assignments
- Use of laptops or computers
- Access to an aide or paraeducator to assist in the classroom and with self-help skills
- Promote and accept assistive technology with an open mind
- Utilize cooperative learning experiences when appropriate

Web Sites

Muscular Dystrophy: www.kidshealth.org/parent/medical/bones/muscular_dystrophy.html

Muscular Dystrophy Association (MDA) USA Homepage: www.mdausa.org

Your Orthopedic Connection: Muscular Dystrophy: www.orthoinfo.aaos.org/topic.cfm? topic=a00384

Resource Book

Title: *Muscular Dystrophy: The Facts*

Author: Alan E. H. Emery

Publisher: Oxford University Press, 2000

Story Profile: This book will answer many of the questions that are often asked about how and why MD occurs, and how it will affect the life of a recently diagnosed child.

(Continued)

(Continued)

Children's Resources

Title: *Martin the Hero Merriweather*

Authors: Bobby Jackson and Michael Carter

Illustrator: Jim Fultz

Publisher: Multicultural Publications, 1993

Story Profile: Because of his physical handicap, Martin struggles to gain acceptance from his classmates, but he finally proves to the whole community that he can be a hero.

Title: *My Buddy*

Author: Audrey Osofsky

Illustrator: Ted Rand

Publisher: Houghton Mifflin Company, 1995

Story Profile: A young boy with MD tells how he is teamed up with a dog trained to do things for him that he cannot do himself.

IMPAIRMENTS FROM OTHER CAUSES

CEREBRAL PALSY (CP)

The United Cerebral Palsy Organization (2008) describes CP as one of the most prevalent physical impairments in children. It is a long-term condition resulting from a lesion to the brain or an abnormality of brain growth. Cerebral palsy is a disorder in which muscular development and control are impaired. The significance of this injury and the effects vary for each person. The brain injury may occur prior to birth from a disease or injury of the mother during pregnancy, during a traumatic birth, or later in life as a result of an infection, disease, or head trauma.

There is no cure for CP; however, it can be treated. The impairment usually does not deteriorate as a child ages. It is not fatal or contagious. Specific effects of CP may include the following:

- Disturbances of voluntary motor functions
- Paralysis
- Extreme weakness
- Poor coordination
- Involuntary convulsions
- Little or no control over their arms, legs, or speech,
- Hearing or vision impairment
- Slow, awkward, jerky movements
- Stiffness
- Weakness
- Muscle spasms
- Floppiness
- Unwanted movements

Educational Considerations for Children With Cerebral Palsy

A multidisciplinary team of individuals will be responsible for determining the treatment of a child with CP. Specific areas of support come from the following.

- Physical therapy
- Speech therapy
- Psychotherapy
- Paraeducators
- Medications
- Mechanical aids (e.g., wheelchairs, walkers)
- Assistive technology

Web Sites

Cerebral Palsy and Special Needs Children's Organization: www.cerebralpalsy.org

United Cerebral Palsy: www.ucp.org

Resource Books

Title: *My Perfect Son Has Cerebral Palsy: A Mother's Guide of Helpful Hints*

Author: Marie A. Kennedy

Publisher: First Books Library, 2001

Story Profile: Marie Kennedy's story of her son's coping with cerebral palsy is one of hope, strength, love, encouragement, and courage. This book provides useful information for anyone, whether an immediate family has been touched by cerebral palsy or not. It is written in a simple style to make it easy for the reader to get the most out of it in the least amount of time.

Title: *Mitchell's Story: Living With Cerebral Palsy*

Author: Jeff Parkin

Publisher: Trafford Publishing, 2006

Story Profile: This book is about a mother who has a touching and somewhat sad tale to tell about her only son who contracted the frustrating disease called cerebral palsy. This book can be of assistance to those who are just now finding out that their son or daughter has this awful disease. The author speaks of obstacles she has encountered that can prepare the new parents of CP kids the challenges that lie ahead.

Children's Resources

Title: *Howie Helps Himself*

Author: Joan Fassler

Illustrator: Joe Lasker

Publisher: Albert Whitman Publishing, 1991

Story Profile: Howie, a boy with cerebral palsy, enjoys life and loves his family; however, he wants more than anything to be able to move his wheelchair himself.

Title: *I'm the Big Sister Now*

Author: Michelle Emmert

(Continued)

(Continued)

Illustrator: Gail Owens

Publisher: Albert Whitman Publishing, 1991

Story Profile: Nine-year-old Michelle describes the joys, difficulties, and special situations involved in living with her older sister, Amy, who was born severely disabled with cerebral palsy.

Title: *Nathan's Wish: A Story About Cerebral Palsy*

Authors: L. Lears and Stacy Schuett

Publisher: Albert Whitman Company, 2005

Story Profile: Nathan lives next door to Miss Sandy, a raptor rehabilitator. She is very busy taking care of injured birds of prey, like owls and hawks. Nathan wishes he could help Miss Sandy with some of her chores, but he is confined to his wheelchair because of cerebral palsy. Then Fire, an owl with a broken wing, comes to Miss Sandy. Fire is desperate to fly, and Nathan can't wait for Fire to get her wish. Nathan desperately searches for a way to help Fire, not realizing that what he finds will help transform his life as well.

Title: *Rolling Along: The Story of Taylor and His Wheelchair*

Author: Jamee Riggio Heelan

Illustrator: Nicola Simmonds

Publisher: Peachtree Publishers, 2000

Story Profile: This book for K–3 students provides a glimpse into the life of a young boy with cerebral palsy. Taylor descries his condition, aspects of his daily activities at home and at school, and his desire for independence.

Title: *Taking Cerebral Palsy to School*

Author: Elizabeth Mary Anderson

Illustrator: Tom Dineen

Publisher: Jayjo Books, 2000

Story Profile: This book is written from the perspective of a child with CP. It answers many of the questions his classmates may have but are too scared to ask. Children, teachers, school nurses, parents, and caregivers will all learn about CP.

BURNS

Burns are the leading type of injury in childhood. Most often burns result from household accidents, but sometimes they are the result of child abuse. Serious burns can cause complications in other organs, long-term physical limitations, and psychological difficulties. Children with serious burn injuries usually experience pain, scarring, limitation of motion, lengthy hospitalizations, and repeated surgeries.

Educational Considerations for Children With Burns

The disfigurement caused by severe burns can affect a child's behavior and self-image, especially if teachers and peers react negatively. When a child is returning to class after a prolonged absence resulting from an extensive burn injury, it may be advisable for the teacher, parents, or other involved persons to explain to classmates the nature of the child's injury and appearance.

Web Site

Burns in Children—Keep Kids Healthy First Aid Guide: www.keepkidshealthy.com/welcome/firstaid/burns.html

---

■ OTHER HEALTH IMPAIRMENT (OHI)

The OHI category includes a broad range of medically diagnosed chronic or acute health conditions that may adversely affect academic functioning and result in the need for special education instruction and related services. The decision that a specific health condition qualifies under the OHI criteria will be determined by the impact of the condition on academic functioning rather than by the diagnostic or medical label given the condition.

To be deemed eligible for special education services under the category area of OHI, there must be a medically diagnosed chronic or acute health condition that is negatively impacting academic functioning. Examples of these medically diagnosed health conditions, including symptoms, treatments, and educational considerations of each are included but not limited to the examples listed below.

ATTENTION DEFICIT DISORDER (ADD) / ATTENTION DEFICIT HYPERACTIVITY DISORDER (ADHD)

ADD describes a child who has difficulty with maintaining attention but is not hyperactive. ADD can be very difficult and problematic for a child. Children with ADD are generally not disruptive in the classroom, and their behaviors are unusually not noticeable or distracting to others. ADD can cause a child to underachieve in the classroom and have low self-esteem.

ADHD describes a child who has difficulty maintaining attention and is inattentive, as described above, and also includes hyperactivity with an impulsivity component.

Symptoms of ADD/ADHD

Inattention

Specific observable behaviors as listed in the DSM-IV for inattention include the following.

- Often does not give close attention to details or makes careless mistakes in schoolwork, work, or other activities
- Often has trouble keeping attention on tasks or play activities
- Often does not seem to listen when spoken to directly
- Often does not follow instructions and fails to finish schoolwork, chores, or duties in the workplace (not due to oppositional behavior or failure to understand instruction)
- Often has trouble organizing activities
- Often avoids, dislikes, or doesn't want to do things that take a lot of mental effort for a long period of time (such as schoolwork or homework)

- Often loses things needed for tasks and activities (e.g., toys, school assignments, pencils, books, or tools)
- Is often easily distracted
- Is often forgetful in daily activities

Hyperactivity

Specific observable behaviors as listed in the DSM-IV for hyperactivity include the following.

- Often fidgets with hands or feet or squirms in seat
- Often gets up from seat when remaining in seat is expected
- Often runs about or climbs when and where it is not appropriate
- Often has trouble playing or enjoying leisure activities quietly
- Is often "on the go" or often acts as if "driven by a motor"
- Often talks excessively

Impulsivity

Specific observable behaviors as listed in the DSM-IV for impulsivity include the following:

- Often blurts out answers before questions have been finished
- Often has trouble waiting one's turn
- Often interrupts or intrudes on other (e.g., butts into conversations or games)

Based on the above stated behaviors, three types of ADHD can be identified.

1. ADHD, Combined Type—behaviors from all three categories are frequently observed

2. ADHD, Predominantly Inattentive Type—behaviors from the inattentive category are frequently observed but not from the other two categories

3. ADHD, Predominantly Hyperactive-Impulsive Type—behaviors from the hyperactivity and impulsivity categories are frequently observed but not from the inattentive category

Treatment for ADD/ADHD

Children and adults with Attention Deficit/Hyperactivity Disorder (CHADD [n.d.]) specifically states that it is "not the role of the teacher or the school to determine if a student has ADD or ADHD." It is a physician who makes the diagnosis and who often requests the teacher to provide a behavior rating of the student as an adjunct to the diagnosis. It is also important to realize that there is no simple test to determine if a person has ADD/ADHD.

Effective treatment for individuals with accurately diagnosed ADD/ADHD generally required three basic components:

1. Medication

2. Behavior management

3. Appropriate educational programs

Medication

Although controversial, medication has been effective with many children. Stimulants are the most widely prescribed type of medication. These drugs stimulate the brain's neurotransmitters to enable it to better regulate attention, impulsiveness, and motor behavior. For children for whom stimulant medication is not effective, antidepressant medication is prescribed.

Behavior Interventions

Many children with ADHD respond well to a reward system with clear consequences for behaviors. Positive behaviors are rewarded with goal of increasing the occurrence of them. Negative behavior may receive consequences with the goal of decreasing them. This type of system is called behavior modification and it has been found to work well with children. The system follows three very simple steps:

1. Identify target behaviors.

2. Identify effective rewards and consequence.

3. Consistently enforce the plan.

Appropriate Educational Programs

ADHD, while not caused by environmental factors, can certainly be influenced by them. A chaotic, unstructured, unorganized setting can exacerbate symptoms. On the flip side, a setting that is structured, predictable, and motivating can greatly help. Some children may benefit most from a special education program for some or all of the day. Others may need only minor adjustments in the general education setting. Still other children may need a special behavior program or counseling services.

Educational Considerations for Children With ADD/ADHD

Seating

- Seat the student with ADD/ADHD away from window and the door.
- Put the student with ADD/ADHD right in front of your desk unless that would be a distraction for the student.
- Have classroom desks in rows with focus on the teacher; this usually works better than having students seated around tables or facing one another in other arrangements.

Information Delivery

- Give instruction one at a time and repeat as necessary.
- If possible, work on the most difficult material early in the day.
- Use visuals, charts, pictures, and color-coding.
- Create outlines for note taking that organize the information as you deliver it.

Student Work

- Create a quiet area free of distractions for test taking and quiet study.
- Create worksheets and tests with fewer items; give frequent short quizzes rather than long tests.
- Reduce the number of timed tests.

- Test the student in the way he or she does best, such as orally or filling in the blanks.
- Show the student how to use a pointer or bookmark to track written words on a page.
- Divide long-term projects into segments and assign a completion goal for each segment.
- Let the student do as much work as possible on the computer.
- Accept late work and give partial credit for partial work.
- Encourage quality rather than quantity.

Organization

- Have the student keep a master notebook—a three-ring binder with a separate section for each subject—and make sure that everything that goes in the notebook has holes punched and is put on the rings in the correct section.
- Provide a three-pocket notebook insert for homework assignments, completed homework, and notes to parents (permission slips, weekly memos, etc.).
- Color-code materials for each subject.
- Allow time for student to organize materials and assignments at the end of the day for home. Post steps for getting ready to go home.
- Make sure the students have a system for writing down assignments and important dates and consistently uses it.

Starting a Lesson

- Signal the start of a lesson with an aural cue, such as an egg timer, a cowbell, or a horn.
- List the activities of the lesson on the board.
- When opening the lesson, tell students what they're going to learn and what your expectations are. Tell students exactly what material they'll need.
- Establish eye contact with students.

Conducting the Lesson

- Keep instructions simple and structured.
- Vary the pace and include different kinds of activities. Many students with ADD do well with competitive games or other activities that are rapid and intense.
- Use props, charts, and other visual aids.
- Have an unobtrusive cue set up with student, such as a touch on the shoulder or placing a sticky note on the student's desk to remind the student to stay on task.
- Allow students frequent breaks.
- Let the student squeeze a Koosh ball or tap something that doesn't make noise as a physical outlet.
- Try not to ask student to perform or answer a question publicly that might be too difficult.

Ending the Lesson

- Summarize key points.
- If you give an assignment, have three different students repeat it, then have the class say it in unison and put it on the board.
- Be specific about what to take home for homework.

Web Sites

ADD/ADHD FAQ, Info and Articles: www.add-adhd.org

Children and Adults With Attention Deficit/Hyperactivity Disorder (CHADD): www.chadd .org

National Attention Deficit Disorder Association (ADDA): www.add.org

Resource Books

Title: *The Gift of ADHD Activity Book: 101 Ways to Turn Your Child's Problems Into Strengths*

Author: Lara Honos-Webb

Publisher: New Harbinger Publications, 2008

Story Profile: This resource offers parents 101 easy and fun tips and activities to help them help their ADHD or spirited child transform his or her challenges into strengths.

Title: *How to Reach and Teach Children With ADD/ADHD: Practical Techniques, Strategies, and Interventions*

Author: Sandra Rief

Publisher: Jossey-Bass, 2005

Story Profile: This fully updated second edition provides management techniques that promote on-task behavior along with strategies to help with language arts, math, writing, and multisensory instruction strategies that maintain student attention and keep students actively involved with learning.

Title: *Learning to Slow Down and Pay Attention: A Book for Kids About ADHD*

Authors: Kathleen G. Nadeau, Ellen B. Dixon, and Charles Beyl

Publisher: Magination Press, 2004

Story Profile: Parents, teachers, and kids will love the checklists found in this book to help children organize their time and daily tasks. This new edition includes more explanations about medication and how it works. In addition, there is an increased emphasis placed on the aspects of ADHD that are troublesome to the children.

Title: *The Organized Student: Teaching Children the Skills for Success in School and Beyond*

Authors: Donna Goldberg and Jennifer Zwiebel

Publisher: Fireside, 2005

Story Profile: Hands on strategies for teaching your disorganized child how to organize for school success! The overstuffed backpack, the missing homework, the unused planner, and the test he did not know about. This practical book is full of hands-on strategies for helping parents identify and teach organizational skills.

Title: *The Survival Guide for Kids With ADD or ADHD*

Author: John F. Taylor

Publisher: Free Spirit Publishing, 2006

Story Profile: What are ADD and ADHD? What does it meant to have ADD and ADHD? How can kids diagnosed with ADD and ADHD help themselves succeed in school, get along better at home, and form healthy, enjoyable relationships with peers? In kid-friendly language and a format that welcomes reluctant and easily distracted readers, this newest survival guide helps kids know they're not alone.

(Continued)

(Continued)

Children's Resources

Title: *Eddie Enough!*

Author: Debbie Zimmett

Publisher: Woodbine House, 2001

Story Profile: Third grader Eddie Minetti is described as a human whirlwind. He is always getting into trouble at school until his ADHD is diagnosed and treated.

Title: *Eukee, the Jumpy, Jumpy Elephant*

Authors: Clifford Corman and Esther Trevino

Publisher: Specialty Press, 1995

Story Profile: This is the story of a young elephant's struggle with ADD. Eukee gets into trouble at home and school because he cannot sit still and follow directions. He gets help at home and from a special doctor and learns ways to succeed.

Title: *Shelley: The Hyperactive Turtle*

Author: Deborah M. Moss

Publisher: Woodbine House, 1989

Story Profile: After his mother takes him to the doctor, Shelley the turtle begins to understand why he feels so jumpy and wiggly inside that he can't sit still.

Title: *Sparky's Excellent Misadventures: My ADD Journal*

Authors: Phyllis Carpenter and Marti Ford

Illustrator: Peter Horjus

Publisher: Magination, 2000

Story Profile: Sparky is a boy with ADD, which makes his life very exciting! With a little help from his family and school and by writing about his ups and downs in his journal, he is figuring out how to "manage his wiggles and keep all of his giggles." Told in a first-person diary format, Sparky's week-in-the-life tale is optimistic and fun and includes many valuable insights and ideas that can help kids with ADD and ADHD gain more control of their lives.

ASTHMA

Asthma is characterized by episodes of narrowing of the bronchial tubes in the lungs. Normally, these tubes narrow only as a protective reaction to prevent harmful substances from entering the lungs. With asthma, the bronchial tubes narrow too much, too often, and too easily in response to a variety of substances, which ordinarily would not damage the lungs. According to kidshealth.com (2008), signs and symptoms of asthma include the following.

- Shortness of breath
- Dry cough
- Tightness of the chest
- Wheezing
- Difficulty speaking
- No known reason

Treatment for Asthma

The American Lung Association (2007) suggests that children with asthma have an asthma action plan developed with the medical doctor indicating the steps to be taken in case of an asthmatic flare-up at school. Because each child's signs and symptoms are unique, the plan should be specifically written for each individual child. The plan should address the following:

- The medication the child takes and dosages
- The child's asthma triggers
- Early symptoms of a flare-up
- What to do if your child is having a flare-up, including when to seek emergency care
- Instructions on how and when to use a peak flow meter (if necessary)
- Recommendations for dealing with exercise-induced asthma

Educational Considerations for Children With Asthma

The American Lung Association (2007) provides the following information regarding asthma.

Handling Flare-Ups at School

- Rescue medication (most often in the form of an inhaler, used to relieve asthma symptoms) should always be immediately available to the child.
- If the child is not old enough to administer the medication himself or herself, the teacher will have it in the classroom, readily available.
- If the school permits and the child is old enough, he or she can be responsible for the inhaler.
- For children who have exercise-induced asthma, the rescue medication should be immediately accessible and available before any strenuous play or exercise.

Triggers in the School Environment

A "trigger" is something in the environment that "brings on" asthma symptoms. It is important for the school to know any triggers that are specific to the children in the school. Possible triggers in the school setting could include any of the following.

- Mold
- Dust mites
- Cockroaches
- Chalk dust
- Perfumes
- Cleaning products or other chemicals
- Animal dander, saliva, or urine

Suggestions That May Assist in Decreasing Possible Flare-ups

- Suggest the use of "dustless" chalk or dry-erase boards.
- Ask the staff to avoid using perfumed cleaning products or soaps.
- Propose the use of air conditioners and dehumidifiers.
- Ask that any classroom where art supplies are used and locker rooms where mold can grow be well ventilated.
- Make sure that the school is vacuumed and dusted regularly, that it's routinely treated by a pest control company, and that it's completely smoke free.

Web Sites

American Lung Association: www.lungusa.org

Asthma in Children: www.everydaykidz.com

Resource Books

Title: *The Complete Kid's Allergy and Asthma Guide: Allergy and Asthma Information for Children of All Ages*

Author: Milton Gold

Publisher: Robert Rose, 2003

Story Profile: This book is filled with the latest information on medications and testing methods, along with the most common allergic conditions and how to diagnose them. It also includes very helpful tips that are recommended for all parents of children with allergies and asthma.

Title: *Control Your Child's Asthma: A Breakthrough Program for the Treatment and Management of Childhood Asthma*

Authors: Harold J. Farber and Michael Boyette

Publisher: Holt Paperbacks, 2001

Story Profile: This book offers parents of children with asthma ways to create an asthma-management plan geared specifically toward the child's needs, incorporating medical, social, and emotional needs in one system. Included in the book is a detailed resource section of organizations dealing with asthma management.

Children's Resources

Title: *All About Asthma*

Authors: William Ostrow, Vivian Ostrow, and Blance Sims

Publisher: Albert Whitman & Company, 1992

Story Profile: The young narrator describes life as an asthmatic, explaining causes and symptoms of asthma and discussing ways to control the disorder to lead a normal life.

Title: *Brianna Breathes Easy: A Story About Asthma*

Author: Virginia L. Kroll

Illustrator: Jayoung Cho

Publisher: Albert Whitman & Company, 2005

Story Profile: When Brianna gets the lead in the Thanksgiving play, she already has a troublesome cough. Then during dress rehearsal, she can't catch her breath, and the school nurse calls an ambulance. At the hospital, a friendly doctor explains that she has asthma and clearly outlines the symptoms, triggers, and treatments of the illness.

Title: *I Have Asthma*

Author: Jennifer Moore-Mallinos

Illustrator: Marta Fabrega

Publisher: Barron's Educational Series, 2007

Story Profile: The child in this story suffers from asthma that sometimes produces frightening attacks. Nevertheless, kids who have asthma learn that with proper medical supervision and treatment, asthma can be kept under control.

Title: *Taking Asthma to School*

Author: Kim Gosselin

Illustrator: Freedman Moss

Publisher: Jayjo Books, 1998

Story Profile: A young boy describes what it is like to have asthma, what happens during an asthma attack, and how his asthma can be treated and controlled.

CHRONIC FATIGUE SYNDROME

Chronic Fatigue Syndrome (CFS) is a complicated disorder characterized by extreme fatigue that does not improve with bed rest and may worsen with physical and mental activity. According to the Department of Health and Human Services Center for Disease Control and Prevention (2006), people with CFS exhibit signs and symptoms much like those of most common viral infections. Unlike normal flu symptoms, which normally subside in a few days or weeks, the signs and symptoms of CFS can last much longer and may come and go with no identifiable pattern.

Because the cause of CFS is difficult to pinpoint, it was determined that a person meets the diagnostic criteria of CFS when unexplained fatigue occurs for six months or more along with at least four of the eight primary signs, as listed below, being present.

1. Loss of memory or concentration
2. Sore throat
3. Painful and mildly enlarged lymph nodes in neck or armpits
4. Unexplained muscle soreness
5. Pain that moves from one joint to another without swelling or redness
6. Headache of a new type, pattern, or severity
7. Sleep disturbance
8. Extreme exhaustion lasting more than 24 hours after physical or mental exercise

Treatment of Chronic Fatigue Syndrome

The Department of Health and Human Services Center for Disease Control and Prevention (2006) states that CFS is a syndrome of symptoms, and in most cases, there is no serious underlying disease causing it. There is no treatment for the syndrome, and in general, doctors aim to relieve the symptoms to help the person feel more comfortable. Treatment may include the following.

- Moderate daily activity—slow down and avoid excess physical activity and stress. The goal is to maintain a moderate level of daily activity and gently increase stamina over time.
- Gradual but steady exercise—begin an exercise program that slowly offers more challenge.
- Cognitive Behavior Therapy—work with a mental health professional to identify negative beliefs and behaviors that might be interfering with recovery and in turn replace them with more positive behaviors.

- Treatment of depression—medications such as antidepressants and SSRI's may be prescribed to help combat depression.
- Treatment of existing pain—over-the-counter drugs such as acetaminophen and ibuprofen may help reduce pain.
- Treatment of allergy-like symptoms—antihistamines and decongestants may relieve allergy-like symptoms such as runny nose.
- Treatment of low blood pressure—drugs may be used to level out blood pressure.
- Treatment for problems of the nervous system—drugs may be prescribed to alleviate anxiety and nervousness.

Educational Considerations for Children With CFS

Students may benefit from the following adaptations and/or modifications.

Related Services

- Physical or occupational therapy
- Counseling services
- Speech or audiology
- Transportation (both to and within the school building)
- Door-to-door transportation
- Individual assistance on or off the vehicle
- Wheelchair or other adaptive device
- Use of the elevator when appropriate

Physical Education

- Modified regular physical education class
- Specially designed physical education class

Testing Modifications (Allow for equal opportunity to demonstrate capabilities)

- Flexible scheduling

  o Extend the time allotted or have no time limit.
  o Administer the test in several sessions during the same day or over several days.

- Flexible setting

  o Administer the test in a separate location with minimal distractions.

- Revised Test Format/Directions

  o Read the directions and/or questions.
  o Provide larger print.
  o Place fewer items on each page.

Use of Support Aids (If students have difficulty or become easily fatigued from writing or memorizing math facts)

- Provide a note taker.
- Use a tape recorder to record answers rather than write them.
- Allow the use of a computer and word processor.
- Allow the use of a calculator or arithmetic tables.

Web Sites

Chronic Fatigue and Immune Dysfunction Syndrome Association of America: www.cfids .org/youth/youth.asp

Chronic Fatigue Syndrome: www.kidshealth.org/parent/system/ill/cfs.html

Chronic Fatigue Syndrome: www.cdc.gov

Resource Book

Title: *Pediatric Chronic Fatigue Syndrome*

Authors: Kenny De Meirleir and Neil McGregor

Publisher: Informa HealthCare, 2007

Story Profile: This book closely examines the potential impact that CFS has on child and adolescent functioning, psychological factors, social factors, and the suffering endured from symptoms. This book will help the family of young CFS sufferers cope with the debilitating illness.

CYSTIC FIBROSIS (CF)

CF is an inherited disease that affects both the respiratory and the digestive systems. According to the Cystic Fibrosis Foundation (2007), CF is the most common fatal hereditary disease in Caucasian children. It occurs in boys and girls equally and is inherited on a recessive basis, which means that a child can have cystic fibrosis only if both parents are carriers of the disease. CF affects the mucus and sweat glands of the body. As a child gets older, chronic respiratory disease may develop, including bronchitis, a collapsed lung due to blockage of airways, pneumonia, or fibrosis of the lung. Advances in research and medical treatments have significantly further enhanced and extended life for children and adults with CF. Many people with the disease can now expect to live into their 30s, 40s, and beyond!

People with CF can have a variety of symptoms, including the following.

- Very salty-tasting skin
- Persistent coughing, at times with phlegm
- Frequent lung infections
- Wheezing or shortness of breath
- Poor growth/weight gain in spite of a good appetite
- Frequent greasy, bulky stools or difficulty in bowel movements

Treatment of Cystic Fibrosis

- Management of problems that cause lung obstruction may include the following.
  o Chest physical therapy (to help loosen and clear lung secretions)
  o Exercise (to loosen mucus, stimulate coughing, and improve overall physical condition)
  o Medications (to reduce mucus and help breathing)
  o Antibiotics (to treat infections)

- Management of digestive problems may involve the following:
  o Appropriate diet
  o Pancreatic enzymes to aid digestion

o Vitamin supplements

o Treatments for intestinal obstructions

- Psychosocial support may help to assist with the following:

o Independence

o Sterility

o Sexuality

o Financial issues

o Relationships

Educational Considerations for Children With Cystic Fibrosis

- Give time during the day to take medicines or do airway clearance therapy.
- Adjust school rules to allow child to take personal medicines, like pancreative enzymes.
- Implement a plan to provide a tutor when the child is ill.
- Provide audio or videotape of missed classes.
- Adjust or waive attendance rules.
- Provide access to a private bathroom, perhaps in the nurse's office.
- Allow use of the bathroom or access to water at any time throughout the day.
- Have a school medical emergency plan in place.

Web Sites

Cystic Fibrosis Foundation: www.cff.org

Cystic Fibrosis Research, Inc. (CFRI): www.cfri.org

Resource Books

Title: *Cystic Fibrosis: Everything You Need to Know*

Author: Wayne Kepron

Publisher: Firefly Books, 2004

Story Profile: An easy-to-understand resource that provides an excellent overview of coping with CF.

Title: *Cystic Fibrosis: The Ultimate Teen Guide*

Author: Melanie Ann Apel

Publisher: The Scarecrow Press, 2006

Story Profile: From diagnosis to death, this book leaves no aspect of CF untold as it includes a description of the illness, causes of the disease, diagnosing the disease, and treatment of the disease.

Children's Resources

Title: *Little Brave Ones: For Children Who Battle Cystic Fibrosis*

Author: Carrie Lux

Publisher: BookSurge Publishing, 2006

Story Profile: See a day in the life, through pictures, of a preschooler with CF.

Title: *Mallory's 65 Roses*

Author: Diane Shader Smith

Publisher: Diane Shader Smith, 1997

Profile: An engaging story of Mallory, an energetic little girl afflicted with CF. She explains her condition and its ramifications in her own words, painting a picture accessible to children and poignant to adults.

Title: *Taking Cystic Fibrosis to School*

Author: Cynthia S. Henry

Illustrator: Tom Dineen

Publisher: Jayjo Books, 2000

Profile: This book is written from the perspective of a child with CF to explain and educate her classmates about her condition. This book is designed to help kids, families, teachers, school nurses, and caregivers to better understand CF.

DIABETES

Diabetes is a disorder of metabolism that affects the way the body absorbs and breaks down sugars and starches in food. It is a common childhood disease and affects about one in 600 school-aged children.

Symptoms of Diabetes

According to the American Academy of Family Physicians (2006), early symptoms of diabetes include the following.

- Extreme thirst
- Extreme hunger
- Frequent urination
- Sores or bruises that heal slowly
- Dry, itchy skin
- Unexplained weight loss
- Blurry vision that changes from day to day
- Unusual tiredness or drowsiness
- Tingling or numbness in the hands or feet
- Frequent or recurring skin, gum, bladder, or vaginal yeast infections

Treatment of Diabetes

- Diet
  - o Eat a consistent and well-balanced diet that is high in fiber, low in saturated fat, and low in concentrated sweets.
  - o A consistent diet that includes roughly the same number of calories at about the same time of day helps the health care provider prescribe the correct dose of medication of insulin.
  - o A consistent diet will help to keep the blood sugar at relatively even levels.

- Exercise
  - o Regular exercise can help reduce the risk of developing complications of diabetes.
  - o Any exercise is beneficial no matter how light of how long; some exercise is better than no exercise.

- Self-monitored blood glucose
  - o Check blood sugar levels frequently, at least before meals and at bedtime.
  - o Keep track of insulin and oral medication doses and times and any significant events of the day (e.g., high or low blood sugar levels and how the problem was treated) in a journal.
- Daily administration of insulin
  - o Insulin must be given as an injection. If taken by mouth, insulin would be destroyed in the stomach before it could get into the blood where it is needed.
  - o It is very important to eat after taking insulin. If the insulin is taken without eating, an insulin reaction could result.

Educational Considerations for Children With Diabetes

- Form a strong and effective team, including the child's parents, school nurse, classroom teacher, specialist teachers, counselor, administrator, medical professionals, food service staff, and any others who are involved with the child to form an Individualized School Healthcare Plan (ISHP).
- Promote a supportive environment for the student with diabetes.
- Provide accommodations for foods at school parties.
- Be aware of the symptoms of hypoglycemia (low blood sugar) or hyperglycemia (high blood sugar).

Signs of Hypoglycemia

Mild	Moderate	Severe
Nausea	Mood changes	Seizures or convulsion
Extreme hunger	Confusion	Loss of consciousness
Feeling nervous or jittery	Blurred vision, dizziness	Coma
Cold, clammy, wet skin	Inability to concentrate	Low body temperature
Excessive sweating	Headache	
Rapid heartbeat	Weakness, lack of energy	
Numbness or tingling of the fingertips or lips	Poor coordination	
Trembling	Difficulty walking or talking	
	Fatigue, lethargy, drowsiness	

The student with hypoglycemia may need to delay schoolwork, as hypoglycemia can impair thinking for several hours.

Signs of Hyperglycemia

Early Signs	Prolonged Signs
Increased thirst	Vaginal and skin infections
Headaches	Slow-healing cuts and sores
Difficulty concentrating	Decreased vision
Blurred visions	Nerve damage causing painful cold or insensitive feet
Frequent urination	Loss of hair on the lower extremities
Fatigue (weak, tired feeling)	Stomach and intestinal problems
Weight loss	Chronic constipation or diarrhea

Provide accommodations such as allowing a water bottle in the classroom, bathroom privileges as needed, and possible omission of physical exercise if needed.

Web Sites

American Diabetes Association: www.diabetes.org

Children With Diabetes Online Community: www.childrenwithdiabetes.com

Resource Books

Title: *487 Really Cool Tips for Kids With Diabetes*

Authors: Bo Loy and Spike Loy

Publisher: American Diabetes Association, 2004

Story Profile: Kids living with diabetes face a world of challenges, and yet, there are few things they can't do. This book is full of tips for kids with diabetes from kids with diabetes.

Title: *My Life as a Pancreas: Reflections on Raising a Child With Diabetes*

Author: Priscilla Call Essert

Publisher: Lulu.com, 2007

Story Profile: An inspirational guide to all parents who are experiencing the trials and tribulations of having a child with diabetes.

Title: *What to Expect When You Have Diabetes: 150 Tips for Living Well With Diabetes*

Author: American Diabetes Association

Publisher: Good Books, 2008

Story Profile: Managing diabetes can be overwhelming, even frightening; however, this handbook offers sounds and steady advice written by experts that will help readers to live with diabetes, not just manage it.

(Continued)

(Continued)

Children's Resources

Title: *The Dinosaur Tamer: And Other Stories for Children With Diabetes*

Authors: Marcia Levine Mazur, Peter Banks, and Andrew Keegan

Publisher: American Diabetes Association, 1996

Story Profile: A collection of twenty-five fictional stories portraying children with diabetes doing usual things such as expressing their emotions, coping with difficulties, and having fun.

Title: *Lara Takes Charge*

Author: Rocky Lang

Publisher: HLPI Books, 2004

Story Profile: Lara, a little girl with diabetes, tells all the things she does that regular kids do—run, swim, dance—and she tells about her insulin pump and doing blood tests.

Title: *Sarah and Puffle: A Story for Children About Diabetes*

Author: Linnea Mulder

Illustrator: Joanne H. Friar

Publisher: Magination Press, 1992

Story Profile: A resource that provides basic diabetes information in an easy-to-understand manner for children.

EPILEPSY

Epilepsy is a chronic condition that is a sign or symptom of an underlying neurological disorder. It consists of recurrent seizures of varying degrees of intensity and duration. According to the Epilepsy Foundation of America (n.d.), a person's consciousness, movement, or actions may be altered for a short time when the brain cells are not working properly.

Symptoms of Epilepsy

Epilepsy is classified by the type of seizure experienced. Epileptic seizures vary in intensity and symptoms depending on what part of the brain is involved.

- Simple partial seizures consists of a wide range of abnormal movements or sensations; however, the person remains fully conscious.
  - Jerking or tingling of extremities
  - Hallucinations that affect seeing, hearing, tasting, smelling
  - Nausea
  - Dizziness
  - Facial numbness
  - Twitching
  - Difficulty talking
  - Drooling

Most simple partial seizures occur at night, and they typically wake the child. Almost all children outgrow these seizures by midadolescence.

- Complex partial seizures can include all of the symptoms of a simple partial seizure; however, consciousness is always impaired to some degree during the episode. In addition to the symptoms of the simple partial seizure as described above, the following symptoms are included.
  - o Automatisms—controlled, repetitive movements, such as lip smacking or fumbling
  - o Confusion
  - o Aggression

These seizures are commonly associated with behavioral problems and developmental delays.

- Absence seizures are formerly known as *petit mal* seizures. They typically occur in children between three and 12 years of age. Symptoms of these include the following.
  - o Abruptly stops whatever he or she is doing
  - o Stares vacantly
  - o Eyelids will flutter
  - o Is unresponsive for five to 10 seconds (length of the seizure)
  - o After the seizure, resumes activity with full consciousness
  - o Has no memory of the seizure
  - o Seizures may occur dozens of times each day
  - o May be preceded by "aura" or a warning sensation

- Generalized tonic-clonic seizures are formerly called *grand mal* seizures; these involve the whole brain and are the most common epileptic seizures of childhood. The following symptoms may be present.
  - o As the seizure begins, child may cry or moan.
  - o Child may alternate between rigid postures and jerking movements.
  - o The child may bite his or her tongue.
  - o Eyes may turn to one side or roll back.
  - o Child may lose control of bladder or bowels.
  - o Secretions may pool in the mouth and airways as the child breathes rapidly and deeply.

Following this seizure the child usually sleeps. Upon awakening, some children report sore muscles and tongue pain.

Treatment for Epilepsy

The Epilepsy Foundation of America (n.d.) suggests that the goal of all epilepsy treatment is to prevent further seizures, avoid side effects, and make it possible for people to lead active lives. Epilepsy cannot be cured, but the symptoms can be treated. There is no single treatment that will work for all seizures.

Medications (Antiepileptic Drugs—AEDs)

Most epilepsy medicines are taken by mouth in tablet, sprinkle, or syrup form. The doctor's choice of which drug to prescribe depends on what kind of seizure a person is having. People react to medications differently and experience side effects differently as well. It often takes time to find exactly the right dose of the right drug for each person. Some of the common drugs prescribed include

Trileptal, Tegretol, Carbatrol, and Zarontin—just a few of the antiepileptic medications available. It is imperative to take the medications as directed, and if the medication is discontinued, it should be tapered slowly rather than stopping suddenly. The medical doctor should closely monitor cessation of the medication.

Dietary Treatment (Ketogenic Diet)

The ketogenic diet has been used as a treatment for children with some types of seizures that do not respond to AEDs. The diet consists of high fat, relatively low carbohydrates, and nutritionally adequate protein. The nutritional content of all meals must be calculated and each food item weighed. AEDs are usually slowly discontinued during dietary treatment if there is a significant improvement in seizure control.

Surgery

Despite numerous medications, 30% to 40% of children continue to have seizures and are not candidates for or do not improve with the ketogenic diet. Surgical treatments may be considered for children who have persistent, frequent seizures that are not controlled after a trial of at least three appropriate medications. The purpose of the surgery would be to remove the abnormal brain tissue that is causing the seizure.

Educational Considerations for Children With Epilepsy

- Form a strong and effective team, including the child's parents, school nurse, classroom teacher, specialist teachers, counselor, administrator, medical professionals, and any others who are involved with the child to form an Individualized School Healthcare Plan (ISHP).
- Promote a positive and comfortable learning environment for the student with epilepsy.
- Be familiar with what to do in case of a seizure.
- Have the steps to follow in case of a seizure written out and easily accessible— do not rely on memory. In case of an emergency, you will need the support of notes.

In Case of a Seizure

- Move anything that can hurt the child out of the way so the child won't be injured.
- Loosen any tight clothing around the neck.
- Put a pillow or something soft under the head.
- Lay him or her on one side.
- Time the seizure.
- Note the events of the seizure so the parents and doctor's know what type of seizure occurred and where in the brain it is coming from.

Things Not to Do During a Seizure

- Do not put anything in the mouth.
- Do not try to hold the child down.
- Don't give mouth-to-mouth resuscitation until the seizure is over.
- Don't call an ambulance during a typical seizure.

Call an Ambulance If These Take Place

- The child was injured during the seizure
- The child may have inhaled water
- The seizure lasted longer than five minutes
- There is no known history of seizures

Web Sites

Epilepsy Foundation: www.efa.org

Epilepsy Treatment of Children: www.mayoclinic.org/epilepsy/children.html

Resource Books

Title: *Children With Seizures: A Guide for Parents, Teachers, and Other Professionals*

Author: Martin L. Kutscher, M.D.

Publisher: Jessica Kingsley Publishers, 2006

Story Profile: This is an excellent handbook and guide for anyone working with children who experience seizures. The book covers important information, including types and causes of seizures and tests and treatments that are available. The information provided will further inform parents and teachers and other professionals on how best to provide support and service for children with seizures.

Title: *Seizures and Epilepsy in Childhood: A Guide*

Authors: John M. Freeman, Eileen P. G. Vining, and Diana J. Pillas

Publisher: The Johns Hopkins University Press, 2002

Story Profile: The book is rich in substance and detail. It provides up-to-date information while conveying a sense of optimism and hope.

Children's Resources

Title: *Dotty the Dalmatian Has Epilepsy*

Editor: Tim Peters Company

Publisher: Tim Peters Company, 1996

Story Profile: This delightful story is about Dotty the Dalmatian who discovers she has epilepsy. At first, Dotty feels embarrassed and afraid. Once she accepts and learns how to control her seizures, however, she helps firefighters save lives.

Title: *Lee, the Rabbit With Epilepsy*

Author: Deborah M. Moss

Illustrator: Carol Schwartz

Publisher: Woodbine House, 1990

Story Profile: Lee is diagnosed as having epilepsy, but medicine to control her seizures reduces her worries as she learns she can still lead a normal life.

Title: *Taking Seizure Disorders to School: A Story About Epilepsy*

Author: Kim Gosselin

Illustrator: Freedman Moss

Publisher: Jayjo Books, 1998

Story Profile: This picture book helps children to understand the condition of epilepsy.

HEMOPHILIA

Hemophilia is a blood disease that does not allow the blood to clot. It is caused by genes that are recessive and sex-linked, so the disorder almost always occurs in boys, not girls. The major problem for people with hemophilia is not superficial external cuts but uncontrolled internal bleeding. Signs and symptoms of hemophilia include the following.

- Large or deep bruises
- Pain and swelling of joints
- Blood in the urine
- Prolonged bleeding from cuts or injuries
- Prolonged nosebleeds

Treatment for Hemophilia

According to Nielsen (2009), there is no cure for hemophilia; however, it can be successfully managed with clotting factor replacement therapy—periodic IV infusions of the deficient clotting factor into the child's bloodstream.

Educational Considerations for Hemophilia

- Form a strong and effective team, including the child's parents, school nurse, classroom teacher, specialist teachers, counselor, administrator, medical professionals, and any others who are involved with the child to form an ISHP.
- Keep the lines of communication open between home and school. Children with hemophilia need all adults in their lives working together.
- Check with the parent to determine which, if any, activities throughout the school day should be restricted.
- Accept and allow the child to be exempt from a sport or game, as children with hemophilia have been taught how to recognize the feelings of internal bleeding.
- If the teacher observes a student limping or not using an arm or hand, or an area is swollen or hot to the touch, notify parents immediately.
- Upon permission from the parents and student, provide open discussion in the class regarding the bleeding disorder.

Web Sites

Comprehensive Information About Hemophilia: www.nlm.nih.gov/medlineplus/hemophilia.html

National Hemophilia Foundation: www.hemophilia.org

Resource Book

Title: *Living With Hemophilia*

Author: Peter Jones

Publisher: Oxford University Press, 2002

Story Profile: A comprehensive guide to hemophilia and related inherited bleeding disorders. Written primarily for families, this book also provides useful information for teachers, physiotherapists, and paramedics.

■ SPECIFIC LEARNING DISABILITY

A Specific Learning Disability is defined by IDEA as a condition within the individual affecting learning relative to potential. A learning disability is a neurological disorder. According to LD Online (2008) in simple terms, a learning disability results from a difference in the way a person's brain is wired. Children with learning disabilities are as smart or smarter than their peers, but they may have difficulty reading, writing, spelling, reasoning, recalling, and/or organizing information if left to figure things out by themselves or if taught in conventional ways.

A specific learning disability is manifested by interference with acquisition, organization, storage, retrieval, manipulation, or expression of information and inhibits the ability of the individual to learn at an adequate rate when provided with the usual developmental opportunities and instruction from a regular school environment.

A specific learning disability is demonstrated by a significant discrepancy between a student's general intellectual ability and academic achievement in one or more of the following areas.

- Oral expression
- Listening comprehension
- Mathematical calculation
- Mathematical reasoning
- Basic reading skills
- Reading comprehension
- Written expression

A specific learning disability is demonstrated primarily in academic functioning but may also affect self-esteem, career development, and life-adjustment skills. A specific learning disability may occur with but cannot be primarily the result of the following.

- Visual, hearing, motor, or mental impairment
- Emotional disorder
- Environmental, cultural, or economic influence
- History of an inconsistent education program

When congress reauthorized IDEA in 2004, the law changed regarding the process used to identify children with specific learning disabilities. The law now states that schools will no longer be required to determine a severe discrepancy between a child's ability and achievement in order to verify eligibility in the area of Specific Learning Disabilities (SLD), and schools have more options for how to evaluate students for SLD. The federal government has now allowed students to be classified with learning disabilities based on documentation of how well the student responds to interventions—a procedure, as described by Bender and Shores (2007), commonly referred to as "RTI" or Response to Intervention. See a more detailed explanation of RTI in Chapter 4.

Symptoms of Specific Learning Disability

There are some common signs of learning disabilities that may indicate potential learning difficulties. It is normal, from time to time, to see one or more of these characteristics in a child. However, if several of the characteristics are observed over a long period of time, it may be appropriate to consider the possibility of a learning disability.

Preschool

- Speaks later than most children
- Pronunciation problems
- Slow vocabulary growth, often unable to find the right word
- Difficulty rhyming words
- Trouble learning numbers, alphabet, days of the week, colors, shapes
- Extremely restless and easily distracted
- Trouble interacting with peers
- Difficulty following directions or routings
- Fine motor skills are slow to develop

Grades K–4

- Slow to learn the connection between letters and sounds
- Confuses basic words (e.g., run, eat, want)
- Makes consistent reading and spelling errors including letter reversals (b/d), inversions (m,w), transpositions (felt/left), and substitutions (house/home)
- Transposes number sequences and confuses arithmetic signs (+, –, ×, /, =)
- Slow to remember facts
- Slow to learn new skills, relies heavily on memorization
- Impulsive, difficulty planning
- Unstable pencil grip
- Trouble learning about time
- Poor coordination, unaware of physical surroundings, prone to accidents

Grades 5–8

- Reverses letter sequences (soiled/solid, left/felt)
- Slow to learn prefixes, suffixes, root words, and other spelling strategies
- Avoids reading aloud
- Trouble with word problems
- Difficulty with handwriting
- Awkward, fist-like, or tight pencil grip
- Avoids writing assignments
- Slow or poor recall of facts
- Difficulty making friends
- Trouble understanding body language and facial expression

High School Students and Adults

- Continues to spell incorrectly, frequently spells the same word differently in a single piece of writing
- Avoids reading and writing tasks
- Trouble summarizing
- Trouble with open-ended questions on tests
- Weak memory skills
- Difficulty adjusting to new setting
- Works slowly
- Poor grasp of abstract concepts

- Either pays too little attention to details or focuses on them too much
- Misreads information

According to Nielsen (2009), characteristics of those who have learning disabilities may vary from individual to individual, but one common aspect is that a person with a learning disability has an average to above-average IQ. There is also a demonstrated discrepancy between intellectual ability and achievement in one or more academic areas.

Educational Considerations for Children With Learning Disabilities

Accommodations are made in the classroom to "level the playing field" and provide equal and ready access to the task at home. Some sample accommodations that can be provided to assist children with learning disabilities in the general education classroom can be sorted into the following six categories.

1. **Presentation**
   - Provide on audio tape
   - Provide in large print
   - Reduce number of items per page or line
   - Provide a designated reader
   - Present instructions orally

2. **Response**
   - Allow for verbal responses
   - Allow for answers to be dictated to a scribe
   - Allow the use of a tape recorder to capture responses
   - Permit responses to be given via computer
   - Permit answers to be recorded directly into the test booklet

3. **Timing**
   - Allow frequent breaks
   - Extend allotted time for a test

4. **Setting**
   - Provide preferential seating
   - Provide special lighting or acoustics
   - Provide a space with minimal distractions
   - Administer a test in a small groups setting
   - Administer a test in private room or alternative test site

5. **Test Scheduling**
   - Administer a test in several timed sessions or over several days
   - Allow subtests to be taken in a different order
   - Administer a test at a specific time of day

6. **Other**
   - Provide special test preparation
   - Provide on-task/focusing prompts
   - Provide an outline of the day's activities on the board
   - Provide kinesthetic opportunities, (i.e., manipulatives)
   - Recognize success no matter how small!

Web Sites

Division for Learning Disabilities (DLD): www.dldcec.org

Learning Disabilities: www.ldonline.com

Learning Disabilities Association of America (LDA): www.ldanatl.org

National Center for Learning Disabilities: www.ncld.org

Resource Books

Title: *Learning Disabilities: From Identification to Intervention*

Authors: Jack M. Fletcher, G. Reid Lyon, Lynn S. Fuchs, and Marcia A. Barnes

Publisher: The Guildford Press, 2006

Story Profile: This book addresses classification, assessment, and intervention for a range of disabilities involved in reading, mathematics, and written expression.

Title: *Teaching Students With Learning Disabilities*

Authors: Roger Pierangelo and George A. Giuliani

Publisher: Corwin, 2008

Story Profile: This resource provides an invaluable set of tools to help teachers create a positive learning environment and foster a sense of belonging for all learners.

Title: *Teaching Students With Learning Disabilities: A Practical Guide for Every Teacher*

Author: James E. Ysseldyke and Robert Algozzine

Publisher: Corwin, 2006

Story Profile: This book is the concise guide to assist in successfully teaching students with learning disabilities.

Children's Resources

Title: *The Don't-Give-Up Kid and Learning Differences*

Author: Jeanne Gehret

Publisher: Verbal Images Press, 1996

Story Profile: As Alex becomes aware of his different learning style, he realizes that his hero, Thomas Edison, had similar problems.

Title: *Thank You, Mr. Falkner*

Author: Patricia Polacco

Publisher: Philomel, 1998

Story Profile: The author shares a personal story in this moving saga of her struggle with a learning disability.

DYSLEXIA

Dyslexia is the most common specific learning disability. The International Dyslexia Association (2008) suggests that dyslexia refers to a cluster of symptoms that result in people having difficulties with specific language skills, particularly reading. Students with dyslexia usually have trouble with other language skills such as spelling, writing, and pronouncing words.

Symptoms of Dyslexia

According to Nielsen (2009), students with dyslexia may exhibit one of more of the following characteristics.

- Inability to learn and remember words by sight
- Difficulty in decoding skills
- Difficulty in spelling
- Lack or organization of materials
- Difficulty in finding the right words for oral and written communication
- No enjoyment of reading independently
- Difficulty writing from dictation
- Reversal of letters and words
- Difficulty in storing and retrieving names or printed words
- Poor visual memory for language symbols
- Erratic eye movement while reading
- Auditory processing difficulties
- Difficulty in applying what has been read to social or learning situations
- Illegible handwriting
- Confusing vowels or substituting one consonant (e.g., "playnate" for "playmate")
- Inadequate fine motor skills

Dyslexia affects 8% of those labeled "learning disabled," and many of the characteristics are similar. Many of the same strategies used to teach students with learning disabilities are appropriate for students with dyslexia as well.

Educational Considerations for Children With Dyslexia

Some accommodation and modification options for children with dyslexia, as listed by Region 10 Education Service Center (2008), include the following.

Books/Reading

- Provide audiotapes/CDs of textbooks and have student follow the text while listening.
- Provide summaries of chapters.
- Use marker or highlighting tape to highlight important textbook sections.
- Assign peer reading buddies.
- Use colored transparency or overlay.
- Review vocabulary prior to reading.
- Provide preview questions.
- Use videos or filmstrips related to the readings.
- Provide a one-page summary and/or a review of important facts.
- Do not require student to read aloud.
- Talk through the material one to one after reading assignments.

Curriculum

- Shorten assignments to focus on mastery of key concepts.
- Shorten spelling tests to focus on mastering the most functional words.
- Substitute alternatives for written assignments (posters, oral/taped or video presentations, projects, collages, etc.).

Classroom Environment

- Provide a computer for written work.
- Set student close to teacher in order to monitor understanding.
- Provide quiet during intense learning times.

Directions

- Give directions in small steps and with as few words as possible.
- Break complex directions into small steps—arrange in a vertical list format.
- Read written directions to students, then model/demonstrate.
- Accompany oral directions with visual clues.
- Use both oral and written directions.
- Ask student to repeat to check for understanding.

Writing

- Use worksheets that require minimal writing.
- Provide a designated note taker, or photocopy another student's or teacher's notes.
- Provide a print outline with videotapes and filmstrips.
- Allow student to use a keyboard when appropriate.
- Allow student to respond orally.
- Grade only for content, not spelling or handwriting.
- Have student focus on a single aspect of writing assignments.
- Allow student to dictate answers to essay questions.
- Reduce copying tasks.
- Reduce written work.

Math

- Allow student to use a calculator without penalty.
- Use visualization and concrete examples.
- Use grid paper to help correctly line up math problems.
- Present information in small increments and at a slower pace.
- Take time to reteach if student is struggling to understand.
- Read story problems aloud.
- Break problems into smaller steps.

Grading

- Provide opportunity to test orally.
- Allow student to type responses.
- Read test to student.
- Evaluate oral performance more than written.
- Avoid penalizing for spelling errors, reversals, and others.

Testing

- Go over directions orally.
- Permit as much time as needed to complete tests; avoid timed testing.
- Read test materials and allow oral responses.
- Separate content from mechanics/conventions grade.
- Provide typed test materials, not tests written in cursive.

- Allow student to respond on tape, with a typewriter, or by dictating answers to a tutor for assessment.
- Allow tests to be taken in a room with few distractions.

Homework

- Reduce reading assignments.
- Accept work dictated by student to a parent/tutor.
- Limit amount of time to spend on homework; have parents verify time spent on assignments.

Web Sites

International Dyslexia Association: www.interdys.org

Northern California Branch of the International Dyslexia Association: www.dyslexia-ncbida.org

Resource Books

Title: *100 Ideas for Supporting Pupils With Dyslexia*

Authors: Gavin Reid and Shannon Green

Publisher: Continuum International Publishing Group, 2007

Story Profile: This book has suggestions to use while assisting students with dyslexia to reach their greatest potential.

Title: *Dyslexia: Action Plan for Successful Learning*

Author: Glynis Hannell

Publisher: Corwin, 2004

Story Profile: This is a comprehensive overview of dyslexia and its effect on concentration, organization, memory, motivation, and confidence.

Title: *What Is Dyslexia? A Book Explaining Dyslexia for Kids and Adults to Use Together*

Authors: Alan M. Hultquist and Lydia T. Corrow

Publisher: Jessica Kingsley Publishers, 2008

Story Profile: This book is a resource to help explain the difficulty to understand the disability of dyslexia.

Children's Resources

Title: *The Alphabet War: A Story About Dyslexia*

Author: Diane Burton Robb

Illustrator: Gail Piazza

Publisher: Albert Whitman & Company, 2004

Story Profile: Adam's struggles and difficult experiences in school will inspire and encourage many youngsters who find themselves in a daily battle in school trying to read.

Title: *It's Called Dyslexia*

Author: Jennifer Moore-Mallinos

Illustrator: Nuria Roca

(Continued)

(Continued)

Publisher: Barron's Educational Series, 2007

Story Profile: The little girl in this story is unhappy and no longer enjoys school. After she discovers that dyslexia is the reason for her trouble, she begins to understand that with extra practice and help from others, she will begin to read and write correctly.

Title: *Lily and the Mixed-Up Letters*

Author: Deborah Hodge

Illustrator: France Brassard

Publisher: Tundra Books, 2007

Story Profile: For Lily, by the time she reaches second grade, school isn't fun anymore due to her trouble reading. After she receives help, she begins to realize what she can do to make things easier.

AUDITORY PROCESSING DYSFUNCTION (APD)

Auditory processing is a term used to describe what happens when the brain recognizes and interprets the sounds around it. The "disorder" part of APD means that something is adversely affecting the processing or interpretation of the information. Nielsen (2009) states that APD is not a specific category of disability but rather an aspect occurring in many disabilities, quite commonly in the category of learning disabilities.

Children with APD often do not recognize subtle differences between sounds in words, even though the sounds themselves are evident. For example, the request, "Tell me how a couch and a chair are alike," could be understood as, "Tell me how a cow and a hair are alike."

Signs of Auditory Processing Dysfunction

Children with APD typically have normal hearing and intelligence; however, they have also been observed to display some of the following characteristics.

- Have trouble paying attention to and remembering information presented orally
- Have problems carrying out multistep directions
- Have poor listening skills
- Need more time to process information
- Have low academic performance
- Have behavior problems
- Have language difficulty (i.e., they confuse syllable sequences and have problems developing vocabulary and understanding language)
- Have difficulty with reading comprehension, spelling, and vocabulary

Treatments for APD

Several strategies are available to help children with auditory processing difficulties in the general education classroom.

- Auditory trainers are electronic devices that allow a person to focus attention on a speaker and reduce the interference of background noise. In classrooms, the teacher will wear a microphone to transmit sound and the child wears a headset to receive the sound.
- Environmental modifications such as classroom acoustics, placement, and seating may help student.
- Exercises to improve language-building skills can increase the ability to learn and use new words and increase a child's language base.
- Auditory memory enhancement is a procedure that reduces detailed information to a more basic representation.
- Auditory integration training may be promoted by practitioners as a way to retrain the auditory system and decrease hearing distortion.

Educational Considerations for Children With Auditory Processing Disorders

- Verbal instruction should be interrelated with visual stimuli and demonstrations.
- Require students to repeat back directions to be sure they understand the expectations.
- Key points given verbally should also be presented visually using the following.

  o Chalkboard
  o Overhead projector
  o Charts
  o Illustrations

- Directions for an assignment should be given in the order in which they should be completed.
- Provide a handout that highlights the key points to be covered in the lesson.
- Briefly summarize the key points at the end of the lesson for additional reinforcement.
- Provide a copy of notes, either from another student or prepared by the teacher.
- Allow the lecture to be tape-recorded for further review.
- Use sight words and the configuration of words when teaching students to read.
- Use frequent visual stimuli such as pictures.

Web Sites

Facts About Auditory Processing: www.nidcd.nih.gov/health/voice/auditory.asp

Learning Disabilities: www.ldonline.org

Resource Books

Title: *Teaching Students With Learning Disabilities*

Authors: Roger Pierangelo and George A. Giuliani

Publisher: Corwin, 2008

(Continued)

(Continued)

Story Profile: This resource provides an invaluable set of tools to help teachers create a positive learning environment and foster a sense of belonging for all learners.

Title: *When the Brain Can't Hear: Unraveling the Mystery of Auditory Processing Disorder*
Author: Teri James Bellis
Publisher: Atria, 2003

Story Profile: APD occurs when the brain cannot process or understand correctly the sounds the ears hear. It is rarely recognized, often misdiagnosed, and poorly understood. This book is the first APD resource book written in easy-to-read language to help parents understand this confusing disorder.

VISUAL PROCESSING DYSFUNCTION

Visual processing dysfunction is the ability to recognize and interpret visual stimuli involving perception, memory, sequencing, and integration. This should not be confused with visual impairment, which deals only with the ability to see. Nielsen (2009) states, "Visual processing, like auditory processing, is not a specific disability category but rather a dysfunction inherent in many disabilities, especially learning disabilities.

Signs of Visual Processing Dysfunction

Spatial-Relationship Dysfunction

This may cause an individual to have difficulty in left-right discrimination, and the individual generally avoids crossing the midline of the body with the hand.

- Poor depth perception
- Reversals and rotations are noted in writing
- Difficulty assembling puzzles and objects
- Difficulty identifying a complete form of a partially exposed picture, word, letter, or number

Figure Ground Deficit

This causes difficulty in differentiating an object from its general sensory background.

- Difficulty isolating a single word or words on a page
- Difficulty scanning for a specific letter, word, or fact
- Difficulty using a dictionary, index, or telephone book
- Difficulty keeping his or her place while reading

Visual Agnosia

This is the inability to recognize objects with adequate sensory information input.

- Difficulty recognizing objects
- Difficulty naming objects

Visual-Sequential Memory Dysfunction

- This causes difficulty with storage and retrieval of information.
- Difficulty remembering the order of letters in a word when attempting to spell the word
- Difficulty remembering the sequence of events or letters in a series
- Difficulty remembering the days of the week or months of the year
- Revisualization of visual clues is very challenging

Educational Considerations for Visual Processing Dysfunction

Intervention and modification ideas are endless when assisting students to utilize strengths to develop challenging areas. Listed below are common interventions and modifications used with children in the general education classroom. Other interventions already described in previous sections are very appropriate to use as well.

Reading

- Enlarge print for books, papers, and worksheets.
- Use a "window" by cutting a rectangle in an index card to keep information focused while blocking out peripheral material.
- When ready, replace the "window" with a straight ruler or a guide underneath the words and eventually have the child point to words with a finger only.

Writing

- Make lines on paper more distinct.
- Use paper with raised lines.
- Simplify worksheets by reducing the amount of material on each page.
- For math, use paper that is divided into distinct sections, or use graph paper to keep larger problems organized.

Web Sites

Learning Disabilities Online: www.ldonline.org

National Center for Learning Disabilities: www.ncld.org

Resource Book

Title: *Visual Perception Problems in Children With AD/HD, Autism, and Other Learning Disabilities: A Guide for Parents and Professionals*

Author: Lisa A. Kurtz

Publisher: Jessica Kingsley Publishers, 2006

Story Profile: This book provides a comprehensive overview of a variety of visual problems most often exhibited by children with ADHD, autism spectrum disorder, and specific learning disabilities. Written in easy to comprehend terms, this book provides an explanation of how vision difficulties are screened and when to seek medical support.

■ SPEECH OR LANGUAGE IMPAIRMENT (SL)

Speech and language impairments refer to problems in communication and related areas such as oral motor function. According to the American Speech-Language-Hearing Association (2007), approximately 10% of school-aged children have a speech or language impairment that is serious enough to require special education services. Speech and language impairments are divided into four separate categories: fluency disorder, voice disorder, articulation disorder, and language disorder. Nearly twice as many boys as girls have speech impairments. Children with articulation problems represent the largest category of speech/language impairments.

Speech impairments refer to difficulties producing speech sounds or problems with voice quality. They might be characterized by an interruption in the flow or rhythm of speech, such as stuttering, which is called dysfluency. Speech disorders can also indicate problems with the way sounds are formed, or they may be difficulties with the pitch, volume, or quality of the voice.

A language disorder is impairment in the ability to understand and/or use words in context, both verbally and nonverbally. Some characteristics may include improper use of words and their meanings, inability to express ideas, inappropriate grammatical patterns, reduced vocabulary, and inability to follow directions. Children may hear or see a word but not be able to understand its meaning. They may have trouble getting others to understand what they are trying to communicate.

Although some speech disorders do have an organic cause, most disorders cannot be attributed to a physical condition. Speech and language impairments that can be attributed only to dialectical, cultural, or ethnic differences or the influence of a foreign language should not be identified as a disorder.

FLUENCY DISORDER

A fluency disorder is the intrusion of repetition of sounds, syllables, and words, prolongation of sounds, avoidance of words, silent blocks, inappropriate inhalation or exhalation, or problems with phonation patterns. These patterns may also be accompanied by facial and body movements associated with the effort to speak. The most common fluency disorder is stuttering.

VOICE DISORDER

A voice disorder is the absence of voice or presence of abnormal quality, pitch, resonance, loudness, or duration in one's voice.

ARTICULATION DISORDER

An articulation disorder is the absence of or incorrect production of speech sounds that are developmentally appropriate.

LANGUAGE DISORDER

A language disorder is a breakdown in communication as characterized by problems in expressing needs, ideas, or information and may be accompanied by problems in understanding.

Educational Approaches for Speech or Language Impairments

Different types of communication disorders require different approaches to remediation. This is usually done one-on-one or in group settings with a specially trained speech and language pathologist. Most of the children with speech disorders attend regular classes and receive the speech therapy throughout the school day for short periods of time. The goal is for the specific activities addressed in the speech and language sessions to be generalized and used in the general education setting as much as possible.

Other educational suggestions for general education teachers include the following.

- Ask questions that require an answer of few words.
- Allow as much time as necessary for an answer to be given.
- Do not require a child with a speech or language impairment to read out loud solo in class.
- In situations where material will be asked to be read aloud, teachers should provide the material so the child can practice at home.
- Concentrate only on the content of what is being said and not the manner in which it is said; do not require children to repeat words correctly.
- Do not hasten a child's attempt to speak; provide as much time as necessary for the child to respond.
- Keep an open and direct relationship with the student's speech and language therapist in order to provide positive and appropriate situations in which the child can practice newly acquired skills.
- Criticism does not help to overcome a speech disorder; understanding and patience are necessary.

Web Sites

A comprehensive resource for speech and language disorders, including articles, links, and online activities: www.angelfire.com/nj/speechlanguage/index.html

American Speech-Language-Hearing Association (ASHA): www.asha.org

Information About Speech & Language Disorders: www.kidsource.com/NICHCY/speech.html

Resource Book

Title: *Speech to Print: Language Essentials for Teachers*

Author: Louisa Cook Moats

Publisher: Brookes Publishing Company, 2000

Story Profile: This book helps explain the organization of written and spoken English and discovers the connection between language structure and how individuals learn to read. The information presented will also enable readers to recognize, understand, and solve the problems individuals with or without disabilities may encounter.

Children's Resources

Title: *Ben Has Something to Say: A Story About Stuttering*

Author: Laurie Lears

(Continued)

(Continued)

Illustrator: Karen Ritz

Publisher: Shen's Books, 2000

Story Profile: An inspirational story about a boy named Ben. He befriends a dog that he feels is being treated unfairly and tries to communicate with the owner about taking better care of his dog but is too ashamed to speak because he stutters. Finally, he builds up enough confidence, overcomes his reluctance to speak, and asks the owner if he can buy the dog. The book has a foreword for adults that lists additional resources that are invaluable for children who stutter or who know someone who does.

Title: *The Bob (Butterbean) Love Story*

Authors: Terry Page and Bob Love

Publisher: Boo Books, 1995

Story Profile: Bob Love, a famous basketball player, tells his story about living with a speech impediment.

Title: *Sarah's Surprise*

Author: Nan Holcomb

Publisher: Jason & Nordic Publishers, 1990

Story Profile: Sarah, a six-year-old who is unable to talk, uses a picture board to communicate. She is working to use an augmentative communication device. With the help of her speech therapist, she gives everyone a surprise at her mother's birthday party.

Title: *The Summer Kid*

Author: Myrna Neuringer Levy

Publisher: Second Story Press, 1991

Story Profile: Karen, a 10-year-old girl who stays at a summer cottage with her grandmother, encounters Tommy, a nine-year-old boy with a severe language disorder.

■ TRAUMATIC BRAIN INJURY (TBI)

According to the National Dissemination Center for Children with Disabilities—NICHCY (2006), "a traumatic brain injury is an acquired injury to the brain caused by an external physical force, resulting in total or partial functional disability or psychosocial impairments, or both, that may adversely affect a child's educational performance and result in the need for special education and related services." The term applies to open or closed head injuries resulting in experiences of a complex array of problems (see table).

Physical Impairments	*Cognitive Impairments*	*Psychosocial-Behavioral-Emotional Impairments*
Speech impairment	Short-term memory deficit	Fatigue
Vision impairment	Long-term memory deficit	Mood swings
Hearing impairment	Slowness of thinking	Denial
Headaches	Limited attention span	Self-centeredness

Physical Impairments	Cognitive Impairments	Psychosocial-Behavioral-Emotional Impairments
Lack of fine motor coordination	Impairments of perception	Anxiety
Spasticity of muscles	Communication impairment	Depression
Paralysis of one or both sides	Impairments of reading and writing skills	Lowered self-esteem
Seizure disorders	Impairments in planning	Sexual dysfunction
Balance	Sequencing impairments	Restlessness
	Judgment impairments	Lack of motivation
		Inability to self-monitor
		Inability to cope
		Agitation
		Excessive laughing or crying

Symptoms of TBI

Any or all of the above impairments may occur to different degrees. The nature of the injury and its attendant problems can range from mild to severe, and the course of recovery is difficult to predict for any given student.

Educational Considerations for Children With TBI

National Dissemination Center for Children with Disabilities (2006) suggests that it is important to recognize that the sudden onset of a severe disability resulting from trauma is very difficult for children to cope with, as children can often remember how they were before the trauma, which can result in a constellation of emotional and psychosocial problems. Careful planning for school re-entry is extremely important in meeting the needs of the child.

- Provide repetition and consistency.
- Demonstrate new tasks, state instruction, and provide examples to illustrate ideas and concepts.
- Avoid figurative language.
- Reinforce lengthening periods of attention to appropriate tasks.
- Probe skill acquisition frequently, and provide repeated practice.
- Use teacher compensatory strategies for increasing memory.
- Be prepared for student's reduced stamina and increased fatigue, and provide rest breaks as needed.
- Keep the environment as distraction-free as possible.

Web Site

Children With Traumatic Brain Injury: www.neuroskills.com

Resource Books

Title: *Children With Traumatic Brain Injury: A Parent's Guide*

Author: Lisa Schoenbrodt

Publisher: Woodbine House, 2001

Story Profile: This book is a comprehensive, must-have reference that provides parents with the support and information they need to help their child recover from a closed-head injury and prevent further incidents. Coping with TBI involves a complex process of readjustment to the changes in a once healthy child and affects everyone in the family.

Title: *The Education of Children With Acquired Brain Injury*

Author: Sue Walker

Publisher: David Fulton Books, 2005

Story Profile: Teachers have to be aware of their students' educational needs. This book describes what an acquired brain injury is and how best to maximize learning opportunities for those with this condition. The book helps the teacher to support pupils by using appropriate teaching methods.

■ VISUAL IMPAIRMENT (INCLUDING BLINDNESS)

The category of visual impairment (including blindness) means a medically verified visual impairment accompanied by a limitation in sight that interferes with acquiring information or interaction with the environment to the extent that special education and related services may be needed. Many children are affected by visual impairments, some much more intrusive than others.

Signs of Visual Impairment

Certain characteristics, as described by Nielsen (2009), of possible visual difficulty may be observed by the teacher and are listed below.

- Holds work too close or too far
- Thrusts head forward to see distant
- Blinks continually when reading
- Tilts head to see better
- Covers one eye
- Holds body tense when reading or looking at distant objects
- Rubs eyes frequently
- Suffers from crusted, red-rimmed, or swollen eyelids
- Has problems with eyes, often watering or appearing bloodshot
- Is sensitive to light
- Has frequent headaches
- Frowns when looking at printed material

If such signs continue to a marked degree over a period of time, the teacher should refer the student for vision screening.

Some vision impairments are refractive errors. Refractive errors include hyperopia, myopia, and astigmatism. Children experiencing difficulties caused by refractive errors generally do not meet eligibility requirements to receive special education services because these impairments can be remedied with corrective lenses.

HYPEROPIA

Also known as farsightedness, this is a condition in which distant vision is better than near vision. Common signs that may indicate that your child or student is experiencing farsightedness include the following.

- Difficulty in concentrating on and maintaining a clear focus on near objects, such as when reading or writing in the classroom
- Eye strain
- Fatigue and/or headaches after close work
- Aching or burning eyes
- Irritability or nervousness after sustained concentration
- Difficulty tracking from one line to the next while reading, or a tendency to read the same line over and over again
- Have difficulty reading
- Have lack of interest in reading
- Have "crossed" eyes

MYOPIA

Also known as nearsightedness, this is a condition in which near vision is better than distant vision. This is a very common vision condition that affects 30% of the United State's population. Common signs that may indicate that your child or student is experiencing nearsightedness include the following.

- Squints or frowns
- Holds books or other objects very close to the face
- Sits at the front of a classroom or theater or close to the TV or computer
- Is not interested in sports or other activities that require good distance vision
- Has reduced athletic performance
- Gets headaches regularly
- Indicates difficulty seeing the blackboard, TV, or movie screen

ASTIGMATISM

This is a condition that causes blurred vision at any distance due to either the irregular shape of the cornea or the curvature of the lens inside the eye. Astigmatism usually occurs with hyperopia or myopia. Common signs of astigmatism include the following.

- Distortions in portions of visual field
- Blurring of vertical, horizontal, or diagonal lines
- Eyestrain or fatigue
- Headaches

School vision screening is most often used to screen for refractive errors; however, traditional school vision screening has focused on the examination of distance vision in order to detect myopia, which is the most common of the visual disorders (Appleboom, 1985). The screening of other visual functions in school, specifically hyperopia, or "near vision," is inconsistent across the states. Ophthalmology and optometry experts strongly support the school screening of near vision in young children to detect hyperopia. Undiagnosed hyperopia can result in reading difficulty, lack of interest in reading, and school failure (Proctor, 2005).

Specific criteria must be met in order to be eligible for special education services under the visual impairment category. There must be a medically verified visual impairment accompanied by limitation in sight that interferes with a child's ability to acquire or gain knowledge. Specific medically diagnosed visual impairments that may or may not require the need for special education services are listed below.

ALBINISM

Albinism is an inherited condition that causes decreased pigment either in the skin, hair, and eyes or in the eyes alone. Albinism is present at birth and does not become worse over time. With corrective lenses, visual acuity usually measures around 20/100 or 20/200, although it may be as good as 20/40. Approximately one in 20,000 children are born with this condition each year.

Medical Treatment for Albinism

Albinism is most often treated with the use of tinted or pinhole contact lenses, absorptive lenses, or optical aids, although these may not always be helpful.

Educational Approaches for Albinism

Adjusting the lighting and conditions for individuals and having them wear sunglasses and seek shade when outdoors are essential for those who are very sensitive to bright lighting.

CATARACT

A cataract is a clouding of the eye lens. Its cause could be the result of heredity, an infection, severe malnutrition, the mother's drug use during pregnancy, or trauma. Symptoms include a whitish appearance of the pupil and blurred vision.

Medical Treatment for Cataracts

The only medical treatment for cataracts is surgery. Cataracts should be removed within the first few months of life if acuity is to develop normally. Contact lenses or glasses may help with vision acuity.

Educational Strategies for Cataracts

A child with a central cataract may have some unusual head positions since the child is essentially "looking around" the cataract to help vision. Magnification is helpful in some cases.

GLAUCOMA

Glaucoma refers to a group of diseases of the eye that cause progressive damage to the optic nerve due to increased pressure within the eyeball. If glaucoma is treated before severe nerve damage results, glaucoma need not cause blindness or severe vision loss. As the optic nerve deteriorates, blind spots develop. If left untreated, the result may be total blindness. Signs and symptoms of glaucoma include blurred vision (usually in one eye), haloes appearing around lights, pain in the eye, and reddening of the eye.

Medical Treatment for Glaucoma

Glaucoma is often treated through surgery. An operation is performed that creates a drainage hole in the iris. This is done by a laser and is very quick, with few repercussions.

Educational Strategies for Glaucoma

Because early treatment of glaucoma will provide the best prognosis, it is important to communicate with the child's parents and doctors to ensure that the treatment plan is being followed as prescribed. Additional educational strategies may be offered by the eye doctor.

NYSTAGMUS

Nystagmus is an involuntary, rhythmical, repeated movement of one or both eyes. Movements may be horizontal, vertical, or circular and are often rapid and jerky. Nystagmus may accompany neurological disorders or may be caused from a reaction to certain drugs.

Medical Treatment of Nystagmus

There is no generally accepted treatment for nystagmus; however, certain types of jerky nystagmus show improvement throughout childhood.

Educational Strategies for Nystagmus

Children with nystagmus may tend to lose their place during reading instruction and may need help. Use of an index card to underline a sentence, or a typoscope (a card with a hole to view one word or line at a time) can be helpful. As children with nystagmus mature, they seem to need these support devices less often, as they tend to compensate in other ways.

RETINITIS PIGMENTOSA (RP)

RP is a condition in which the retinas in both eyes slowly deteriorate. There is often no apparent reason for its occurrence. As the disease progresses, night vision deteriorates and peripheral vision is lost, producing "tunnel vision." This often leads to legal blindness.

Medical Treatment of RP

There is no known treatment for RP.

Educational Strategies for RP

A variety of optical aids, such as magnifiers, telescopes, and prism lenses, may be helpful and effective.

Educational Strategies for All Visual Impairments

Teachers of children with visual impairments need specialized skills along with knowledge and creativity. There is no intellectual impairment associated with vision disorders, and a person's intelligence is not related to the person's ability to see. Most children who receive special education services due to visual impairments will receive all educational programming with appropriate accommodations and support within the general education classroom.

Most children who are blind learn to read using Braille. In most cases, mobility is an issue as well, and therefore, a white cane is used to help people gain information about their environment. Guide dogs are also used to assist people who are visually impaired. They may also learn to type and use special equipment for mathematics, social studies, and science, as well as learn to feel and read regular print while listening to it on a taped recording. Children with low vision should learn to use their residual vision as efficiently as possible. They may use optical aids and large print to read regular type. Encourage all visually impaired children to develop and utilize their listening skills.

Zoom Text software, as described by Nielsen (2009), is designed to assist individuals with visual impairments by magnifying any handwritten or printed reading material or pictures from two to 32 times its original size. It will also speak the text that is typed, enabling the student to hear what has been written.

Mobility and orientation are of greatest concern, and therefore, the student with a visual impairment should be encouraged and given adequate opportunity to become familiar with the room arrangements and classroom setup. Once the student is familiar with it, the room arrangement should not be changed. A buddy can also be selected to help guide and assist the student, which not only helps the student but also fosters an understanding and acceptance of the student and increases self-confidence as well. The teacher should provide a safe and comfortable environment that promotes positive relationships among students. Learning social skills is extremely challenging for children with visual impairments because it is difficult for them to read facial cues and expressions to help them understand social situations.

Web Sites

American Council of the Blind: www.acb.org

National Association for the Visually Handicapped: www.navh.org

National Library Service for the Blind and Physically Handicapped: www.loc.gov/nis/

Resource Books

Title: *Including Children With Visual Impairments in Mainstream Schools: A Practical Guide*

Author: Pauline Davis

Publisher: David Fulton Books, 2003

Story Profile: This book is a guide that aims to provide inclusive teaching practices to support staff and teachers in mainstream schools. A framework is included that encourages critical reflection on teaching practices regarding the inclusion of children with visual impairments in the general education classroom setting.

Title: *Look at It This Way: Toys and Activities for Children With Visual Impairment (Play Can Help Series)*

Author: Roma Lear

Publisher: Butterworth-Heinemann, 1988

Story Profile: This is one volume out of the "Play Can Help" series that has been derived from the fourth edition of *Play Helps*. This book is dedicated to children with visual impairment and will add an element of fun and variety to the playtime of children with special needs.

Title: *A Parents' Guide to Special Education for Children With Visual Impairments*

Author: Susan Laventure

Publisher: AFB Press, 2007

Story Profile: This is a handbook for parents, family members, and caregivers that explains the special education services to which children with visual impairments will most likely be entitled and how to ensure they will receive them.

Children's Resources

Title: *Do You Remember the Color Blue?: The Questions Children Ask About Blindness*

Author: Sally Hobart Alexander

Publisher: Puffin, 2002

Story Profile: Sally Hobart Alexander lost her sight at the age of 26 and has written this book to help people feel more comfortable around blind people. In this book, Sally responds to personal questions that children and teens have asked her.

Title: *The Secret Code*

Author: Dana Meachen Rau

Publisher: Children's Press, 1998

Story Profile: Oscar, a blind boy in the story, explains to his classmates that his book is not written in a secret code, but in Braille. The Braille alphabet is introduced throughout the story so children can begin to recognize and learn the letters.

Title: *Taking Visual Impairment to School (Special Kids in School)*

Author: Rita Whitman Steingold

Publisher: Jayjo Books, 2004

Story Profile: A girl with visual impairments describes how she finds her way around school, knows where her clothes are in her closet, and even plays baseball.

2

The Special Education Process

■ SPECIAL EDUCATION PROCESS FLOW CHART

Special Education Process Flow Chart

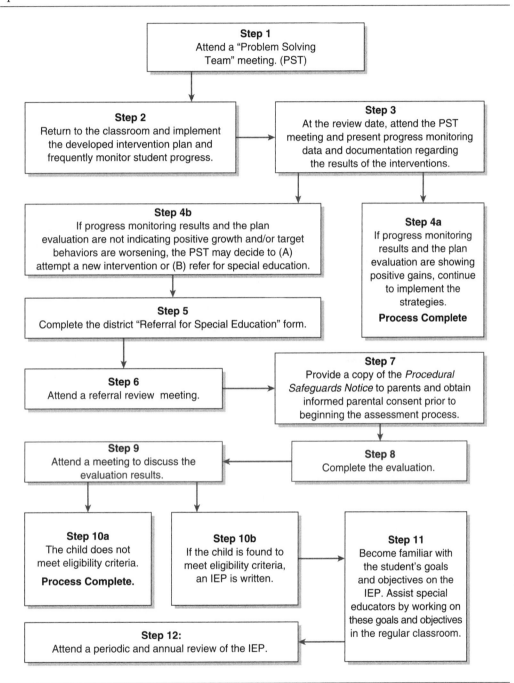

Step 1
Attend a "Problem Solving Team" meeting. (PST)

Step 2
Return to the classroom and implement the developed intervention plan and frequently monitor student progress.

Step 3
At the review date, attend the PST meeting and present progress monitoring data and documentation regarding the results of the interventions.

Step 4b
If progress monitoring results and the plan evaluation are not indicating positive growth and/or target behaviors are worsening, the PST may decide to (A) attempt a new intervention or (B) refer for special education.

Step 4a
If progress monitoring results and the plan evaluation are showing positive gains, continue to implement the strategies.
Process Complete

Step 5
Complete the district "Referral for Special Education" form.

Step 6
Attend a referral review meeting.

Step 7
Provide a copy of the *Procedural Safeguards Notice* to parents and obtain informed parental consent prior to beginning the assessment process.

Step 9
Attend a meeting to discuss the evaluation results.

Step 8
Complete the evaluation.

Step 10a
The child does not meet eligibility criteria.
Process Complete.

Step 10b
If the child is found to meet eligibility criteria, an IEP is written.

Step 11
Become familiar with the student's goals and objectives on the IEP. Assist special educators by working on these goals and objectives in the regular classroom.

Step 12:
Attend a periodic and annual review of the IEP.

From Maanum, Jody L. (2005). *The General Educator's Guide to Special Education* (2nd Ed.). Thousand Oaks: Corwin. Reprinted with permission.

■ EXPLANATION OF THE SPECIAL EDUCATION PROCESS

Since education is a state function, state statutes as well as federal law govern the special education process. The state's special education laws must be consistent with federal laws; however, there will be differences between states. Some states have provisions that go beyond what is required by IDEA and may provide students with additional disability rights and protections under state statutes. If there is a conflict between the two laws, the federal law supersedes the state law. The guidelines listed here are based on IDEA 2004 and comparisons of several state statutes. The timelines for your state may be slightly different.

The following information explains each step of the special education process. The numbered items correspond directly to the flow chart shown on the previous page.

Keeping Parent(s) Informed

It is imperative to keep the parent(s) informed of the child's progress in school. If you have not yet discussed your concerns with the parents, you need to contact them at this time before attending the initial Problem Solving Team (PST) meeting. Throughout this publication, the term "parents" will be used to indicate the primary caregiver and the one responsible for making educational decisions for the child.

Step 1: Attend a "Problem Solving Team" (PST) meeting.

General education teachers can effectively meet the needs of many students with learning and behavior problems within the general education classroom. Situations arise, however, when a teacher needs a support system to help with students who present unique learning and/or behavioral challenges. The intervention team is a committee formed to assist regular education teachers who have concerns about students who are struggling to learn or whose behaviors are interfering with their own or affecting other students' ability to learn in the general education classroom. Depending upon the school district, the intervention team may be referred to as the Child Study Team (CST), Pre-Placement Team (PPT), Pre-Referral Team (PRT), Student Support Team (SST), or perhaps the Building Intervention Team (BIT). For the purpose of this publication, the term Problem Solving Team (PST) has been selected. Regardless of the name used, the function of this team is to screen students and provide early intervention ideas before making any recommendations for special education referrals.

If you have a concern about a specific student, you will need to make a request for assistance. Well-developed teams require you to complete a form prior to the intake meeting. At the initial meeting, you will need to be prepared to share information relating to the academic and/or behavioral concerns in the classroom and about the progress, lack or progress, or regression seen throughout the school year. You will also be asked to disclose any additional information such as parental concerns or medical information that will help the PST better understand the student.

An effective team will be one that focuses on solving problems in order to improve student performance. The goal for each student is to decrease the discrepancy between what is expected of the student and what is actually occurring. The collaborative problem solving method developed by Bergen and Kratchowill (1990) is an excellent example that the PST can utilize in an effort to facilitate the intervention process.

The above mentioned problem-solving model consists of the following steps.

- Problem identification
- Problem analysis
- Plan development
- Plan implementation
- Problem plan

Effectively completing the five problem-solving steps will not occur in just one meeting. It is important to work efficiently and thoroughly through each step of the process to ensure positive outcomes.

Problem identification—what is the discrepancy between what is expected and what is occurring?

This step will take place at the initial intake meeting. It may be helpful to answer any of the following questions that would be pertinent to the specific problem you are attempting to identify.

- What is the student doing or not doing that has caused us to perceive a problem?
- What behaviors would we like to see maintained, and what behavior would we like to eliminate?
- What environmental and personality factors are contributing to the problem situation?
- What behaviors would we like to see the student engaging in or not engaging in?
- What is the student's current level of performance, and what level of performance will the student need to reach to meet expectations?

It is important to use a variety of information and sources to answer these questions. Review data from

- school and medical records,
- student work samples,
- teacher and parent interviews, and
- direct observations.

The problem needs to be precisely stated and defined in concrete terms in order to be readily observed and easily measured. The goal is for the target behaviors or academic skills that are expected to increase or decrease because of intervention efforts to be clearly defined by the team.

Problem analysis—why is the problem occurring?

The purpose of this step is to formulate reasons why the problem is occurring so that appropriate interventions can be developed. It may be helpful to answer any of the following questions to help analyze the problem.

- How are environmental and personality factors contributing to the mismatch that exists between actual and desired levels of performance?
- In what settings is the problem behavior occurring, and in what settings is performance better?

- What assessment methods are most appropriate for determining factors that contribute to the problem situations, and how do these methods relate to intervention design?
- What resources are available to help resolve this problem situation?

Plan development—what is the goal?
What is the intervention plan to address this goal?

During this process, intervention strategies will be selected that have a strong likelihood for success. It is important to set your goal before you determine the intervention.

1. Set a goal.

2. Specify a time frame (e.g., end of year, end of semester, certain number of weeks). Give the intervention enough time to work and for the team to gather good data.

3. Specify measurement conditions (i.e., measurement material to be used and setting in which the intervention will take place).

4. Specify the desired behavior (i.e., Are you trying to increase a desired behavior or decrease an undesired behavior?).

5. Specify criterion for success (be realistic; state the final level of expected performance).

Plan implementation—how will
implementation integrity be ensured?

The larger the discrepancy between what is expected and what is occurring, the more intense the intervention should be. Bender and Shores (2007) suggest considering the following questions when making decisions regarding intervention implementations.

- What strategies/procedures will be used? To ensure effective results, research-based intervention strategies should be selected. For specific research-based intervention ideas, refer to the intervention strategy section.
- When and how often will the intervention occur? More frequent with less time is better than less frequent with more time.
- Where will the intervention take place? Choose the least restrictive environment whenever possible.
- Who is responsible for implementation? Consider all resources available. To ensure effective implementation, be sure the person delivering the intervention is properly trained.
- Start date—when will the intervention begin. Consider the time it will take to prepare materials and if necessary to train staff.

Before adjourning the meeting, a review date of three to six weeks will be set to review the progress the student is making and to review the appropriateness of the intervention.

Keeping Parents Informed

After the initial PST meeting, notify parents and share with them the intervention plan that will be in place for their child.

*Step 2: Return to the classroom and implement
the developed intervention plan and frequently monitor
student progress.*

As the classroom teacher, it is essential that you ensure the integrity of the intervention implementation. Follow the plan specifically and frequently monitor progress by gathering data that will be used to determine the effectiveness and appropriateness of the intervention.

Here are some details to consider when monitoring student progress.

- How will the data be collected?
  - Review (incident reports, attendance data)
  - Observe (time on task, frequency of behavior, out of seat)
  - Test (Curriculum-Based Measurement [CBM], running records)

- What materials will be used to collect data and monitor progress?
  - Is it skills specific?
  - Is it standardized (i.e., given the same way each time)?
  - Can it be given repeatedly?
  - Is it easy to administer?
  - Is it time efficient?
  - Can you compare the scores to the performance of other students?
  - Does it provide you with useful data?

- Where will the data be collected?
- When and how often will data be collected?
- Who will collect the data?

*Step 3: At the review date, attend the PST meeting
and present progress monitoring data and documentation
regarding the results of the interventions.*

At the meeting, progress monitoring data of the specifically followed intervention will be reviewed. Bring all pertinent and beneficial information with you to the meeting, including anecdotal recordings, observations, graphs, timings, and other appropriate data.

Plan evaluation—is the intervention plan effective?

During problem evaluation, it is important to ask the following questions.

- How well is the intervention working?
- Is the problem resolved, or does the intervention need to continue?
- If the intervention was not successful, is it certain that the integrity of the intervention was maintained?
- Should this problem cycle through the problem-solving process again?

Keeping Parent(s) Informed

Before returning to the PST meeting, inform the child's parents of the results of the intervention strategy. Let them know that you will be attending another meeting to discuss the results and will notify the parents of the decision made at the next PST meeting.

Step 4a: If progress monitoring results and the plan evaluation are showing positive gains, continue to implement the strategies.

If improvement and progress is noted, the PST will probably decide that a special education referral is not necessary at the present time. A follow-up review meeting will be scheduled for six to eight weeks to further review and ensure continual student progress and growth. As long as the intervention is in place, frequent, weekly progress monitoring should be occurring in the classroom.

Keeping Parents Informed

It is important to inform the child's parents that the intervention strategy has produced positive results and that you will continue to use the strategy with their child in the classroom and that there will be no need for a special education referral at this time. Also, ensure parents that monitoring of progress and growth will be ongoing to continually evaluate the effectiveness of the intervention in place.

Step 4b: If progress monitoring results and the plan evaluation are not indicating positive growth and/or target behaviors are worsening, the PST may decide to do the following:

A. Attempt a different intervention strategy; if so, refer to Step 1 to begin the process again.

Or

B. Refer the child for a special education evaluation.

Step 5: Complete the district "Referral for Special Education" form.

You will need to complete the district referral form. The results of the pre-referral intervention strategies, student-specific demographic information regarding name, age, grade, parent's name, and other pertinent information may be listed on this form. Once the form is complete, sign it and submit it to the appropriate person for an administrative signature. You will be notified when the referral review meeting will take place. With the implementation of the RTI mode, many districts have only one team and the referral review committee is the same as the PST.

Keeping Parents Informed

Notify the parents that you have completed and submitted the referral form and that a meeting will be held to discuss the next step in the special education referral. The parents have the right to be informed in advance of the date and time of this meeting. Encourage the parents to make every effort to attend this first meeting, as their input is critical and openly welcomed.

Step 6: Attend a referral review meeting.

After the district referral form has been signed, the school psychologist and special education staff will be informed of the referral. As mentioned previously, it is likely that the PST will be the ones initiating the evaluation plan. At the meeting, the team will discuss the issues and concerns surrounding the student and will develop an evaluation plan to be followed during the referral process.

The student's team will consist of the student's parent(s), classroom teacher, school psychologist, principal, and one or more of the special education staff who will be involved in the assessment process. The special education staff is determined by the needs of the student. If academic concerns are the issue, a learning disabilities teacher is involved; if behaviors are the issue, the emotional and behavioral disorders teacher is involved; if speech or language is a concern, the speech and language teacher is involved, and so forth. If there is a combination of issues, two or more specialists will be invited to the meeting.

At the meeting, the referral review form will be completed as well as an assessment plan. The following information will be discussed and documented on the referral review form.

Referral Review Form

Student's present level of performance

The team will discuss and review the student's performance in the following areas.

Intellectual functioning

This section refers to the student's cognitive ability or IQ.

Academic performance

This area discusses the student's academic performance in the classroom. Specific information related to the curriculum will be addressed. The general education teacher will be asked to provide information regarding the student's academic performance in the classroom.

Communicative status

This area examines the student's ability to communicate with others, including age-peers, teachers, and adults in order to get his or her needs met. Parent(s) and classroom teachers will be asked to provide information in this area.

Motor ability

Discussion in this area includes both fine and gross motor skills. Fine motor skills such as handwriting and cutting may be discussed. In the area of gross motor skills, physical education activities such as running, jumping rope, and skipping may be discussed. Parent(s) and classroom teachers will be asked to provide information in this area.

Vocational potential

Transition services are intended to be a coordinated set of activities, provided to the student by the school and sometimes other agencies to promote a successful transition from high school to postsecondary education or employment. Transition planning must be included in the first IEP that will be in effect when the child turns 16 years of age. Four areas of transition will be considered: training, education, employment, and independent living skills. The area of vocational potential will rarely be utilized for elementary students.

Sensory status

This area includes both the visual and hearing components. Any concerns regarding a student's sight or hearing abilities will be discussed. Information gathered from the student's parent(s) will be essential.

Physical status

A student's overall health condition and general health will be noted in this section. Parental input will be critical for this area.

Emotional and social development

This section covers the child's interactions with peers and adults in social situations as well as how the child is able to emotionally handle different situations and feelings.

Behavior

The student's overall behavior is noted here. Behavior concerns in the classroom, the community, and at home are addressed in this section. Input from teacher(s) and parent(s) is important for this section.

Functional skills

Functional skills include information related to how the student is able to care for him or herself and how the student independently performs daily living skills. Issues such as toilet training, dressing, feeding, and self-care will be discussed. Other functional skills will include caring for pets, keeping personal space clean, bathing and showering, and other areas of concern. Parental input will be imperative.

Keeping Parent(s) Informed

It is essential that the student's parent(s) be involved in this initial referral review meeting. The student's parent(s) most adequately provide crucial information regarding the student's communicative status, physical status, emotional and social development, behavior, functional skills, and medical information.

Development of the Evaluation Plan

After the referral review is completed and all of the above present levels have been discussed, an evaluation plan should be developed. An evaluation is an assessment of a student's strengths and weaknesses by using different testing instruments. It is important for the team to use a variety of assessment tools, both formal and informal, to gather relevant, functional, and developmentally appropriate information about a student. This information can be gathered in a variety of ways.

- *Traditional assessments* are formal, standardized tools designed to test the student's level of functioning in specific areas. The assessments are used to gather in-depth information relating to a student's capabilities and performance. The results gathered during formal assessments are used to compare the student's level of performance to the performance of other students of the same age and grade level. The tests provide information that will help to determine if the student is performing above, below, or at the same level as other students of the same age and grade level.
- *Nontraditional assessments* are additional means to gather valuable information. These assessments are informal methods of gathering systematic information about a student's functioning in a particular setting. Systematic progress monitoring is a quick, efficient, informal way of monitoring a child's progress. Other informal ways include class work samples, observations in multiple settings, student portfolios, and any other additional ways to gather information that will help to learn more about the student.

Special Education Staff Responsibility

After the team determines the necessary assessments, the team members must decide who is responsible for administering the assessments. A case manager will be determined indicating who will then be responsible for distributing the appropriate forms at the targeted time.

Completion of the "Notice of Education Evaluation/Reevaluation" Form

All information discussed at this meeting, including the assessment methods used and the special education staff responsibility, will be documented on the *"Notice of Education Evaluation/Reevaluation"* form.

Step 7: Provide a copy of the Procedural Safeguards Notice to parents and obtain informed parental consent prior to beginning the assessment process.

The *Procedural Safeguards Notice* is given to the parents after which a copy of the Notice of Education Evaluation/Revaluations must be provided to the parent(s) of the student. A parent must sign the form giving consent before any assessments can begin. The school *cannot* proceed with an initial assessment without signed, informed parental consent.

Keeping Parent(s) Informed

Parents will be provided with the Procedural Safeguards Notice. Explain to the parents that the safeguard notice is a formal document that describes the rights and protections of their child and themselves under IDEA. Once the parents have read and understood their rights, it is necessary to obtain informed parental consent on the Notice of Education Evaluation/Revaluation form before the evaluation can begin. It is imperative that parents know that giving consent to evaluation *does not mean* that the parent is giving consent for the child to *receive* special education services. It only means that the special education team is given permission to evaluate the child. If the parents have any further questions related to the evaluation, you are advised to encourage that the parent contact the school psychologist, the administrator, or the special education teacher(s) listed on the form.

Step 8: Complete the evaluation.

Immediately upon receiving the signed Notice of Education Evaluation/ Reevaluation form, the assessment period begins. Many states have established specific time frames in which a student evaluation must be completed. It is important to know if the specified time frames are in calendar days or school days. If you are conducting evaluations in a state that does not have an established timeline for completing an evaluation, IDEA 2004 requires that the evaluation be conducted within 60 calendar days of receiving parental consent. When the assessments are complete, the special education team will compile the findings from the formal and informal assessment and summarize the information on the *Evaluation Report*. The report will include test results and interpretations, present level of performance in the areas assessed, and the team's judgment regarding eligibility for services. The *Evaluation Report* must be dated and have all involved team members' names and titles listed.

Keeping Parent(s) Informed

Inform the parents that once the assessment is complete, a meeting will be arranged to discuss the results of the assessments. The parent(s) will receive a written notice from the special education department regarding the upcoming meeting date and time. They should be notified early enough so that they have adequate time to arrange to attend. It may be appropriate to call the parents several days before the meeting as a reminder and to be sure they understand the importance of the meeting. The results of the testing data will be presented, and the special education team will make recommendation of how to proceed. Meetings do not have to be face-to-face, and alternative ways of meeting, such as through telephone conference calls or video conferences, are acceptable.

Step 9: Attend a meeting to discuss the evaluation results.

During this meeting, each team member who has assessed the student will describe the evaluation procedure and discuss the results. If at any time you do not understand the terminology or the information presented, be sure to ask for clarification. If you do not understand, it is likely that the parents may not understand either. Once all assessment results have been shared, the team will determine whether the results indicate if appropriate and necessary eligibility criteria have been met in order for the student to qualify to receive special education services. The evaluation results must be summarized on the Evaluation Report, and all team members must agree upon the eligibility conclusion. If a child is deemed eligible to receive services, the decision must be recorded on the Evaluation Report.

An example agenda of the meeting may include the following.

- Introductions of those attending
- A review of evaluation results
- A review of any material that the parents want to have included as part of the determination
- Discussion of evaluation results
- Determination of eligibility and the educational needs of the student

Keeping Parent(s) Informed

Parents are invited to bring other individuals with them to the meeting; however, the law does require that the other individuals attending must have knowledge or special expertise regarding the child. Individuals that may attend the meeting might include educational advocates, private evaluators, private tutors, and other professionals who have experience with the child. If necessary, a translator will be provided by the school district.

Step 10a: If the child does not meet eligibility criteria, the process is complete.

If the evaluation results indicate that the child *does not* meet required criteria necessary for a child to receive special education or related services under any one of the 13 categories, the special education process is complete. No further special education action can be taken.

Keeping Parent(s) Informed

If a child is not found to meet required criteria to receive special education services, parents may inquire about other ways through which their child might obtain additional educational assistance—perhaps targeted instruction (small group), Title 1 services, or a plan allowed under Section 504 of the Rehabilitation Act.

Step 10b: If the child is found to meet eligibility criteria, an IEP is written.

If the evaluation results indicate that the child *does* meet required criteria necessary for a child to receive special education or related services under any one of the 13 categories, an Individualized Education Plan (IEP) must be written. If time permits, the IEP may be written immediately after the assessment results have been discussed and eligibility is determined. The second option is to schedule a separate meeting. An IEP must be developed within 30 calendar days of the determination that the child is eligible for special education services. Services may not be provided until an IEP has been developed and the parents have provided informed consent. It is encouraged that the IEP meeting take place at the same time and place as the evaluation meeting to avoid having to schedule an additional meeting.

When writing the IEP, all team members must be present. Required team members include the parent(s), student (if appropriate), special education teacher(s), general education teacher, a representative of the school district (a special education administrator or school administrator), and any additional people at parental or district discretion.

Keeping Parent(s) Informed

Encourage parent(s) to ask questions that they may have. You want to be sure they understand the information discussed and the plan developed for their child. Be aware the parents have received a large amount of information already. Often, once the information is reread at home, questions will arise.

Developing the IEP

The IEP is tailored to each student's unique educational needs, and decisions are made by the child's team to ensure this is true. Most states and/or local school districts have developed forms to make the IEP process run smoothly. These forms contain all of the elements required by IDEA and may also contain additional state and/or district level elements.

An IEP is the result of a process to ensure that individuals with disabilities receive appropriate education planning to accommodate their unique instructional needs and that these needs are met in an appropriate learning environment. An IEP is a written legal document that is developed, reviewed, and revised as needed. The IEP is reviewed annually, and the student's needs must be reevaluated every three years to ensure continued need for special education services.

Writing the IEP

The IEP must include specific components to ensure that all areas of the student's education will be addressed. Pierangelo and Giuliani (2007) identify 12 required steps when writing an IEP. The 12 steps are as follows.

1. Formulation of Present Level of Academic Achievement and Functional Performance

2. Consideration of Special Factors

3. Determination of Measurable Annual Goals

4. Reporting Progress to Parents

5. Determine the Extent to Which the Student Will Not Be Able to Participate in General Education Programs (LRE Explanation)

6. Determine Placement Options

7. Determine Related Services, Program Modifications, Accommodations, Supplementary Aids, and Services

8. Determine the Need for Assistive Technology Devices and Services

9. Determine the Ability of a Student to Participate in State and District Assessments

10. Determine Extended School Year (ESY) Services

11. A Statement of Secondary Transition Service Needs and Needed Transition

12. Develop a Statement of Transfer of Parental Rights to the Student Upon Reaching the Age of Majority

1. **Formulation of Present Level of Academic Achievement and Functional Performance (PLOP—Present Level of Performance)**

   The team develops a statement describing the child's present levels of academic and functional performance. This statement should be drawn from a variety of information and data, including input from the general education teacher and parents. The PLOP statement must include information on how the child's disability affects his or her involvement and progress in the general education curriculum. The PLOP establishes the starting point or baseline that will be used to develop the IEP's measurable annual goals and objectives, so it is important that objective information such as recent test scores and other evaluation data be included in this statement.

2. **Consideration of Special Factors**

   The team must consider a list of "special factors" that might require additional elements in the IEP. These factors include the following.

   - The use of positive behavioral interventions and strategies to address a child's behavior that gets in the way of his or hear learning or that of others

     Key question: Is the student's behavior affecting his or her learning or that of others?

   - The language needs of a child with limited English proficiency

     Key question: Does the student's level of English language proficiency affect special education and related services the student needs? If so, to what extent?

   - Instruction in Braille for a child who is blind or visually impaired

     Key question: What are the student's future needs for instruction in Braille?

   - The language and communication needs for a child who is deaf or hard of hearing

     Key question: Does the student need to learn or use special communication and language skills and strategies? If yes, do the student's annual goals and short-term objectives or benchmarks address affected areas?

   - The need for assistive technology devices and services for all children with disabilities (e.g., special computer software, calculators, audio books)

Key question: What, if any, assistive technology devices and services does the student need to achieve her or his annual goals, including benchmarks or short-term objectives?

3. Determination of Measurable Annual Goals

At least one annual goal must be written for each of the needs identified in the PLOP. For each goal, short-term objectives must be written as well.

Annual goals: statements that identify what knowledge, skills, and behaviors a student is expected to be able to demonstrate within a period of time from the time the IEP is implemented until the next scheduled review. Annual goals must be identified to meet the student's needs, as identified in the present levels of performance.

Short-term objectives are derived from the annual goals but represent smaller, more manageable learning tasks a student must master on the way to achieving the goals. The purpose of short-term objectives is to enable teachers to monitor progress during the school year and revise the IEP with the student's instructional needs. In most cases, at least two objectives should be written for each annual goal.

(The requirement for short-term objectives for students other than those with significant cognitive disabilities was eliminated in IDEA 204; however, some states may choose to continue to require such interim steps as part of annual goals.)

4. Reporting Progress to Parents

The IEP team will describe how the student's progress toward meeting the annual goals and short-term objectives (if appropriate) will be measured and reported to parents. The description must include when and how often the progress will be reported to parents. Reports to parents should not rely on any one single measure but should include results gathered by curriculum-based measurement, standardized tests, teacher observations, and grades. Teacher observations and grades are just a portion of the appropriate measures used to monitor and report student progress.

5. Determine the Extent to Which the Student Will Not Be Able to Participate in General Education Programs (LRE Explanation)

The IEP must include a statement that describes how much time the student will spend outside of the regular education classroom and away from students who do not have disabilities. This requirement is designed to protect the student's right to be educated in the least restrictive environment (LRE) as required by IDEA.

The student should have full access to the general education curriculum regardless of where he or she receives special education and related services. If special education services, such as reading instruction, will be provided in a separate location such as a resource room, the IEP should indicate exactly what the student will be missing in the regular education classroom at that same time. The same program options and nonacademic services that are available to student without disabilities must be available to students with disabilities. Program options typically include art, music, industrial arts, clubs, home economics, sports, field trips, and vocational education. Nonacademic services and extracurricular activities typically include athletics, health services, recreations activities, and special interest groups or clubs.

6. Determine Placement Options

The IEP team must provide a written justification for the decision to place a student in any setting outside of the regular classroom. Providing services outside of the general education classroom shall occur only when the nature or severity of the student's needs is such that education in the regular classes with the use of supplementary aids and services cannot be achieved satisfactorily.

A written description of the options considered and the reasons for those options to be rejected must be provided for each placement consideration. The IEP must also contain written description of the option accepted and reasons the option was accepted.

The IEP must state the special education program or services needed by the student. This statement of special education services is the school's commitment of resources to the student that will allow him or her to reach the measurable annual goals developed by the IEP team. Such programs and services include the following.

- Special classes
- Resource rooms
- Direct and indirect consultant teacher services
- Travel training
- Home instruction
- Special teacher, including itinerant teachers
- Adaptive physical education

Projected starting date and anticipated frequency, duration, and location of services must be indicated for each special education and related services. The date must include the month, day, and year and have a duration of no more than a year from the date of the meeting.

7. Determine Related Services, Program Modifications, Accommodations, Supplementary Aids, and Services

The IEP team must develop a statement about the program modifications, accommodations, supplementary aids, and services provided to the student. As justified in the IEP, these services must enable the student to do the following.

- Advance appropriately toward reaching the annual goals
- Be involved in and make progress in the general education curriculum, extracurricular, and other nonacademic activities
- Be educated and participate with children who do not have disabilities

Further description modifications, accommodations, and supplementary aids are listed in Chapter 3.

8. Determine the Need for Assistive Technology Devices and Services

The IEP must describe the student's needs for assistive technology devices needed for the student to benefit from education. The IEP should also state whether the student requires the use of a school-purchased assistive technology device in the student's home or in other settings in order for the student to receive a free appropriate public education. Specific examples of assistive technology devices can be found in Chapter 3.

9. **Determine the Ability of a Student to Participate in State and District Assessments**

The IEP team reviews the student PLOP and annual goals to decide what the student should know and be able to do before determining the assessment needs of the student. The IEP team will need to determine what modifications will be made that will allow the student to participate in the assessment requirements. If the team makes the determination that the student will not participate in the state or district assessment, a statement of why that assessment is not appropriate, including an explanation of how the student will be assessed, must be clearly stated in the IEP. Specific assessment accommodations are listed in Chapter 3.

10. **Determine Extended School Year (ESY) Services**

Pierangelo and Giuliani (2007) define ESY services as being provided to students with a disability beyond the normal school year in accordance with the student's IEP and at no cost to the parents of the student. The goal of an ESY program is to assist students with disabilities in the general areas of emerging skill, regression or recoupment, and self-sufficiency. A team must make specific justification for a student to receive ESY services. Specific documentation must be collected and reported on to assist the determination for ESY.

11. **A Statement of Secondary Transition Service Needs and Needed Transition**

Beginning when the student is turning 16, the law requires that the IEP include plans for the student's successful transition from high school to postsecondary education or employment. This important process must include a statement of appropriate measurable postsecondary goals based upon age-appropriate transition assessment related to training, education, employment, and where appropriate, independent living skills. Further details regarding transition planning can be found in Chapter 3.

12. **Develop a Statement of Transfer of Parental Rights to the Student Upon Reaching the Age of Majority**

The IEP must include a statement that the student has been informed and is aware that upon reaching age 18, all rights under IDEA 2004 will be transferred over to the student. This statement must appear in the IEP at least one year prior to the student reaching age 18.

The IEP must be written and agreed upon by all team members. Upon completion of the IEP, parents will be asked to sign the document, which will serve as signed informed consent for the school to begin to provide special education services for the student. Services should begin as soon as possible once the IEP is finalized.

Keeping Parent(s) Informed

A parent's signature on the IEP will indicate consent and that services can begin immediately. Encourage parents to share any questions or concerns that they may have.

Step 11: Become familiar with the student's goals and objectives on the IEP. Assist special educators by working on these goals and objectives in the regular classroom.

A classroom teacher must be familiar with a student's IEP contents, especially the goals, objectives, accommodations, and modifications that must be implemented in the general education classroom.

Step 12: Attend a periodic and annual review of the IEP.

The student's progress toward the IEP goals and objectives must be reviewed at least two times during the year. A periodic review is scheduled *at least* one time (often more frequent) during the year to discuss the student's progress. The periodic review is most often held during a parent-teacher conference. An annual review must be completed within one year of the date on the IEP. At the annual review, the IEP is reviewed, revised, and rewritten. If the student has met some or all of the goals and objectives on the IEP, new goals and objectives must be written to address the current educational performance needs. It is at the IEP annual review that the team also determines whether or not the student continues to exhibit a need for special education services.

Keeping Parent(s) Informed

Encourage the parents to attend both the periodic review and annual review meetings, as their input is essential. Parents do have the right to request an IEP meeting at any time if they feel one is necessary. For example, if the parent believes their child is not progressing satisfactorily or there is a problem with the current IEP, it would be appropriate for the parent to request a staffing. A student who receives special education services must be reassessed every three years to ensure that the student continues to meet the eligibility criteria and continues to exhibit a need for special education services.

■ TRADITIONAL FORMAL ASSESSMENTS

This section includes an overview of some of the most common assessment tools used. Some assessment tools must be administered by the school psychologist, whereas others are administered by a special education teacher. The person who administers the test is also responsible for interpreting the assessment and sharing the results with the IEP team.

■ EXPLANATION OF TEST SCORES

Assessment Terminology

Specific terminology is used when reporting assessment results. Listed below in alphabetical order are the most common terms used. It is important to be familiar with these terms before attending the IEP evaluation summary meeting.

Age Equivalents

An age-equivalent score is a very general score used to compare the performance of children at the same age with one another. These scores express test performance in terms of the familiar units of chronological age. For example, if a student receives an age score of 7.6 (seven years, six months) on an assessment, it means that the student has performed as well as the average seven-year, six-month-old child.

Grade Equivalents

A grade-equivalent score is a general score used to compare the performance of children in the same grade with one another. The scores express test performance in terms of grade levels. For example, a student who receives a score of 4.5 is performing as well as the average student in the fifth month of fourth grade.

Percentile Ranks

Percentile ranks represent the percentage of individuals within the norm group who achieved this raw score or a lower one. If a student earns a percentile rank of 62, it can be said the student performed at a level equal to or greater than 62% of the norm group and at a level lower than that of the remaining 28% of the norm group.

Raw Scores

The first step in scoring an assessment is to determine the raw score. The raw score normally indicates the number of items correctly answered on a test.

Scaled Scores

Scaled scores most frequently refer to subtest scores. Most often, scales place the average score at 10, thus if a student receives a scaled score of 10, the student is performing in the average range when compared to the norm group of the same age. Students who receive a scaled score of 19 would fall in the above-average range, whereas students who receive a scaled score of three fall in the below-average range.

17 and above	**Above Average**
14 to 16	**High Average**
7 to 13	**Average**
4 to 6	**Low Average**
3 and below	**Below Average**

Standard Scores

Standard scores are often used to report overall test performance and are useful for comparing several different test scores for the same student. Standard scores transform the raw score to fit a normal curve. Normally, standard scores have a mean score of 100 and a standard deviation of 15. This means that if a student received a standard score of 100, the student's score could range between 85 and 115. This score would fall in the average range.

130 and above	**Above Average**
116 to 129	**High Average**
85 to 115	**Average**
71 to 84	**Low Average**
70 and below	**Below Average**

Intellectual Functioning Assessments

WECHSLER INTELLIGENCE SCALES FOR CHILDREN—FOURTH EDITION (WISC-IV)

This test is administered individually to children ages 6.0 to 16.11 years. It assesses general intellectual functioning. The results of this battery of tests will also provide information regarding the student's strengths and weaknesses in specific areas of ability. The test consists of 15 subtests, but only 10 subtests are required to be administered in order to determine IQ scores. The test is divided into four main sections: the *verbal index* that consists of five subtests, the *perceptual reasoning index* that consists of five subtests, and the *working memory index* and the *processing speed index,* each consisting of three subtests.

When determining results of the WISC-IV, four composite scores are calculated. The full-scale IQ is based on the performance of all combined scales.

The global IQ scores are just like standard scores and can be interpreted using the standard score criteria. Four factor-based index scores are also produced by combining various subtests. The index scores are the same as standard scores as well and can be interpreted using the standard score criteria. Individual subtest scaled scores are provided.

WECHSLER ABBREVIATED SCALE OF INTELLIGENCE (WASI)

This test is administered to individuals ages 6.0 to 89.0 years old. This is an abbreviated scale which meets the demand for a quick, reliable measure of an individual's verbal, nonverbal, and general cognitive functioning in any setting. Two different formats can be administered. A four-test format (Vocabulary, Similarities, Block Design, Matrix Reasoning) provides full-scale IQ, verbal IQ, and performance IQ scores, or a two-test format (Vocabulary and Matrix Reasoning) provides an estimate of general cognitive ability (full-scale IQ).

WECHSLER PRESCHOOL AND PRIMARY SCALE OF INTELLIGENCE—THIRD EDITION (WPPSI-III)

This is a test administered individually to children ages 2.6 to 7.3 years old. The results of this battery of tests will provide information regarding the student's strengths and weaknesses in specific areas of ability. There are four core subtests and one supplemental verbal subtest for children ages 2.6 to 3.11. For children ages 4.0 to 7.3, there are seven core subtests with two verbal and performance supplemental subtests. The test takes approximately 35 minutes for younger children and 50 minutes for older children. Results from the subtest given are used to provide information regarding a child's verbal and nonverbal fluid reasoning, receptive versus expressive vocabulary, and processing speed.

When determining results of the WPPSI-III, age-specific scaled scores and IQ score are provided. The global IQ scores can be interpreted using the standard score criteria. Individual subtest scaled scores are also provided.

WOODCOCK-JOHNSON PSYCHO-EDUCATIONAL BATTERY III—TEST OF COGNITIVE ABILITY (PART 1)

The Woodcock-Johnson test has two parts. The first part measures a student's cognitive ability, and the second part measures the student's performance or achievement. Part 1 of this test is used to determine a student's intellectual ability. This test is administered individually and usually takes less than one hour to administer the entire standard battery. The test can be used for individuals ages 2.0 to 90+ years old and has scoring norms for Grades K–12 and college (undergraduate and graduate level).

Seven subtests make up the standard battery, and 14 supplemental subtests comprise the extended battery. The entire standard battery must be administered. Depending on the purpose and extent of the assessment, one, several, or all of the extended battery tests may be administered. This battery is difficult to administer and should be administered by the school psychologist.

This assessment battery produces many results. The broad ability scale summarizes the student's performance on the standard battery. A broad ability extended scale takes into account all of the standard battery subtests as well as seven of the supplementary subtests. Results can also be reported by subtest, cognitive factor, and areas of scholastic aptitude. More than 35 subtest and area results are produced, and each result can be expressed as an age-equivalent, grade-equivalent, standard score, and percentile rank.

STANFORD-BINET INTELLIGENCE SCALE: FIFTH EDITION (SB5)

The Stanford-Binet Intelligence Scale: Fifth Edition is considered to be a standard tool of many school psychologists. This test, unlike the Wechsler version, provides multiple IQ scores instead of one single IQ score. This test offers a comprehensive measurement of five factors, including fluid reasoning, knowledge, quantitative reasoning, visual-spatial processing, and working memory.

The SB5 is appropriate to be used as an initial vocabulary test that, along with the student's age, determines the number and level of subtests to be administered. The total testing time ranges from 45 to 90 minutes. Raw scores are based on the number of items answered and converted into a standard age score, similar to an IQ measure. The testing results can be expressed as an age-equivalent and scaled score.

Academic Achievement Assessments

These assessments measure a student's academic level in reading, mathematics, written language, social studies, and science. Results of these tests are used to determine a student's achievement of school skills as compared to other age or grade-level peers.

WOODCOCK-JOHNSON PSYCHO-EDUCATIONAL BATTERY III—REVISED TESTS OF ACHIEVEMENT (PART 2)

The Test of Achievement is the second part of the two-part Woodcock-Johnson Psycho-Educational Battery, Revised. The first part assesses a student's cognitive ability and is described in the Intellectual Functioning Assessments section. Part 2 of this assessment is designed to assess and provide information about four areas of the curriculum: reading, mathematics, written language, and knowledge (social studies, science, and humanities). The standard battery contains nine subtests, and the supplemental battery contains five additional subtests.

This achievement assessment can adequately assess skills in people ages 2 to 90+. This assessment is easy to administer and is designed for use by professionals such as special education teachers who are trained in the administration and interpretation of individual tests. The test is administered using an easel-style notebook. The test administrator uses a test protocol to record student's answers.

Results produced by the Woodcock-Johnson Test of Achievement can be reported by subtests, academic areas, and subskills. More than 30 subtest and academic area results are produced, and each result can be expressed in a variety of scores including age equivalents, grade equivalents, standard scores, and percentile ranks.

WECHSLER INDIVIDUAL ACHIEVEMENT TEST, SECOND EDITION (WIAT-II)

This academic achievement test is the only achievement battery empirically linked with the Wechsler Intelligence Scale for Children, Fourth Edition (WISC-IV) and the Wechsler Preschool and Primary Scale of Intelligence, Third Edition (WPPSI-III). The WIAT-II provides a rich source of information about an individual's academic skills and problem-solving abilities that can be used to guide appropriate intervention. It is a comprehensive yet flexible measurement to use for achievement skills assessment, learning disability diagnosis, special education placement, curriculum planning, and clinical appraisal of children, adolescents, college students, and adults ages 4 to 85.

The WIAT-II contains nine subtests. Three subtests assess reading (nonsense word decoding, word reading, and reading comprehension), two assess math (numerical operations and mathematics reasoning), two assess written language (spelling and written expression), and two assess oral language (listening comprehension and oral language.)

A school psychologist most often administers the WIAT-II, as the manual recommends that only professions with graduate-level training in the use of individually administered assessment instruments are qualified to administer and interpret the test results. The results of the WIAT are best used to identify curriculum areas where a student is performing significantly below his or her age or grade peers.

Results are provided using standard scores, percentile ranks, and age-equivalent and grade-equivalent scores for all subtests administered. These same scores are also provided for the five composite scores given (reading, mathematics, language, writing, and total). The total composite score reflects all eight subtests combined.

KAUFMANN TEST OF EDUCATION ACHIEVEMENT, SECOND EDITION (KTEA-II)

The KTEA-II is an individually administered battery that provides a flexible, thorough assessment of the key academic skills in reading, math, written language, and oral language.

There are two forms of the KTEA-II, a brief form and a comprehensive form. The brief form can be utilized for individuals ages 4.6 to 90 years old and provides subtests in the areas of reading, math, and written language. It takes approximately 20 to 30 minutes to administer.

The comprehensive form can be administered to anyone between the ages of 4.6 to 25 years old and assesses the areas of reading, math, and written and oral language. The administration times vary depending upon the age of the student. Approximate times are 30 minutes (preK–K), 20 minutes (Grades 1–2), and 80 minutes (Grades 3+).

Results produced from the KTEA-II include grade-equivalent scores, standard scores, and percentile rank for each subtest as well as for the total test score. For each subtest given and for the total reading cluster, grade-equivalent and age-equivalent scores are provided as well as percentile ranks and standard scores.

PEABODY INDIVIDUAL ACHIEVEMENT TEST–REVISED (PIAT-R/NU)

The PIAT-R/NU is an individually administered measure of academic achievement. This revised edition includes normative updates (NU). The test is designed to provide a wide range of screening measures in six content areas. The test may be administered to student ages 5.0 to 22.11 and in kindergarten through 12th grade. The six content areas assessed by the PIAT-R/NU are as follows. The mathematics section measures knowledge and application of mathematical concepts and facts. The reading recognition section measures the initial pre-reading items, the ability to recognize the sounds associated with letters, and in later items, oral reading of words. The reading comprehension section measures the student's understanding of what is read. The initial items in the spelling section measure the student's recognition of standard spellings. The general information section measures general encyclopedic knowledge. The final written expression is divided into two levels and measures story-writing skills. The total battery can be administered in approximately 30 to 40 minutes. Six individual domain scores are produced from each of the content areas as well as a total reading composite, written language composite, and a total test score. All subtest domain scores as well as the total reading and total test composites can be reported using grade-equivalent and age-equivalent scores, percentile ranks, and standard scores.

DIAGNOSTIC ACHIEVEMENTS BATTERY-3 (DAB-3)

The DAB-3 is an individually administered battery that uses 14 short subtests to determine a child's strengths and weaknesses across several areas of achievement. The 14 subtest areas include story comprehension, characteristics, synonyms, grammatical completion, alphabet/word knowledge, reading comprehension, capitalization, punctuation, spelling, contextual language, story construction, math reasoning, math calculation, and phonemic analysis. The assessment may be administered to students ages 6.0 through 13.0 and can be administered in approximately 45 to 60 minutes. Eight composite scores are produced including total achievement, listening, speaking, reading, writing, mathematics, spoken language, and written language. Subtest and composite scores can be reported using standard scores, percentile ranks, age equivalent, and grade equivalent.

WIDE RANGE ACHIEVEMENT TEST 4 (WRAT-4)

The WRAT-4 is an individually administered battery that is used to measure the basic academic skills necessary for effective learning, communication, and thinking. It includes four subtests: word reading, sentence comprehension, spelling, and math computation. This assessment can be administered to those ages 5.0 through 94.0. Administration time varies depending upon the age, skills, and behavioral style of the individual being tests. For children (ages eight years and older) and adults, the administration time is between 30 to 45 minutes. For younger children (ages five to seven years) the administration time is between 15 to 25 minutes.

Scores for the WRAT-4 are produced and reported using age equivalents, grade equivalents, standard scores, percentile ranks, stanines, normal curve equivalents, and scaled scores.

Adaptive Behavior Assessments

Adaptive behavior is related to both personal independence and social responsibility. Expected adaptive behavior varies with the age of the individual. Preschool children are expected to learn to walk, talk, and interact with family members. School-aged children are expected to widen their circle of acquaintances and add academic skills to their repertoire. A student's adaptive behavior is assessed when a student is suspected of being mild-moderate or moderate-severely mentally impaired or suspected of having autistic characteristics.

Adaptive behavior is usually not measured directly. Instead, the student's parents or teachers are used as informants about the student's current nonacademic functioning. The parents are usually interviewed, and the teachers often complete written questionnaires.

AAMR ADAPTIVE BEHAVIOR SCALE—SCHOOL (2ND ED.) (ABS-S:2)

The ABS-S:2 is an indirect measure of adaptive and maladaptive behavior. This test can be used with children and young adults ages 3.0 to 21.0 with mental impairments. It may also be used with children and teenagers without mental impairments between the ages of 3.0 to 18.0. Results of the ABS-S:2 can be used to identify strengths and weaknesses in adaptive behavior, can determine if a student shows below average performance, and can document student progress. ABS-S:2 is a questionnaire and can be completed by professionals such as teachers. If the professional is unable to make judgments regarding the student's skill level, the scale may be administered by a trained professional in an interview format with a parent or other adults who know the student well. Part 1 of the ABS-S:2 addresses adaptive behavior skills related to personal independence; Part 2 is concerned with social behaviors. The assessment includes 16 domains. The 16 domains are separated into five factors. The five factors are personal self-sufficiency, community self-sufficiency, personal-social responsibility, social adjustment, and personal adjustment.

Results of the ABS-S:2 are reported using percentile ranks and scaled scores for each of the 16 domains as well as the five factor scores. A quotient or overall test score can be explained using percentile ranks and standard scores. Age-equivalent scores can be obtained for Part 1 factors (Factors 1, 2, and 3) only.

VINELAND ADAPTIVE BEHAVIOR SCALES, SECOND EDITION (VINELAND-II)

The Vineland Adaptive Behavior Scales, Second Edition, provides a measure of personal and social skills from birth to adulthood. The assessment contains four separate scales: two interview editions (a survey form and an expanded form), a parent/caregiver rating form, and a teacher rating form. The interview editions are used by trained interviewers with parents or others who know the student well. The survey form includes fewer items than the expanded interview form and consequently requires less administration time. The Vineland-II has an expanded age range encompassing birth to age 90 when using the survey interview, expanded interview, and the parent/caregiver rating forms and ages 3 to 21.11 when using the teacher rating form.

Use of the Vineland-II aids in diagnosing and classifying mental retardation and other disorders such as autism, Asperger syndrome, and developmental delays. The content and scales of the Vineland-II are organized within a four-domain structure encompassing communication, daily living, socialization, and motor skills as well as an optional maladaptive behavior index that provides more in-depth information.

Standard scores are used to report results of the Vineland-II. These standard scores are available for each of the four adaptive behavior domains as well as for the total test, which summarizes the domains.

SCALES OF INDEPENDENT BEHAVIOR (SIB-R)

The Scales of Independent Behavior (SIB-R) is a comprehensive assessment of adaptive and maladaptive behavior. The assessment contains three separate scales: a full scale, a short form, and an early development form. The SIB-R has an age range of infancy to 80+ years and requires 45 to 60 minutes to administer the full scale and 15 to 20 minutes to administer the short or early development forms.

The content and scales of the SIB-R are 14 adaptive behavior clusters that are divided into a four-domain structure encompassing motor skills, social interaction and communication skills, personal living skills, and community living skills.

Scores for the SIB-R are reported using standard scores, percentile ranks, age equivalents, and support scores.

Reading Assessments

Early Reading

TEST OF EARLY READING ABILITY—THIRD EDITION (TERA-3)

The TERA-3 is an individually administered assessment for children ages 3.6 to 8.6 years. The entire test can be administered in 15 to 30 minutes. The TERA-3 assesses a child's mastery of early developing reading skills. The three subtests provided include alphabet, which measure the child's knowledge of the alphabet and its uses; conventions, which measures the child's knowledge of the conventions of print; and meaning, which measures the construction of meaning from print. Standard scores are provided for each subtest. An overall reading quotient is computed using all three subtest scores. Age- and grade-equivalent scores are provided for ages 3.6 through 8.6.

The TERA-3 results can be used to identify children who are significantly different from their peers in the early development of reading. Results from this assessment indicate children who are having reading problems and identify children who are performing significantly above their peers.

Phonemic Awareness (PA)

COMPREHENSIVE TEST OF PHONOLOGICAL PROCESSING (CTOPP)

The CTOPP was developed to aid in the identification of individuals from kindergarten through college who may profit from instructional activities to enhance their phonological skills. The CTOPP assesses phonological awareness, phonological memory, and rapid naming. Children with deficits in one or more of these phonological processing abilities may have more difficulty learning to read than those who do not. The first version of the test is developed for individuals ages five and six (primarily kindergartners and first graders) and contains seven core subtests and one supplemental test. The subtests include elision (substitution and deletion), rapid color naming, rapid object naming, blending words, sound matching, nonword repetition, and memory for digits.

The second version of the test, for individuals ages seven through 24, contains six core subtests and eight supplemental tests. The subtests for phonological awareness include elision (substitution & deletion) and blending words. Phonological memory includes memory for digits and nonword repetition. Rapid naming includes rapid digit naming, rapid letter naming, rapid color naming, and rapid object naming. The other subtests are blending nonwords, phoneme reversal, segmenting words, and segmenting nonwords. These supplemental tests are provided to allow the examiner to more carefully assess specific phonological strengths and weaknesses. Both versions are individually administered, taking about 30 minutes to administer the core subtests.

Scores are reported using percentiles ranks, standard scores, age equivalents, and grade equivalents.

TEST OF PHONOLOGICAL AWARENESS— SECOND EDITION PLUS (TOPA-2+)

The TOPA-2+ is an individual or group administered measure of phonological awareness for children ages five through eight. There are two versions: a kindergarten version, which is suitable for administration any time during the kindergarten year, and the early elementary version, which is suitable for first- and second-grade children. Either version takes approximately 20 minutes to administer. The assessment measures young children's ability to isolate individual phonemes in spoken words and understand the relationships between letters and phonemes in English.

The test is divided into subtests. Those subtests include rhyming, segmentation, isolation, deletion, substitution, blending, graphemes, decoding, and invented spelling. The scores from the subtests are reported using age equivalency, percentile ranks, and standard scores.

Decoding

WOODCOCK READING MASTERY TESTS—REVISED (WRMT-R/NU)

The Woodcock Reading Mastery Tests—Revised is used to pinpoint students' strengths and weaknesses in the specific reading decoding areas of word attack and word identification. There are two forms of the WRMT-R/NU: Form G and Form H. Form G is a complete battery made up of four tests of reading achievement and a readiness section; Form H is a condensed form that contains only alternate forms of the reading achievement tests.

The four subtests common to both forms are as follows: word identification, in which students are shown individual words and must pronounce each word; word attack, in which students are asked to pronounce nonsense works and syllables; word comprehension, in which students are asked to identify antonyms, synonyms, and analogies; and passage comprehension, in which students are shown a brief passage with one word omitted and then asked to supply the missing word. Form G contains all of the previously mentioned measures as well as three measures of reading readiness that include visual-auditory learning, letter identification, and supplementary letter checklist.

The WRMT-R/NU is designed for students from kindergarten through college and ages 5.0 thorough 75+, but young children and nonreaders may experience success only on the readiness subtests. Each cluster of tests should take between 10 to 30 minutes to administer.

The WRMT-R/NU offers a variety of scores. For each subtest given and for the total reading cluster, grade-equivalent and age-equivalent scores are provided, as are percentile ranks and standard scores.

TEST OF WORD READING EFFICIENCY (TOWRE)

The Test of Word Reading Efficiency (TOWRE) for ages six through 24 measures word reading accuracy and fluency. It can be administered individually in five to 10 minutes and provides an efficient means of monitoring the growth of two kinds of word-reading skills that are critical: the ability to accurately recognize familiar words as whole units and the ability to sound out words quickly.

The TOWRE contains two subtests: the Sight Word Efficiency (SWE) subtest and the Phonetic Decoding Efficiency (PDE) subtest. The SWE assesses the number of real printed words that can be accurately identified within 45 seconds. The PDE assesses the number of pronounceable printed nonsense words that can be accurately decoded within 45 seconds. Each subtest has two forms (Forms A and B) that are of equivalent difficulty, and either one or both forms of each subtest may be given depending up the purposes of the assessment.

Results of the TOWRE are reported through percentile ranks, standard scores, and age and grade equivalents. Standard scores are provided for each subtest as well.

Fluency

GRAY ORAL READING TESTS—FOURTH EDITION (GORT-4)

The Gray Oral Reading Tests, Fourth Edition, provides an efficient and objective measure of growth in oral reading and an aid in the diagnosis of oral reading difficulties. The test consists of two parallel forms, each containing 14 developmentally sequenced reading passages with five comprehensive questions that can be given to students ages six to 19. The GORT-4 provides a fluency score that is derived by combining the reader's performance in rate (time in seconds taken to read each passage) and accuracy (number of deviations from print made in each passage).

Scores are reported in standard scores, percentile ranks, grade equivalents, and age equivalents. The fluency score and the oral reading comprehension score are combined to obtain an oral reading quotient. The GORT-4 is administered individually and takes approximately 20 to 30 minutes.

GRAY DIAGNOSTIC READING TESTS—SECOND EDITION (GDRT-2)

The GDRT-2 assesses students ages six to 14 years who have difficulty reading continuous print and who require an evaluation of specific abilities and weaknesses. Two parallel forms are provided to allow you to study a student's reading progress over time. The information received is very useful and efficient in gauging reading skills progress. The test is administered individually and takes approximately one hour.

The GDRT-2 has four core subtests, each of which measures an important reading skill. The four subtests are letter/word identification, phonetic analysis, reading vocabulary, and meaningful reading. The three supplemental subtests—listening vocabulary, rapid naming, and phonological awareness—measure skills that are helpful in diagnosing or teaching of developmental readers or children with dyslexia.

DYNAMIC INDICATORS OF BASIC EARLY LITERACY SKILLS (DIBELS)

DIBELS is a reading fluency and comprehension measure for students in kindergarten through third grade and fourth through sixth grade. This test can be used for benchmark assessments in the fall, winter, and spring to monitor progress (more frequent assessment of lower achieving students).

The measures are designed to be short (one minute) and used regularly to monitor the development of pre-reading and early reading skills. There are seven fluency measures: Initial Sounds Fluency (ISF), Letter Naming Fluency (LNF), Phoneme Segmentation Fluency (PSF), Nonsense Word Fluency (NWF), Oral Reading Fluency (ORF), Retell Fluency (RTF), and Word Use Fluency (WUF). Assessment results are reported as at risk, some risk, low risk or deficit, emerging, and established.

Vocabulary (May also be tested in a speech and language evaluation)

PEABODY PICTURE VOCABULARY TEST—FOURTH EDITION (PPVT-4)

The PPVT-4 is an individually administered test of receptive vocabulary designed for ages 2.6 to 90 years and older. The administration of this test only requires 10 to 20 minutes. In this test, a student is shown a page containing four drawings. The administrator reads a word and the student points to or says the number of the drawing that represents the word. The PPVT-4 is quick and easy to administer. This can be used as both a test of achievement (because it assesses the acquisition of English vocabulary) and as an aptitude test (because it assesses verbal skills).

The PPVT-4 is not divided into subtests, and only one result is obtained—a total test performance index. This total can be reported using several types of scores. Standard scores, percentile ranks, and age- and grade-equivalent scores can be obtained.

EXPRESSIVE VOCABULARY TESTS, SECOND EDITION (EVT-2)

The EVT-2 is an individually administered test of receptive vocabulary designed for ages 2.6 to 90 years and older. The administration of this test only requires about 10 to 15 minutes. The EVT-2 is often used in conjunction with the PPVT-4 and is effective for comparing receptive and expressive vocabulary. In this test, a student is asked to label 38 items. The examiner points to a picture or part of the body and asks a question. There is also a synonym section where the examiner presents a picture and stimulus words within a phrase. The examinee responds for each item with a one-word answer.

The EVT-2 results can be reported using standard scores, percentile ranks, stanines, and age-equivalent scores.

EXPRESSIVE ONE-WORD PICTURE VOCABULARY TEST (EOWPVT)

The EOWPVT is an individually administered test that provides an assessment of an individual's English-speaking vocabulary. It is available for use with children ages 2.0 through 18.11. This edition is conformed to the Receptive One-Word Picture Vocabulary Test (ROWPVT) so that meaningful comparisons can be made between an individual's expressive and receptive language.

To administer the test, the examiner presents a series of pictures each of which depicts an object, action, or concept. The examinee is asked to name each picture. Total time for administration and scoring is typically 15 to 20 minutes. Raw scores can be converted to standard scores, percentile ranks, and age equivalents.

RECEPTIVE ONE-WORD PICTURE VOCABULARY TEST (ROWPVT)

The ROWPVT is an individually administered norm-referenced test that provides an assessment of an individual's English-hearing vocabulary. It is available for use with children ages 2.0 through 18.11. This edition is conformed to the EOWPVT so that meaningful comparisons can be made between an individual's expressive and receptive language.

To administer the test, the examiner presents a series of test plates; each shows four pictures. The examiner orally presents a stimulus work, and the examinee must identify the illustration that depicts the meaning of the word. Total time for administration and scoring is typically 15 to 20 minutes. Raw scores can be converted to standard scores, percentile ranks, and age equivalents.

OWLS LISTENING COMPREHENSION SCALE (LCS) AND ORAL EXPRESSION SCALE (OES)

OWLS is an individually administered assessment of receptive and expressive (both oral and written) language for children and young adults ages three through 12 years (five though 21 years for written expression). OWLS consist of three scales: Listening Comprehension (LC), Oral Expressions (OE), and Written Expression (WE).

The LC scale is designed to measure the understanding of spoken language. The OE scale is designed to measure the understanding and use of spoken language. The WE scale is designed to measure the ability to communicate meaningfully using written forms.

The LC scale consists of three examples and 111 items and takes approximately five to 15 minutes to administer. The OE scale consists of two examples and 96 items and takes approximately 10 to 25 minutes to administer. The WE scale consists of 39 items divided into four overlapping item sets each designed for a specified age level and takes approximately 10 to 40 minutes to administer. Results of individual scales can be reported through age-equivalent, grade-equivalent, percentile ranks, and stanine scores. Composite scores can be reported using standard scores, percentile ranks, stanines, and age-equivalent scores.

TEST OF LANGUAGE DEVELOPMENT PRIMARY: THIRD EDITION (TOLD-P:3) AND TEST OF LANGUAGE DEVELOPMENT INTERMEDIATE: THIRD EDITION (TOLD-I:3)

The TOLD-3 primary and intermediate versions are individually administered tests used to assess oral language and vocabulary. The primary version is used for preschool and early elementary grade children ages 4.0 to 8.11 years. The intermediate version is used for older elementary grade students ages 8.6 to 12.11 years. The TOLD-P:3 consists of seven subtests that assess receptive and expressive phonology, syntax, and semantics skills. TOLD-I:3 consists of six subtests that assess receptive and expressive syntax and semantics skills. The purpose of both versions of the TOLD-3 is to identify a student's strengths and weaknesses in oral language development.

In oral language, speech is the expressive component of language, whereas listening skills are the receptive components. *Phonology* focuses on combining the features of sound into significant speech sounds (phonemes). *Syntax* is the ability to form combinations of words into acceptable phrases, clauses, and sentences. *Semantics* is the understanding and ability to make sense of the meaning of the words in sentences.

Administration of the TOLD-3 primary and intermediate tests is quite easy. Not all subtests are required to be administered in order to get scores.

For the TOLD-P:3, percentile ranks and scaled scores are available for each of the seven subtests. Standard scores are also provided for six composite areas. The spoken language quotient is a summary of performance on all subtests. The other composite areas are listening quotient, speaking quotient, and quotients for semantics, syntax, and phonology.

For the TOLD-I:3, percentile ranks and scaled scores are available for the six subtests. Standard scores are also provided for five composite areas. The spoken language quotient is a summary of the performance on all subtests. The other composite areas for this assessment are listening quotient, speaking quotient, semantics quotient, and syntax quotient.

BOEHM TEST OF BASIC CONCEPTS—THIRD EDITION (BOEHM-3)

The Boehm-3 is an individually administered assessment for children ages 3.0 to 5.11 and is designed to evaluate young children's understanding of the basic relational concepts important for language and cognitive development as well as for later success in school. The results of the Boehm-3 can be used to identify students with weaknesses in receptive vocabulary and to identify basic concepts that students have not yet mastered. With this assessment, the student responds to a total of 50 test items. The test can be administered to an individual or a group of students.

Results of the Boehm-3 are reported as raw scores and percentile ranks.

Comprehension

GRAY SILENT READING TEST (GSRT)

The purpose of the GSRT is to quickly and efficiently measure an individual's silent reading comprehension ability. The test can be used independently or as an adjunct to the Gray Oral Reading Test, Fourth Edition. (GORT 4). The test consists of two parallel forms, each containing 13 developmentally sequenced reading passages with five multiple-choice questions. It can be given individually or to groups seven years through 25 years of age. Each form of the test yields raw scores, grade equivalents, age equivalents, percentile ranks, and a silent reading quotient.

TEST OF READING COMPREHENSION, THIRD EDITION (TORC-3)

The TORC-3 does not attempt to measure all aspects of the reading process. Instead, it emphasizes comprehension skills, silent reading, and knowledge of word meanings.

The TORC-3 contains eight subtests. It is not necessary to administer all eight subtests to receive an index of general reading comprehension ability. The general comprehension core consists of the following four subtests. The first is general vocabulary where students are presented with three words that are related. They are then given four additional words from which to choose one word that best relates to the first three words. The second, syntactic similarities, requires students to read five sentences and select the two that are most similar in meaning. The third, paragraph reading, requires students to read six one- or two-paragraph selections and then answer five multiple-choice questions about each. The fourth, sentence sequencing, gives students five sentences in random order, and the student must determine the sequence of the sentences in order to construct a meaningful paragraph.

The TORC-3 is designed for students ages 7.0 to 17.11. Students must be able to work independently and read silently. The assessment time is approximately 30 minutes for each subtest. Results of the TORC-3 are reported with subtest scaled scores and then an overall reading comprehension quotient (standard score) that is indicative of the student's overall skills level in reading comprehension. Percentile ranks are also given for each individual subtest.

Written Language Assessment

TEST OF WRITTEN LANGUAGE— THIRD EDITION (TOWL-3)

The TOWL-3 is designed to identify students who perform significantly below their peers in written expression; it will help to determine a student's strengths and weaknesses in writing. It is also used to provide directions for further educational assistance. The TOWL-3 is a completely revised edition used to document the presence of deficits in the written-language area of literacy.

The test has two assessment forms. Each form assesses three components of language: the rules for punctuation, capitalization, and spelling; the use of written grammar and vocabulary; and the conceptual component that suggests the ability to produce written products that are logical, coherent, and sequenced. When administering this test, writing is elicited by means of contrived and spontaneous formats. Spontaneous formats are assessed when students are asked to produce writing samples.

The eight subtests of the TOWL-3 measure a student's writing competence through both essay-analysis (spontaneous) formats and traditional test (contrived) formats. This assessment requires the student to have reading and writing skills. During several subtests, the student must be able to read words or sentences that prompt the writing task. This test can be administered individually or in a group setting. It is appropriate for students between the ages of 7.0 and 17.11 years. It takes approximately 90 minutes to administer the complete assessment.

Results for each subtest on the TOWL-3 can be reported through percentile ranks and scaled scores. Three global scores (contrived writing quotient, spontaneous writing quotient, and overall written language quotient) are reported using percentile ranks and standard scores.

TEST OF EARLY WRITTEN LANGUAGE— SECOND EDITION (TEWL-2)

The TEWL-2 is an individual assessment instrument for children ages 3.0 to 10.11 years. The assessment has two forms, A and B. Each form includes a basic writing and a contextual writing subtest. The basic writing quotient is a measure of a student's ability in the areas of spelling, capitalization, punctuation, sentence construction, and metacognitive knowledge. Forms A and B each consist of 57 items. The contextual writing quotient measures the student's ability to construct a story when provided with a picture prompt. This subtest measures areas such as story format, cohesion, thematic maturity, ideation, and story structure. Each form consists of 14 items and scores.

A global writing quotient is formed by combining the standard scores from each subtest. The global writing quotient is the best indicator of a child's general writing ability.

The TEWL-2 provides standard score quotients, percentile ranks, and age equivalents. It allows items to be profiled for diagnosis of strengths and weaknesses and provides direction for instructional assistance.

TEST OF WRITTEN EXPRESSION (TOWE)

The TOWE is an individual or group administered assessment for children ages 6.6 through 14.11. It uses two assessment methods to evaluate a student's writing skills. The first method involves administering a series of 76 items that tap different skills associated with writing. The second method requires students to read or hear a prepared story starter and uses it as a stimulus for writing an essay. Results of the test are reported in raw scores and standard scores.

Math Assessments

KeyMath 3

The KeyMath 3 is an individually administered test designed to provide a comprehensive assessment of a student's understanding and application of important mathematical concepts and skills. This assessment is appropriate for students ages 5.0 to 22.0 years old and for students in Grades K–12. The test consists of 13 subtests that are organized into three major areas of mathematics: basic concepts (foundation knowledge), operations (computation skills), and applications in mathematics (the use of knowledge and computational skills).

The results from the KeyMath 3 help evaluators determine the student's current achievement in basic mathematics concepts, computational operations, and applications such as problem solving, estimation, time, money, and measurement. The KeyMath 3 is most useful as a screening device to identify possible mathematical strengths and weaknesses.

For each subtest given, results are expressed using both percentile ranks and scaled scores. Grade-equivalent and age-equivalent scores, percentile ranks, and standard scores are given for the overall total test as well as for the three major areas assessed (basic concepts, operations, and applications).

Test of Mathematical Abilities— Second Edition (TOMA-2)

The TOMA-2 attempts to assess the attitudes a student might have toward mathematics, the understanding of the vocabulary used in a mathematical sense, and the understanding of how information related to mathematics is used. This test will effectively assess students ages 8.0 to 18.11 years and requires 60 to 90 minutes to administer. The TOMA-2 contains five subtests: attitude toward math, vocabulary, computation, general information, and story problems.

The results of the test may be reported in standard scores, percentile ranks, grade-equivalent scores, or age-equivalent scores. The standard scores of the core battery are combined to comprise a total score called the math quotient.

Speech and Language Assessments

Articulation Assessments

Articulation is the way of saying things more clearly. A student who is hard to understand as he or she speaks may be told to articulate more clearly. This simply means that the person should speak the words more precisely to be better understood.

Clinical Assessment of Articulation and Phonology (CAAP)

The CAAP is the only instrument that assesses the articulation and phonology of preschool and school-age children. The test will effectively assess students ages

2.6 to 8.11. The articulation portion of the test can be administered in 15 to 20 minutes and results provide standard scores, percentile ranks, and age-equivalents and a critical-difference scores.

GOLDMAN-FRISTOE TEST OF ARTICULATION—SECOND EDITION (GFTA-2)

The GFTA-2 measures a child's articulation of consonant sounds and is available for the age range of two to 21. The GFTA-2 results provide information necessary to assess a child's articulation ability with 39 consonant sounds and blends. Age-based standard scores are results of the scoring.

THE PHOTO ARTICULATION TEST—THIRD EDITION (PAT-3)

To administer the PAT-3, the examiner simply points to each consecutive numbered photograph and asks the child, "What is this?" The child's response is scored indicating the presence or absence of errors. The elicited sounds are arranged by age of acquisition. All sounds that are tested are written; in addition, consonant sounds are differentiated into the initial, medial, and final positions within the stimulus word. Testing time is 20 minutes on an individual basis for ages 3.6 to 9.0.

ARIZONA ARTICULATION PROFICIENCY SCALE—THIRD REVISION (ARIZONA-3)

The Arizona-3 is a precise assessment of articulatory skills in children. The scale is designed for children from 1.5 through 18 years of age. Although norms stop at age 18, the Arizona-3 can be used with older individuals as well. It is a comprehensive, simple, and brief assessment that covers all major speech sounds in the English language, including initial and final consonants and blends, vowels, and diphthongs. It can be administered to most children in less than three minutes and generates a clear-cut total score, which indicates severity of articulatory deviation.

Result scores are provided in several formats, including percentile rankings and standard scores.

Oral Language Assessments

CLINICAL EVALUATION OF LANGUAGE FUNDAMENTALS—THIRD EDITION (CELF-3)

The CELF-3 is a diagnostic test that contains 11 subtests that assess syntax, semantics, and memory. This assessment is designed for students ages 5.0 to 16.11 years. The battery provides several measures of receptive and expressive syntax (forming sentences in appropriate order) and semantics (understanding what the words are telling).

Results of the CELF-3 can be provided using individual subtest scaled scores and three global standard scores. The three standard scores are given in the areas of receptive language, expressive language, and total language. An age-equivalent score is available for the total language global score.

TEST OF NARRATIVE LANGUAGE (TNL)

Examiners are able to assess children's ability to remember and tell stories in three formats: stories with no picture cues, stories that correspond to sequenced pictures, and stories that correspond with a single picture of a scene. This test is designed to examine how well children use their knowledge of the component of language as they engage in functional discourse. Examiners audiotape record their administration of the TNL and later score the children's stories as they listen to the tape. The TNL is easy to administer on an individual basis to children ages five to 12 years and measures story comprehension and oral narration in 15 to 20 minutes.

Auditory Processing Assessments

TEST OF AUDITORY PROCESSING SKILLS—THIRD EDITION (TAPS-3)

The TAPS-3 offers coverage for ages four through 18 years and for individuals preK through adult. The TAPS-3 measures what a person does with what is heard and is intended to be used along with other tests. The order of the subtests reflects the developmental progression of tasks from easiest to most difficult. The subtests focus on the concepts of word discrimination, word memory, phonological segmentation, sentence memory, phonological blending, auditory comprehension, numbers forward, auditory reasoning, and numbers reversed. In addition to one overall score, individual subtest scores are combined to derive three cluster scores: basic auditory skills, auditory memory, and auditory cohesion.

The TAPS-3 is an untimed test and can be completed in about one hour. Individual subtests are reported as scaled scores, while cluster scores and the overall score are reported as standard scores, percentile ranks, and age equivalents.

Occupational Therapy Assessments

MOTOR FREE VISUAL PERCEPTION TEST—3 (MVPT-3)

The MVPT-3 assesses an individual's visual perceptual ability without any motor involvement needed to make a response. It is utilized for those between the ages of 4.0 and 70+. The MVPT-3 takes approximately 25 minutes to administer on an individual basis. Raw scores are gathered first and converted to standard scores and percentile ranks.

PEABODY DEVELOPMENT MOTOR SCALES—SECOND EDITION (PDMS-2)

The PDMS-2 is an early childhood motor development assessment that provides remediation of gross and fine motor skills. The assessment is composed of six subtests that measure interrelated motor abilities that develop early in life. It is designed to assess the motor skills of children from birth through 5.0 years of age. Subtests include reflexes, stationary, locomotion, object manipulation, grasping, and visual-motor integration. The subtests yield a gross motor quotient, a fine motor quotient, and a total motor quotient.

BRUININKS-OSERETSKY TEST OF MOTOR PROFICIENCY—SECOND EDITION (BOT-2)

This motor proficiency tests measures gross and fine motor skills in children ages four through 21 years. Eight subtests assess fine motor precision, fine motor integration, manual dexterity, bilateral coordination, balance, running speed and agility, upper-limb coordination, and strength.

BOT-2 covers a broad array of fine and gross motor skills, providing composite scores in four motor areas and one comprehensive measure of overall motor proficiency. These composite areas are fine manual control, manual coordination, body coordination, strength and agility, and total motor composite.

BEERY-BUKTENICA DEVELOPMENT TEST OF V-MI—5TH EDITION (BEERY VMI-5)

The Beery VMI-5 helps assess the extent to which individuals can integrate their visual and motor abilities. The short form, often used with children ages two to eight years and the full format for ages two to 18 years, presents drawings of geometric forms arranged in order of increasing difficulty that an individual is asked to copy.

The short and full format tests can be administered individually or to groups in 10 to 15 minutes. The supplemental visual perception and motor coordination tests are designed to be administered individually after results from the short or full format tests have been obtained.

Results are reported as standard scores and percentile ranks.

Behavioral Assessments

A wide variety of rating scales and checklists are available for assessing student's behavior in school, at home, and in the community.

BEHAVIOR EVALUATION SCALE—THIRD EDITION (BES-3)

The BES-3 is designed to identify strengths and weaknesses in five behavioral domains of students in Grades K–12. There are 76 behavior descriptors that the informant must rate according to frequency of those behaviors occurring. There are seven frequency-rating choices, ranging from "never or not observed" to "continuously throughout the day." The 76 specific behaviors are divided into the five types of behavior disorders: learning problems, interpersonal difficulties, inappropriate behavior, unhappiness/depression, and physical symptoms/fears.

It is recommended that the teacher observe the student for at least one month before completing the rating scale. The informant should be the teacher who has the primary instructional responsibility and the most contact with the student to ensure that precise completion is occurring.

Subscale scaled scores and percentile ranks are distributed for the five behavior disorders areas named above. Standard scores and percentile ranks are used to describe the overall behavior quotient that combines all five subscales for a total behavior score.

BEHAVIOR RATING PROFILE—SECOND EDITION (BRP-2)

The BRP-2 attempts to provide a comprehensive overview of a student's current behavioral status. It is appropriate for students between the ages of 6.6 and 18.6 years of age and for students in Grades 1–12. Information for this assessment can be gathered from four types of informants: the student, teacher, parents, and peers. The student's behavior at home and school as well as the student's interpersonal relationships can be assessed.

The BRP-2 consists of four profiles. The student rating scale is completed by a classroom teacher who knows the student well enough to provide accurate information. The parent rating scale is completed by a parent who can provide accurate information regarding the student in the home environment. Finally, a peer scale is completed, which is a sociometric technique used for the student's classmates. The purpose of the BRP-2 is to identify students with possible behavior disorders who may be in need of further assessment.

Results of the BRP-2 are described using scaled scores and percentile ranks. Several scores are available, depending on the scales administered. If the student completed the student rating scale, three separate scores are reported: home, school, and peer. There is one score for each teacher and each parent who rated the student, and each sociometric question answered by the student's peers produces a score.

ATTENTION DEFICIT DISORDERS EVALUATION SCALE, THIRD EDITION (ADDES-3) (HOME VERSION AND SCHOOL VERSION)

The ADDES-3 is a rating scale designed for use with school-aged children and adolescents ages 4.0 to 18.0 years old. Both a school and home version are available, and it asks about specific behaviors that reflect inattention, impulsivity, and hyperactivity. The school version can be completed in approximately 15 minutes and includes 60 items easily observed and documented by educational personnel. The home version can be completed by a parent or guardian in approximately 12 minutes and includes 46 items representing behaviors exhibited in and around the home environment. The informant is asked to rate each specific behavior according to the frequency with which it occurs. The Likert Scale consists of a range of five behavior ratings.

Two types of results are produced by the ADDES-3. Three subscales (inattentive, impulsive, and hyperactive) receive separate scaled scores. The overall total scale, which combines the three subscales, is described by a percentile rank.

CONNERS' RATING SCALE—REVISED (CRS-R)

The Conners' Rating Scales consists of three versions—the Conners' Parent Rating Scale (CPRS), Conners' Teacher Rating Scale (CTRS), and Conners-Wells' Adolescent Self-Report Scale (CASS). All three versions consist of both a long form and short form. This assessment is used to assess attention-deficit/hyperactivity disorder in children and adolescents. This rating scale can be used to rate the behavior of children ages 3.0 to 17.0 years old. Results are reported with both scaled scores and percentile ranks for the scales.

BEHAVIORAL AND EMOTIONAL RATING SCALE—SECOND EDITION (BERS-2)

The BERS-2 helps to measure a child's emotional and behavioral strengths in five subscales. The five subscales include interpersonal strengths, family involvement, intrapersonal strengths, school functioning, and affective strengths. The measure assesses children ages 5.0 through 18.11. The BERS-2 is a multimodal assessment system that measures the child's behavior from three perspectives of the child (youth rating scale), parent (parent rating scale), and teacher or other professional (teacher rating scale.)

The scale can be completed in approximately 10 minutes.

SELF ESTEEM INDEX (SEI)

The SEI is a self-report rating scale for students 8.0 to 18.11 years old. It can be administered individually or as a group assessment. The index contains 80 statements that students rate on a Likert Scale. The ratings are always true, usually true, usually false, or always false. Each statement fits into one of the following four self-esteem scales: perception of familial acceptance, perception of academic competence, perception of peer popularity, and perception of personal security.

Results of the SEI are described through scaled scores and percentile ranks for the four self-esteem scales. Scores on the four scales are combined to produce a total test self-esteem quotient. This quotient is provided through a percentile rank and a standard score.

■ NONTRADITIONAL AND PROGRESS MONITORING ASSESSMENTS

The previous assessments described will be administered by the special education team. As the classroom teacher, you have a wealth of information about the student that will help determine educational needs. The following information can be compiled and then added to the assessment data. These nonstandardized forms of assessment are very helpful when determining the IEP goals and objectives as they are tied directly to the classroom curriculum.

Curriculum-Based Progress Monitoring Assessment

This is a direct evaluation tied to the curriculum content. For example, reading rate and fluency information may be gathered by asking the student to read aloud from curriculum-based materials. Classroom assessments may be analyzed for errors. Student progress in the areas of reading and math is monitored and recorded to ensure growth and progress. Research has shown that listening to a child read a graded passage aloud for one minute and calculating the number of words read correct per minute provides a highly reliable and valid measure of general reading achievement, including comprehension for most students.

Commercially based products are available to assist teachers in collecting, organizing, and analyzing student-achievement data. Two of the frequently used commercial systems are AIMSweb and DIBELS (Dynamic Indicators of Basic Early Literacy Skills).

One screening procedure utilized by both AIMSweb and DIBELS is the Reading Curriculum-Based Measurement Oral Reading Fluency passage.

AIMSweb: www.aimsweb.com

AIMSweb is a formative assessment system that informs the teaching and learning process. Teachers are provided with continual student performance data and reporting to enable evidence-based evaluation and data-driven instruction. The hope is that this data will help teachers individualize their instruction to better meet the educational needs of all of their students.

Specific AIMSweb screenings include the following.

READING CURRICULUM-BASED MEASUREMENT (R-CBM)

AIMSweb screenings include sets of standard reading assessment passages for Grades K–8 as part of the AIMSweb system. Typically there are over 30 equivalent passages at each grade level.

A Spanish version of this measurement is also available.

MAZE CURRICULUM-BASED MEASUREMENT (MAZE-CBM)

This is specifically used when comprehension problems are suspected. Maze reading can be used as a corroborative measure to provide more complete picture of a students' reading skills. Maze is a multiple-choice or closed task that students complete while reading silently. The first sentence of a 150- to 400-word passage is left intact. Thereafter, every seventh word is replaced with three words inside parentheses. One of the words is the exact one from the original passage. Science-based research has shown that this provides a reliable and valid measure of reading comprehension.

TEST OF EARLY LITERACY (TEL)

The National Reading Panel (National Reading, Panel 2000) has identified some critical pre-reading skills that should be assessed in kindergarten and early Grade 1. These specific skills include phonemic awareness and elements of phonics (letter names and sounds and ability to read nonreal [nonsense] words).

A Spanish version of this measure is available as well.

SPELLING CURRICULUM-BASED MEASUREMENT

Science-based research has shown that dictating grade-level words aloud at a prescribed pace for two minutes and counting the number of correct letter sequences provide a valid and highly reliable measure of general spelling proficiency.

TEST OF EARLY NUMERACY (TEN)

The four AIMSweb TEN assessment are used to identify students at risk and monitor the progress of students in kindergarten and early first grade as they move on the pathway to good math skills. Students orally count, identify numbers, identify the bigger number from a pair, and identify the missing number from a number line. Each task is one minute and designed to represent a critical early numeracy skill for kindergarten and first-grade students.

Written-Expression Curriculum-Based Measurement (WE-CBM)

Being able to communicate thoughts and ideas in writing is a fundamental basic skill that is valuable throughout life. Progress can be monitored by having students write a story for three minutes given an age-appropriate story starter.

Math-Curriculum-Based Measurement (M-CBM)

AIMSweb provides M-CBM probes based on expected computational skills for Grades 1–8 with 40 alternate forms per grade. Research has shown that having students write answers to grade-level computational problems for two to four minutes is a reliable and valid general outcome measure of general mathematics computation.

The Dynamic Indicators of Basic Early Literacy Skills (DIBELS)

DIBELS: www.dibels.uoregon.edu

DIBELS is a set of individually administered measures of early literacy development. The measures are designed to be short (one minute) fluency measures used to regularly monitor the development of pre-reading and early reading skills.

Specific DIBELS screenings include the following.

Initial Sound Fluency (ISF)

The ISF measure assesses a child's ability to recognize and produce the initial sound in an orally presented word. The ISF measure takes about three minutes to administer and has over 20 alternate forms to monitor progress. Recommended administration of this measure is during the preschool and kindergarten years.

Letter Naming Fluency (LNF)

This measurement presents student with a page of randomly placed uppercase and lowercase letters, and students are asked to name as many letters as possible. The student is allowed one minute to produce as many letter names as he or she can, and the score is the number of letters named correctly in one minute. Recommended administration of this measure is kindergarten and beginning of first grade.

Phoneme Segmentation Fluency (PSF)

The PSF assesses a student's ability to segment three- and four-phonemes words into their individual phonemes. The student is presented a word with three or four phonemes and asked to verbally segment the word into individual phonemes. For example, the word *sat* would be segmented into /s/ /a/ /t/—for a total of three points. The examiner continues to present words for one minute. Recommended administration for this measure is middle of kindergarten through the end of first grade.

Nonsense Word Fluency (NWF)

The student is presented with a paper with random Vowel Consonant (VC) and Consonant Vowel Consonant (CVC) nonsense words and asked to "read" the nonsense work. The student is allowed one minute to produce as many letter sounds or words as possible. Recommended administration for this measure is middle of kindergarten through the end of first grade.

DIBELS Oral Reading Fluency (DORF)

Student's performance on the oral reading fluency is measured by having the student read a passage aloud for one minute. The number of correct words read per minute from the passage is the oral reading fluency rate. Recommended administration of this measure is from the middle of first grade through the end of third grade.

Retell Fluency (RTF)

RTF is intended to provide a comprehension check for the DORF assessment. This measure will help to recognize children whose comprehension is not consistent with their fluency. Recommended administration of this measure is from the middle of first grade through the end of third grade.

Consistently utilizing AIMSweb or DIBELS measures to provide benchmark scores and monitor progress and interventions is considered best practice and used to improve general education achievement.

Informational Assessment

Information gathered through the Problem Solving Team including data collected from attempted interventions and strategies.

Environmental Assessment

Observe the student in various learning environment and settings where the student routinely operates to determine how the environment may affect the student's performance.

Portfolio Assessment

Collect and analyze work samples from the student, including classroom-based assessments, daily work, homework assignments, and projects.

Diagnostic Teaching Assessment

Implement the results from diagnostic teaching methods or other systematic methods of instruction.

Learning-Style Inventory Assessment

Assess the student's learning style to determine how the student learns and solves problems.

Information Gathering Assessment

Interview people who can provide key information about the student (e.g., student, parent, previous teachers).

■ SECTION 504

In order for students to qualify for special education services under the IDEA, specific eligibility requirements must be met. While eligibility requirements differ with each disability category, documentation must indicate that the disability is interfering with the child's ability to make educational progress and growth in order for the child to meet eligibility requirements under any of the current 13 special education categories. There are times, however, when students may require support services due to a "handicapping" condition that does not impede educational growth. Although the child may not meet eligibility criteria under IDEA, it is possible that the child could receive support under Section 504 of the Rehabilitation Act of 1973.

According to Jan Baumel (2008a), Congress passed Section 504 of the Rehabilitation Act in order to protect people with disabilities by eliminating barriers and allowing full participation in areas such as education and the workplace. Although the law does not provide any funding to agencies to which the law applies, federal funding can be withheld if agencies do not comply. Because public schools receive federal tax dollars, Section 504 applies to them.

> Section 504 provides that no qualified individual with a disability should, only by reason of his or her disability, be excluded from the participation in, be denied the benefits of, or be subjected to discrimination under any program or activity receiving Federal financial assistance. (Section 504(a) of the Rehabilitation Act 29 U.S.C. §794(a) (1973))

All students with IEP's are covered automatically under Section 504. Because necessary accommodations are included in the IEP, there is no need to write an additional Section 504 plan for these students.

An estimated 1% to 2% of children may be eligible under Section 504 alone. For example, a child with diabetes may need help from the school staff to monitor blood sugar levels but have no problems with the education program itself. Criteria for support will not be met through IDEA; however, receiving support through Section 504 may be available if the Section 504 team, after a complete assessment, determines that the child has a substantial and pervasive impairment to make him or her eligible under this federal law. Most school districts have a process to follow to make Section 504 determinations. If a child is found to be eligible under Section 504, a plan will be developed in order to give the child access to the general education curriculum. This often means that the child will receive reasonable accommodations to help experience success in the general education classroom. Because every school district applies this law differently, it is important to know the process and policy of Section 504 in your district.

■ SPECIAL EDUCATION ACRONYMS AND ABBREVIATIONS

ABI	Acquired Brain Injury
ADD	Attention Deficit Disorder
ADHD	Attention Deficit Hyperactivity Disorder
AE	Age Equivalent
ALD	Assisted Listening Device
APE	Adapted Physical Education
ASHA	American-Speech-Language-Hearing Association
ATD	Assistive Technology Devices
AUT	Autism
AYP	Adequate Yearly Progress
BD	Behavior Disorder
BL	Blind
BST	Building Support Team
CATS	Career and Transition Services
CBA	Curriculum-Based Assessment
CEC	Council for Exceptional Children
CF	Cystic Fibrosis
CMI	Chronic Mental Illness
CP	Cerebral Palsy
CRT	Criterion Referenced Test
CST	Child Study Team
DAPE	Developmental Adapted Physical Education
DBL	Deaf/Blind
DCD	Developmental Cognitive Disability
DD	Developmental Disability
DEA	Deaf
DH	Developmentally Handicapped
D/HH	Deaf/Hard of Hearing
DI	Differentiated Instruction
DIS	Designated Instructional Services
E/BD	Emotional or Behavioral Disorder
ECSE	Early Childhood Special Education
ED	Emotional Disturbance, Emotionally Disturbed
ED/LD	Educationally Handicapped/Learning Disabled
ELL	English Language Learner
EMR	Educable Mentally Retarded
ER	Educable Retarded
ER	Evaluation Report
ESY	Extended School Year
FAPE	Free Appropriate Education
FAS	Fetal Alcohol Syndrome
FH/FFH	Foster Home/ Family Foster Home
GATE	Gifted and Talented Education
GE	Grade Equivalent
HI	Hearing Impaired
HOH	Hard of Hearing
HQ	Highly Qualified
IDEA	Individuals with Disabilities Education Act

IDEIA	Individuals with Disabilities Education Improvement Act of 2004
IDT	Interdisciplinary Team
IEP	Individualized Education Plan
IFSP	Individual Family Service Plan
INT/D	Interpreter/Deaf
IPP	Individual Program Plan
ITP	Individualized Transition Plan
IWEN	Individual With Exceptional Needs
IQ	Intelligence Quotient
LAS	Language/Speech Impaired, Language and Speech
LD	Learning Disabled/Learning Disability
LH	Learning Handicapped
LRE	Least Restrictive Environment
MD	Muscular Dystrophy
MDT	Multi-Disciplinary Team
MH	Multihandicapped
MMMI	Mild-Moderate Mentally Impaired
MR	Mental Retardation/Mentally Retarded
MS	Multiple Sclerosis
MSMI	Moderate—Severe Mentally Impaired
NCLB	*No Child Left Behind Act of 2001*
NTD	Neural Tube Defect
OH/ORT	Orthopedically Handicapped
OHD	Other Health Disability
OHI	Other Health Impaired
OSEP	Office of Special Education Programs
OT	Occupational Therapy/Occupational Therapist
PARA	Para-Educator
PCA	Personal Care Attendant
PD	Physically Disabled/Physically Handicapped
PI	Physically Impaired
PL	Public Law
PLEP	Present Level of Educational Performance
PLOP	Present Level of Performance
PS	Partially Sighted
PSEN	Pupil with Special Education Needs
PT	Physical Therapy
RSP	Resource Specialist Program
RST	Resource Specialist Teacher
RTI	Response to Intervention
SED	Seriously Emotionally Disturbed
SH	Severely Handicapped
SLD	Specific Learning Disability
SLP	Speech or Language Pathologist
SMI	Severely Multiply Impaired
SST	Student Success Team
TAT	Teacher's Assistance Team
TBI	Traumatic Brain Injury
TDD	Telecommunications Device for the Deaf
TMR	Trainable Mentally Retarded
VH/VI	Visually Handicapped/Visually Impaired

3

Access to the General Education Curriculum

Accommodations, Modification, Strategies, and Assistive Technology

Access to the general education curriculum refers to the education and participation of students with disabilities in the academic, extracurricular, and other activities of the schools they attend. It also refers to their progress in the general education curriculum, which occurs through the *adaptation* of the curriculum (what students learn) and *modification* of the methods of instruction (how students learn) (Nolet and McLaughlin, 2005).

■ ACCOMMODATIONS

What Are Accommodations?

Accommodations are made to allow a student access to the general education curriculum and demonstrate learning. Accommodations do not change the instructional level of the curriculum or the performance criteria (Pierangelo & Giuliani, 2007).

With accommodations, the students are working on the same instructional objectives and content as the other students; however, how the student learns and the ways they demonstrate what they have learned may be different from that of their peers. Accommodations are not intended to take the place of real learning or instruction in basic skills; instead, they provide ways for kids with learning problems to take in information or help them express their knowledge. Accommodations can include changes in the following.

- Presentation and/or response format and procedures
- Instructional strategies
- Time and scheduling
- Environment
- Equipment
- Architectures

It is important to remember that accommodations are appropriate and should be made available for use for children in elementary and secondary settings. Listed below are accommodations categorically listed as ideas to assist students to have better access to the general education curriculum.

■ MODIFICATIONS

What Are Modifications?

Modifications are substantial changes in what a student is expected to learn and demonstrate. Changes may be made in the instruction level, the content, or the performance criteria. Such changes are made to provide a student with meaningful and productive learning experiences, environments, and assessments that are based on that individual's needs and abilities.

Modifications require a change in the type and amount of work expected of the students. For example, a student may be working at a lower level than other students in the class. In other instances, the student may be working on a skill related to the skills upon which other students are focusing (Pierangelo & Giuliani, 2007).

Modification might include changes in the following.

- Instructional level
- Content
- Performance criteria

Accommodation and Modification Options

Physical Arrangement of the Classroom

- Provide preferential seating (e.g., seated near the front of the room and away from distraction); such a location helps the student maintain better focus.
- Stand near the student when giving instructions.
- Have the daily routine in writing where it is easy to see.
- Include opportunities for physical activity in the schedule.
- Room decoration should directly relate to current curriculum being taught—allow students to make and post as much of the material as possible.
- Provide student with a stimuli-reduced environment.

Instruction

- Allow tape recording of lectures.
- Provide a written outline of material covered.
- Use overhead and other visual media with oral instruction.
- Incorporate technology (e.g., computers, calculators, videos).
- Provide the student with visuals as part of the discussion (e.g., films, tapes, flash cards).
- Accept typed or word-processed assignments.
- Allow oral or audiotaped assignments.
- Individualize assignments (e.g., length, number, due date, topic).
- Use peer tutoring.
- Teach specific study skills (e.g., organization, note taking).
- Establish and maintain eye contact for all oral directions.
- Pause and create suspense by looking around before asking a question.
- Stand close to the student during the discussion.
- Use a personal listening device to help the student focus more on the teacher's voice and less on extraneous noises.
- Provide handouts in appropriate media (e.g., Braille, tape, large print, tactile representation).
- Keep the *Closed Captioning* option on when showing videos or TV segments so that all students can listen to and read the information.

Discussion and Questioning

- Make sure that you have the student's attention before asking a question.
- Ask questions that are as concrete as possible.
- Ask questions that can be answered with words or a phrase instead of long, essay answer.
- During discussion, use speech literally, avoiding the use of idioms, double meanings, sarcasm, and nicknames.
- Break lengthy questions into separate components.
- An Assistive Listening Device (ALD) may be worn by the teacher to increase the volume and clarity of the class lecture or discussion.
- If student is in need of an interpreter, teacher should present lecture at an appropriate speed for the interpreter to keep pace.
- Allow the interpreter time to translate to the class what the student signs.
- Reward the child for exhibiting good turn-taking skills.
- Establish a cue with student to provide him with feedback (nonverbally) regarding his or her on-task behavior, turn taking, level of movement.
- Give a written copy of the questions that are going to be asked during the discussion for students who need additional processing time.
- Emphasize key words in the questions by inflection or deliberate pausing to help students focus on the main idea.

Note Taking

- Suggest that the student color-code notebooks with texts.
- Allow student to receive copied notes from the teacher or peer.
- Provide students with a paper to copy notes from instead of the overhead.
- Provide students with an outline of key points prior to the lecture.

Independent Work Time

- Allow physically active students to kneel or stand by their desks as long as they are not disrupting others.
- Allow the students to isolate themselves if they are too distracted.
- If there are many items on a page, fold the paper so only a small amount shows at a time.
- Emphasize accuracy instead of speed.
- Photocopy sections of assignments and present the work to the child in part to avoid feeling overwhelmed.
- Provide a place for the student to consistently place completed work.
- Provide the student with worksheets that are uncluttered (e.g., four math problems on a page rather than 20).
- Use a highlighter to highlight spaces for answers.
- Visually divide the worksheet with lines, boxes, and different colored areas.
- Prioritize for the students which tasks need to be completed first, second, third, and so on.
- Provide self-checking and/or self-monitoring experiences for their work.

Testing

- Mark correct answers rather than mistakes.
- Base grades on modified standards (e.g., IEP objectives, effort, amount of improvement, content rather than spelling).
- Specify the skills mastered rather than give a letter grade.
- Offer untimed testing.
- Allow student to take an oral test instead of written.
- Provide limited choices for multiple choice and matching tests.
- Provide the student with an answer list for fill in the blank questions.
- Teach memory techniques for student to study for test.
- Highlight the directions to the test so that the student will focus on them.
- Highlight important sections of a book to help the student study.
- Provide the student with a written outline of the material that will be covered on the test.
- Provide the student with short-answer tests; avoiding essay tests.
- Allow the student to actively move during assessments (walk, jump, chew gum).
- Allow open book tests; provide practice questions for the student to study.
- If matching vocabulary with definitions, color-code the test (definitions = blue paper; words = green paper).
- Cut test into strips so the child can match one blue strip with one green strip until the test is completed.

Homework

- Limit homework to a certain amount of time spent productively rather than an amount of work to be completed.
- Give modified assignments.
- Allow extra credit assignments.
- Allow student to work on homework at school.
- Provide written explanation of homework assignments.
- Select a "study buddy" who can copy assignments or clarify by phone.

- Give reminders about due dates for long-term assignments.
- Develop a reward system for work completed and turned in.
- Assist the student in underlining the key words in the directions before beginning the task.

Long-Term Assignments or Projects

- Have a "count down" until projects are due.
- Short, frequent assignments in an orderly sequence are preferable to long-term projects.
- Give the student and parent a checklist describing what is due and when it is due.
- Provide flexibility regarding the student's response to the assignment (medium used, display type, illustrations, models, and oral versus written presentations).
- Provide students with multimedia desktop publishing application.
- Provide student with outlining or webbing software application for brainstorming and organization.
- Provide student with work processing application (standard or talking) with word prediction software.
- Provide examples and specific steps to writing a report.
- Use samples or pictures of finished products to show the student what needs to be done.
- Allow students to work with a peer.
- Allow the student to prepare a taped presentation on an oral report rather than having to do it "live."
- Limit the child's "choices" for projects to ideas that he or she has had prior experiences with until the child has shown an ability to assimilate, organize, and transfer new information so that the child may complete a satisfactory project with ease.

Home-School Communication

- Develop a daily or weekly home–school communication system, (e.g., notes, checklists, voice mail, or email).
- Mail assignment sheets directly to home.
- Hold periodic student–teacher meetings.
- Schedule regular parent–teacher meetings.

Organization

- Assist the student to color-code notebooks with texts.
- Post materials needed for each activity in a prominent place and remind the student ahead of time to gather the needed items.
- Stand in front of the student with the needed item (a sample) in your hand as you are asking the class to get out the needed item.
- Use a buddy or partner system with every child and change buddies every two to three weeks to help the student get out and organize work materials.
- Have a checklist by the door for typical things that need to be taken home, to the next class, or whatever is needed.
- Tape (student-developed) behavior and organizational reminders on the student's desk to encourage self-monitoring.

- Use an assignments sheet or calendar to help a student monitor upcoming due dates and what needs to be done as homework with listed materials.
- Give the student a cubbyhole or place on a shelf to store items only used in your class. Utilize a container to hold the items and remind the student that only needed items can be kept in it.

Computers

- Place the computer keyboard close to the screen so that the keyboard and screen can be seen simultaneously.
- Use a roller ball or tracking ball with a separate button (track ball mouse).
- Allow the student to use Intellikeys, which often help reduce visual distractions.
- Encourage the student to wear headphones to minimize distraction and maximize clarity of sounds.
- Consider the use of bold key labels and primary keyboards in alpha order if keyboard awareness skills are not developing using the standard equipment.
- Use a desktop security program to prevent the student from accessing prohibited areas while completing schoolwork.
- Ensure that the monitor is at eye level.
- Allow the student plenty of time to "over-learn" task through repeated drills before moving onto a new task. This applies to software applications as well.

Group Work

- Require the student to stay in the group for the activities that are meaningful to them.
- Provide the student with a transition warning before group activities begin.
- Allow the student to leave the group before becoming frustrated.
- Provide the student with a sequence for the group activities (written or pictures).
- Make sure the student can complete the activity independently before moving to the shared activity group situation.

Academics

Reading

- Allow student to have a second set of books at home.
- Utilize books on tape as well as having the parent or peer tape record the reading assignment so that the student can read and listen at the same time.
- Use unison reading when having student read out loud.
- Utilize interactive CD reading program, making sure that the program doesn't require too many tasks at one time.
- Provide student with a talking handheld spell checker or dictionary for identifying unknown words.
- Reduce the amount of pictures in reading material for students who are visually distractible.
- Read poetry, songs, or other pieces to the student with strong rhythm and rhyme.
- Use pre-reading materials that will tie into the student's prior knowledge of a related subject.
- Use "advance organizers" to help the child transfer and maintain new skills.
- Choose stories with lower vocabulary requirements that are age and ability appropriate for the child that will present minimal frustration for the student.

Writing

- Allow student to use word processors or computers.
- Allow student to work at the chalkboard to increase level of participation.
- Allow the student to dictate the responses to a teacher or peer for recording as an alternate to writing.
- Allow student to utilize any method of output, even if there is a mix of manuscript with cursive writing.
- Allow student to use recommended writing support like alternate paper, alternate utensils and added grips, word processors, form-filling software to complete worksheets and tests, text to speech support, word prediction, and grammar and spellcheckers.
- Allow the student to dictate responses to an audio tape recorder.
- Use a slant board to provide compensation for vestibular difficulties (a four-inch binder works well).
- Use letters of various textures such as plastic, wood, or foam. This allows the student to feel the letters.
- Allow the student to use a vibrating, weighted, or felt-tip pen.
- Provide raised line paper.
- Allow student to write about favorite topics whenever possible.
- Use pre-writing strategies to help the student to think about what they are going to say before they write their ideas.
- Use graphic organizers, Venn diagrams, webs, and brainstorm sheets to help organize student's thought.
- Have the student practice "SSSH":

  S = sharpened pencil ready with paper

  S = straightened work area

  S = sitting correctly

  H = have "listening" ears on

- Offer story starters to promote creative writing.

Math

- Don't worry about "perfect calculations" when teaching a new concept; focus on the process first.
- Provide student with an easy to read math dictionary of required math terms.
- Include drawings and examples to illustrate the meaning of terms.
- Highlight similar math operations to help students focus on the operation (e.g., multiplication in blue, division in green).
- Introduce concepts using real-life examples whenever possible.
- Teach fact families and build fluency with games and challenges.
- Teach students to highlight each operation in mixed-operation worksheets.
- Model math problems using manipulatives whenever possible.
- When teaching about the number line, use tape or draw a number line on the floor for student to walk on.
- Enlarge worksheets and assignments on copier to give more writing space.
- Put boxes around each problem to visually separate them.
- Use manipulatives whenever possible (coins, counters, grouping rings).
- Allow use of one-inch graph paper when completing longer computational problems, writing one number in each box to keep place value lined in right spots.

- Allow the use of number lines.
- Allow the use of a multiplication chart.
- Turn lined paper vertically so the student has ready-made columns.
- Allow the use of calculators.

■ ASSISTIVE TECHNOLOGY

According to Pierangelo and Giuliani (2007), assistive technology devices are any items—piece of equipment or product system—that may be used by a person with a disability to perform specific tasks, improve functional capabilities, and become more independent. The level of guidance or support necessary for each student in the classroom may vary greatly; the student may need anything from physical, verbal, or visual prompts to high-technology devices and services. "No" technology and "low" technology devices that do not require electronic equipment are usually readily available and are cost effective. "High" technology requires a high-maintenance electronic system and hence is more costly (Purcell & Grant, 2002). Listed below is a simple sampling of the wide variety and endless possibilities of Assistive Technology Devices available.

Assistive Technology Devices

Assistive Technology for Vision (aids students who are blind or have low vision)

Low-Tech Devices

- Eyeglasses
- Large-print books
- Books on tape
- Magnifying glass
- Slate and Braille
- Stylus
- Stencil
- Tape recorder
- Cassettes
- Stereo headphones
- Lighting contrasts
- Adapted paper (e.g., raised surfaces, highlighted lines, various colors, sizes)
- Pen lights
- Calculator with large keys or large display
- Talking calculators
- Self-sticking notes (such as Post-it Notes)
- Highlighters
- Color-blind aids
- Computer screen magnifier
- Glare reduction screens
- Talking electronic dictionary, thesaurus, spell checker
- Video magnifiers

- Voice amplification or voice projector
- Screen reader

High-Tech Devices

- Braille writer (to take notes, store information, print in various formats)
- Braille translation software (translates inputted text that can be Brailled)
- Braille printer
- Computer with speech output or feedback
- Operating system special-accessibility options (screen enlargement, adjustment of keyboard, sound, display, mouse)
- Closed-circuit television
- Letter- or word-magnification software
- Voice-output screen-reading software

Assistive Technology for Communication (aids students who have difficulty in communicating effectively)

Low-Tech Devices

- Adapted common tools (e.g., big pencils)
- A roller-ball pointing device with a separate button for clicking
- Adapted handles (e.g., pencil grips)
- Scotch tape to hold paper in place (Velcro, slant borders)
- Adapted book-page turners or fluffers
- Adapted paper (different sizes)
- Built-up stylus
- T-bar to assist with typing (a single axis "put and stay" joystick)
- Switches
- Head pointers
- A mouth stick to press keys on the keyboard
- Arm support
- Slant board
- Tilt board
- Book holders
- Key guards
- Touch-sensitive colored lights

High-Tech Devices

- Joysticks
- Adapted mouse
- Typewriting
- Foot pedals or hardware switches (instead of a mouse) to operate a technology device
- On-screen keyboards
- Voice input or output devices
- Voice-recognition software (turns the spoken word into the typed word)
- Eye controlled computer-input devices
- Computer access modification software or hardware
- Touch window
- Portable word processor

- Adaptive switches
- Alternative keyboards

Assistive Technology for Hearing (assists students who are deaf or hard of hearing)

Low-Tech Devices

- Hearing aids
- Signaling devices
- Vibrotactile switch
- Pictures, photographs, objects
- Communication boards
- Phonic ear
- Headphones (to keep the listener focused, adjust sounds, etc.)
- TDD/TTY for phone service
- Closed-captioning television
- Real-time captioning
- CD-based (text) books, electronic books
- Audio-voice amplification device for teachers
- Telecaption decoders

High-Tech Devices

- Assistive listening devices (e.g., amplified phone system)
- Vibrotactile systems

Assistive Technology for Learning and Studying (aids students with high incidence disabilities—including learning, behavior, and cognitive disabilities—to increase, maintain, or improve their functional capabilities)

Low-Tech Devices

- Highlighting tape
- Sticky notes
- Picture schedule
- Written schedule
- Social stories
- Written or picture-supported directions
- Aids to help find materials (e.g., color tabs)
- Editing devices: correction fluid (such as Liquid Paper or White Out) correction tape, correction pen, highlight tape
- Sentence windows
- Graphic organizers to visually help in developing and structuring ideas
- Single-word scanners (reading pens) or handheld scanners
- Close-captioned television

High-Tech Devices

- Portable word processors
- Talking word processors
- Handheld computers

- Voice-recognition products
- Software for organizing ideas and studying
- Electronic organizers or reminders
- Word-prediction software (assist in spelling and sentence construction)
- Multimedia software for production of ideas (e.g., PowerPoint)
- Talking electronic device or software to pronounce challenging words
- Graphic organizer software
- Software for concept development, manipulation of objects, math computations
- Portable word processor to keyboard instead of write
- Text-reading software
- Tactile of voice-output measuring devices

Assistive Technology for Motor/Self-Care (assists student in mobility and caring for self)

Low-Tech Devices

- Stander
- Manual wheelchair
- Walker
- Supportive classroom chair
- Positioning device
- Cane or crutches
- Adapted commode
- Braces or supports

High-Tech Devices

- Power wheelchair
- Bus lift
- Lift for transfers

4

Meeting the Needs of All Students

Response to Intervention

When a classroom teacher enters his or her fourth-grade classroom on any given day, he or she is greeted with the following:

Johnny, one of 30 students in the class, sits quietly at his desk and appears to be intently reading from his basal reader. Appearances can be deceiving, however; although Johnny "looks" as if he is reading, in reality, Johnny reads at a first-grade level and cannot decode or comprehend anything that is being presented in the fourth-grade text.

Sally, sitting right next to Johnny, has her nose in a library book. She finished the basal story within a few minutes of starting and can recall the fine details of the story and describe all story elements, including the problem and solution. She loves to read and could successfully join the tenth-grade literature class at the high school if given the opportunity.

Jose, seated across the room, has finished his math problems, including the extra credit options. He loves math and has been described as a math "whiz," but at this moment, he is struggling to complete writing a three-sentence paragraph in English because he is much more comfortable writing in Spanish, his native language.

Jane, seated at the other corner of the room, has her hand raised and is waiting for the teacher's help. She is correcting her math assignment from yesterday: story problems that require the use of addition, subtraction, multiplication, or division to solve. Jane is very quick at recalling the basic facts and loves to play the flashcard games because she always wins. Jane, however, only solved two out of the 18 problems on yesterday's assignment correctly. As a beginning reader and attempting to read the fourth-grade math problem independently, Jane was unable to understand what the problem was asking her to do and therefore was uncertain which operation to use to solve the problem. The two problems that she did solve correctly were lucky guesses.

As you are reading this, I am certain you can relate with each scenario regardless of the grade level or content area that you teach, as you have these students in your classroom as well. There are 26 students in this hypothetical 30-student classroom that I have yet to describe, and each of those children has individual needs just as the others. This is educational diversity at its finest and is consistently a significant part of American education. As educators, we are required to ensure that "no child is left behind," and we are held accountable for each student to make adequate yearly progress. Meeting the needs of all learners can be a daunting and difficult task. Fortunately, with the careful planning, consultation, and collaboration of all individuals involved in leading and supporting our young learners, there is hope!

Response to Intervention (RTI) was initially put into place to support eligibility determination of students with learning disabilities. According to Bender and Shores (2007), the effects of RTI are much broader and can easily make an impact on every child and teacher in the nation. The implementation of RTI in the general education classroom will enhance instruction and offer a renewed emphasis on "best practice" instruction for all students.

By utilizing RTI, teachers will be better able to tailor their instruction directly toward any identified academic deficits. A huge benefit of RTI is the fact that effective implementation will result in increased understanding of the academic skills of each student in the classroom. The model promotes early identification of students at risk for academic failure and therefore replaces the "wait-to-fail model" under which we have worked in the past. Appropriate learning experiences and interventions are implemented as soon as the need is identified. The RTI process will also promote the collaboration efforts of the general and special education teachers as they work together to provide individualized support and interventions in the general education classroom before initiating a referral to special education services too soon.

There is no one correct way to implement the RTI model in a school district. There are a few basic steps to follow, and the fine details can be determined based on the needs of individual districts. The purpose of this section is not to present an RTI implementation model or format for your district to adopt and follow. If your school district is moving forward with implementing the RTI model, many excellent resources are available to assist in the process development. Two excellent resources that I have found to be incredibly helpful include *The RTI Toolkit: A Practical Guide for School* by Jim Wright and *Response to Intervention: A Practical Guide for Every Teacher* by William N. Bender and Cara Shores.

The purpose of this section, however, is to encourage and promote the effective collaboration and utilization of all educators (general and special educators, support staff, and paraeducators) as they work toward meeting the individual needs of students. Children in the schools can no longer be thought of as your kids and my kids, but they need to all be considered "our kids."

■ THE "VERY BASIC" STEPS OF RTI

The "very basic" steps of RTI as described by Wright (2007) include the following.

1. Implement schoolwide screening measures (fall/winter/spring benchmark screenings)—DIBELS and AIMSweb are suggested to assist in progress monitoring measures.

2. Use data from the benchmark screenings to determine needs.

3. Follow the three-tier system to make decisions regarding interventions.

Tier 1 includes 75% to 85% of the student population. Progress is monitored three times a year for these students. Interventions and strategies take place in the general education classroom.

Tier 2 includes 10% to 15% of the student population. Interventions become more individualized and more intense; however, they still take place in the general education classroom. Support from Title One teacher or reading specialists may occur. Progress must be monitored at least monthly.

Tier 3 includes 5% to 10% of the student population. Alternative programming is appropriate and usually takes place in a special education setting.

4. Ensure systematic monitoring of progress to gather data to assist in determining the effectiveness of the intervention.

5. Use the data from progress monitoring measures to make educational decisions (if data indicate no progress is being made while utilizing a specific intervention, change the intervention).

■ THREE-TIER SYSTEM

A three-tier pyramid system is used as a basis for understanding the RTI model. Many districts in many states have developed their own system of tiers that may involve many more than three levels. The three-tier model, however, is common across most states and for initial purposes; the three-tier pyramid is very effective. A student's placement in the tiers will help determine which intervention(s) to implement. It will also determine the frequency that progress will be monitored to verify the effectiveness of the interventions in place.

Three-Tier System

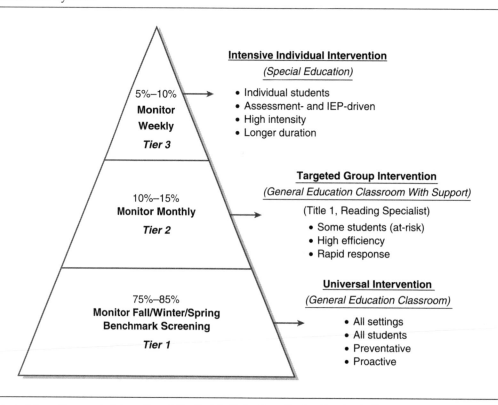

Adapted from *Response to Intervention: A Practical Guide for Every Teacher* (Bender & Shores, 2007).

■ INTERVENTION STRATEGIES

Educational decisions made for children placed in Tier 1 and Tier 2 are ultimately the responsibility of the general education teacher. Making decisions regarding specific interventions or strategies to attempt with a student can be difficult. It is also appropriate to receive support and intervention ideas through your child study or problem solving team. Listed below are varieties of interventions and strategies that can be utilized to help improve progress in a specific area of need. Interventions are not limited to academic areas. Behavioral and social areas are included as well as difficulties in these areas that can certainly interfere with academic progress.

Interventions can range from less restrictive to more restrictive. Less restrictive interventions are ones that can be utilized in a group setting and more restrictive interventions are those that are more effective when utilized with a small group or on an individual basis.

Many of the interventions mentioned below have been compiled and offered for use through Jim Wright's Web site (www.interventioncentral.org). This Web site is a one-stop shop for teachers who are looking for ideas and interventions to assist with promoting progress and growth in children. Jim Wright, the creator of Intervention Central, is a school psychologist and school administrator from central New York. Listed below are only samplings of interventions that are available on his Web site. I invite you to utilize www.interventioncentral.org on a regular basis.

Consistent implementation of interventions is essential to ensure that the integrity of the intervention is maintained. If the intervention is presented in a different format each time when monitoring progress, it will be difficult to determine if it truly was the intervention that did or did not support the growth or change. Intervention integrity checklists are also very helpful for the person implementing the intervention. They help to monitor the sequence of the intervention as well as document the consistency and frequency with which the intervention is being implemented.

■ LANGUAGE ARTS STRATEGIES

Reading Decoding

The National Reading Panel (2000) concluded that phonics instruction produces significant benefits for children from kindergarten through sixth grade and for children having difficulty learning to read. Systematic phonics instruction is appropriate for assisting in reading decoding; however, no one approach will work for all children. The objective is to increase decoding skills to assist in word recognition.

Phoneme Segmentation

The act of decoding involves recognizing and saying the sounds in words. Phoneme segmentations provides students the opportunity to practice this skill. Using three-letter Consonant Vowel Consonant (CVC) words initially, the teacher models the strategy by saying, "I will say the sounds in this word; with each new sound, I'll hold up another finger. The word is *cat*." The teacher says, "C," (holds up pointer finger), "A" (holds up middle finger), and "T" (holds up ring finger) to indicate the three sounds in the word cat. Now, it is the child's turn. As the child says the sounds in the word *hit*, the teacher will hold up the fingers for each sound. Child says, "H" (teacher holds up pointer finger), child says, "I" (teacher holds up middle finger), and the child says, "T" (teacher holds up ring finger). Move onto the next word (e.g., *tag*) and follow the same procedure. Go back and review *hit* and *tag* before moving on to the next word. As the child becomes comfortable with CVC words, expand the number of letters in the words that you are using.

Phoneme Blending

Use letter cubes, magnetic letters, letter tiles, or any other type of manipulative to spell a word. For an example, see the figure below.

Say the word *cat* and have the child repeat the word back to you. Next, the teacher will model by saying the sounds in cat and while saying the sounds, push the appropriate tile or cube up on the table: /c/ /a/ /t/. Have the child repeat after you. Move on to the next word. For example, present the appropriate cubes or tiles for *fig*. The teacher will say the sounds first while physically moving the tiles or cubes up on the table: /f/ /i/ /g/. Then, the child will do the same. Next, have the child independently follow the procedure with the first two words *cat* and *fig* before moving onto the word.

Reading Fluency

Students who can decode text accurately, read at an acceptable rate, and read aloud with appropriate expression are said to be *fluent* readers. Research indicates that readers become more fluent when they are given lots of opportunities to practice their reading either independently or with guidance and assistance from a more accomplished reader. Reading-fluency interventions can pay surprising dividends—not only do those strategies help children to read more fluently, but they also improve readers' *accuracy* and *reading comprehension* (National Reading Panel, 2000). The objective is to increase reading fluency.

■ WHOLE CLASS STRATEGIES

Model Fluent Reading

In order to read fluently, students must first hear and understand how fluent reading should sound. From there, they will be more likely to transfer those experiences into their own reading. The most powerful way for you to help your students is to read aloud to them often and with great expression. Choose the selection carefully. Expose them to a wide variety of genres, including poetry, excerpts from speeches, and folk and fairy tales with rich, lyrical language. Choose texts that will spark your students' interests and draw them into the reading experience.

Following the read-aloud session, ask your students the following question: "After listening to how I read, can you tell me what I did that is like what good readers do?" Encourage students to share their thoughts. Also, ask your students to think about how a fluent reader keeps the listener engaged.

Repeated Reading in Class

As indicated by Cunningham and Allington (2006) in their book *Classrooms That Work,* repeated readings are a way to help students recognize high frequency words more easily, thereby strengthening their ease of reading. Having students practice reading by rereading short passages aloud is one of the best ways to promote fluency.

Choose a short poem or shorter passage, preferably one that fits into your current unit of study and place it onto an overhead transparency. Make a copy of the poem or passage for each student. Read the poem or passage aloud several times while your students listen and follow along. Intentionally discuss your reading behaviors such as *phrasing* (the ability to read several words together in one breath), *rate* (the speed at which we read), and *intonation* (the emphasis we give to particular words or phrases).

Next, ask students to engage in an "echo reading" in which you read a line and all the students repeat the line back to you. Following the echo reading, have students read the entire poem together as a "choral read." Doing group reading like these can be effective strategies for promoting fluency because all students are actively engaged and they may be less apprehensive about making a mistake because they are part of a community of readers rather than standing alone.

Phrased Reading in Class

Fluency involves reading phrases seamlessly as opposed to word-by-word. To help students read phrases better, begin with a poem. Write the lines of the poem onto sentence strips with each line on its own sentence strip. This will serve as a cue to show students how good readers cluster portions of text rather than saying each word separately. Hold up strips one at a time and have students read the phrases together.

Reader's Theater in Class

Reader's theater is an oral performance of a script and is one of the best ways to promote fluency. In the exercise, meaning is conveyed through expression and intonation. The focus thus becomes interpreting the script rather than memorizing it.

To begin, give each student a copy of the script. Read it aloud as you would any other piece of literature. After your read aloud, do an "echo read" and a "choral read" of the script to involve the entire class. Once the class has had enough practice, choose students to read the various parts. Put together a few simple props and costumes and invite other classes to attend the performance.

For the presentation, have readers stand in front of the room and face the audience. Encourage students to make eye contact with the audience and one another before they read. Once they start, they should hold their scripts at chest level to avoid hiding their faces and look out at the audience periodically.

Reading Together to Increase Fluency

Explicit Modeling

This type of modeling helps children learn to think about what they already know while they are reading. Explain to children that you are going to think aloud while reading. As you read a short passage aloud, talk about your thinking process—what you do to get meaning from the words and understand the text. For example, "That's a new word. It begins with *cl*. I don't know how to pronounce the next part—*ue*. Harriet is a spy. It must be *clue* because spies look for clues."

Implicit Modeling

This type of modeling also helps children think while they read. In this case, you would demonstrate how to use thinking skills without describing what you are doing. When a child is stuck on a word, you can suggest strategies he or she can use to figure it out. The child can use these strategies immediately and when reading in the future. You might ask any of the following questions.

"Try reading the sentence again."

"Try reading the next sentence."

"Where did the boy go at the beginning of the story?" or

"Where do you think he might be going now?"

Choral Reading

This strategy helps children become more fluent and confident readers. Ask the child to sit beside you or slightly in front of you. Hold the book together and ask the child to read along with you. Begin reading in a voice that is slightly louder and faster than the child's. As the child becomes more comfortable with reading the text, lower your voice and slow down your reading speed. If the child slows down, increase you loudness and speed again.

Echo Reading

This is another way to help a child develop confidence and fluency. Read aloud a line of text. Ask the child to read the same line. With a young child, point to the line of text as you are reading and encourage the child to do the same. Continue taking turns reading and rereading the same lines. When the child begins to read with more expression and fluency, suggest that he or she read aloud on his or her own.

Paired Reading

Paired reading is a technique that allows teachers to vary the amount of support they provide to a child while reading aloud together. Explain to the child that sometimes you will read aloud together—duet reading—and sometimes he or she will read alone—solo reading. Agree on two signals the child can use to switch back and forth from solo to duet reading. When the child gives you the duet signal, you will begin reading together. When the child feels ready for solo reading, he or she will give the solo signal, and you will stop reading. You can nod your head or give some other simple sign of encouragement for solo reading. Continue paired reading until the book or passage is completed.

Repeated Reading

In repeated reading, children work on reading as they would work at making music. They continue working with each text until it is fluent. Repeated reading works best with readers who have reached at least a primer instruction level. Use a passage of 100 words or so at the instructional level. The text should be decodable, not predictable. The reader might select a favorite from among familiar books.

Graph how fast students read with a one-minute read. Graphing is motivating because it makes progress evident. Emphasize speed rather than accuracy. Set a reachable but challenging goal. Have the student read for one minute. Count the number of words read and graph the results with an easily understood chart.

Tape-Assisted Reading

In tape-assisted reading, students read along in their books as they hear a fluent reader read the book on an audiotape. For tape-assisted reading, you need a book at a student's independent reading level and a tape recoding of the book read by a fluent reader at about 80–100 words per minute. The tape should not have sound effects or music. For the first reading, the student should follow along with the tape, pointing to each word in her or his book as the reader reads it. Next, the student should try to read aloud along with the tape. Reading along with the tape should continue until the student is able to read the book independently without the support of the tape.

■ READING COMPREHENSION

Text comprehension can be thought of as the interaction of reader and text. That is, readers must construct meaning by interpreting information presented in the reading through the lens of their own prior knowledge of the topic or events that make up the content of that passage (National Reading Panel, 2000). Constructing meaning from text begins before, during, and after reading. According to Laverick (2002), there are seven areas that can be linked to an effective reader, and these areas occur before, during, and after reading a passage or story. *Predicting, visualizing,* and *connecting* are areas that are implemented as before reading strategies. *Questioning* and *clarifying* are areas implemented during reading, and *summarizing* and *evaluating* are implemented as after reading strategies. The goal of the teacher is to help students apply comprehension reading strategies to become an effective reader.

Before Reading Strategies

Predicting, visualizing, and connecting are before reading strategies used in activities to spark an interest in reading. These strategies help to activate prior background knowledge so that the learner can begin to make a connection to the reading. Good learners always begin a text with a purpose or reason for reading (D'Arcangelo, 2002).

Word Splash

This strategy emphasizes vocabulary skills and is best used when implemented at the beginning of a new story. Begin this activity by "splashing" a collection of key terms or concepts from the reading selection on an overhead. Ask the students to write complete sentences that predict how the terms are related to the topic.

K-W-L Charts

This strategy will activate students' prior knowledge by asking students what they already *know* about the topic; then students as a group will set specific goals regarding what they *want* to learn; and after reading, students discuss what they have *learned*. This will help them use higher order thinking skills to construct meaning from what they have read. (A sample is provided on page 183.)

Anticipation Reading Guide

To activate prior knowledge of a topic, students complete a brief questionnaire on which they must express agreement or disagreement with "opinion" questions tied to the selection to be read. The instructor first constructs the questionnaire. Each item on the questionnaire is linked to the content of the upcoming article or story. All questionnaire items use a "forced-choice" format in which the student must simply agree or disagree with the item. After students have completed the questions, the teacher reviews responses with the class and allows the students an opportunity to explain their rationale for their answers. The students then read the article or story (Merkley, 1996).

During Reading Strategies

Questioning and clarification are strategies used by readers that will help reinforce their comprehension and maintain self-interest. These particular strategies help readers engage personally, respond to the text, consolidate ideas, and find a reason for the sequence of information. Examples of these strategies include making graphic organizers, semantic maps, marginal notes, and drawing pictures (D'Arcangelo, 2002).

Sticky Note Symbols

Students use sticky notes during the reading process to write down questions or comments about what they are reading. They place the sticky note in the particular area of question or comment and draw an arrow to indicate the spot on the page. This activity teaches students to focus on what they are reading and to depend on their understanding.

Selective Highlighting

This is a strategy that helps students select what is important in the text. Specific steps should be taught to assist students to distinguish critical from non-critical information. Students can learn to highlight sentences, paragraphs, or words that they have questions about, or they can highlight answers to the pre-reading questions they have asked during the K-W-L session.

After Reading Strategies

Laverick (2002) indicates that summarizing and evaluating are strategies used by the students to thoroughly understand what they have just read. Students should be led to begin recalling information from the text, allowing the evaluation process to occur.

Picture This

This strategy emphasizes visual representation. Students work together as a team to think about the text they have read and organize their thoughts to create a visual representation of the text. Students can make book jackets to illustrate their understanding of the story.

Graphic Organizers

Graphic organizers give the student graphic representations of the relationship that links together facts, vocabulary, and concepts of texts. Graphic organizers come in many variations and are designed to organize abstract ideas into a concrete form. Listed below are a few samples of the many graphic organizers that can be used. Many educational Web sites offer graphic organizers that can be customized to your specific needs. An excellent teacher resource that provides excellent access to a wide variety of organizers is www.edhelper.com. Listed below are a few examples of graphic organizers that can be used to assist students in summarizing and evaluating what they have read.

Story Charts or Maps

Identify the characters, setting, problem, sequence of events, and the resolution of the conflict of a story by using charts and maps. Primary grades will use a slightly modified chart compared to the chart used by upper-elementary grade levels. (A sample is provided on page 180.)

Storyboard

Divide the chalkboard or a piece of paper into sections (six to eight sections depending on the length of the story). Have the students draw, write, or dictate for the teacher to record the story events in sequence in each box or section. (A sample is provided on page 181.)

Character Web

Put the character's name in the center of the web, and then have students report traits and descriptions of that character in the outer sections of the web. (A sample is provided on page 182.)

Plot Profiles

After reading a book or story, choose a number of events and produce a class graph of events students found to be the most exciting. Plot on a large graph the majority opinion of the class regarding how exciting each event was. (Have the students show hands or applaud when you mention the part of the story that they thought was most exciting.)

Wanted Posters

Have the students create posters by drawing a picture of and writing about identifying characteristics of a character in the book.

Venn Diagram

Use the circular diagram to compare and contrast two similar books, stories, or pieces of literature. Compare two versions of a story, a book with its movie version, or two characters within a book.

STORY CHART

Use this chart to identify the different elements of the story you just read. You can draw a picture or write words to describe the elements.

Title:

Author:

Illustrator:

Characters:

Setting:

Story Summary:

STORYBOARD

Draw pictures or write sentences about the story events in the order the events occur.

Story Title:_____

Author:_____

Illustrator:_____

1.   2.

3.   4.

5.   6.

CHARACTER WEB

Write the character's name in the center of the web. Fill in the outer section of the web with traits that describe the character.

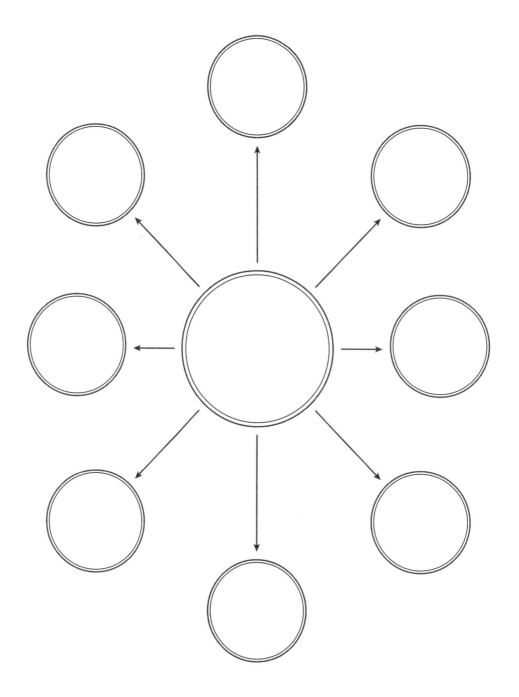

K-W-L CHART

K	W	L
What I **K**now	What I **W**ant to Know	What I **L**earned

■ WRITTEN EXPRESSION STRATEGIES

Writing is very difficult for many students, especially when they are expected to "just write." For many, determining a topic about which to write and then gathering ideas about that topic is very troublesome. These students struggle to place their ideas on paper in an interesting and descriptive way. Here are some strategies to present to students in your class who have difficulty with writing.

Copy Change

Rasinski and Padak (2000) explain the purpose of this strategy is to provide a framework for writing. Students use another author's patterns as a framework for their own writing. For example, young children might use Bill Martin Jr.'s *Brown Bear, Brown Bear, What Do You See?* to create their own version: "Fierce eagle, fierce eagle, what do you see?" Or Mr. Jones, Mr. Jones, what do you see?"

Dialogues

The purpose of this strategy is to provide an opportunity for students to react to ideas and extend their thinking about the material being studied and to permit students to think about conflicts and possible solutions. Students write a dialogue between two or more persons, historical figures, or characters being studied. These conversations might reflect a historical event or a problem that needs to be solved. The dialogue could also include the students themselves.

Helping Students in the Writing Process

Clark, Fuerstenberg Gabler, Goethel, and Milne (1994) reiterate to teachers how intimidating and overwhelming it can be for children when faced with the daunting task of taking a piece of written work "through the writing process." They offer this suggestion to assist children through the writing process.

Follow these steps:

1. Prewriting
   - Use a brainstorming device such as one of the following:
     - The "I remember" list
     - "I used to _____ but now I _____" exercise
     - Feeling exploration: "I feel happy that _____"
   - Do the exercise first; then share it with your students to encourage trust and stimulate ideas.
   - Encourage students to do the writing as much as possible.
   - Work in class together or assign writing for the student to do at home.

2. Drafting
   - Emphasize that spelling, grammar, and punctuation do not matter in the first draft. Concentrate on the flowing ideas.
   - Try these techniques:
     - List details before putting together sentences; arrange them in connecting circles or as lists grouped for similarity.
     - Student and teacher each writes a draft (teacher model).
     - Student dictates and teacher/tutor writes.

3. Responding to First Draft
   - Have your student read the draft aloud to you.
   - Concentrate on content, not mechanics. You will correct that later.
   - Ask questions that help the student focus. You want the piece to be clearly stated, complete in detail, and interesting to read.
   - Suggested techniques include the following:
     o Be positive; point out the things you like about the piece.
     o "Say back"; summarize the main idea in your own words.
     o Ask for more detail in specific areas.
     o Make one or two suggestions to improve content. Do this in the "What if . . . ?" mode, which lets the writer decide whether to make the change or not.
     o Occasionally ask for the student's opinion on your own writing. Your willingness to do this shows the student that acceptance of criticism and rewriting are part of the process for all writers.
     o Depth of revision will vary. Some students will want to write many short pieces and move on. Others will prefer to add on to and revise the same piece for several weeks. The main thing is to do some writing every day.

4. Revising the Draft
   - Revision may be done during school or assigned as homework depending on the length and purpose of the piece.

5. Editing for Correctness
   - Use the editing process to teach matters of spelling, punctuation, and grammar.
   - Focus on only one or two editing skills so that the students are not overloaded with or discouraged by corrections.
   - Produce a clean copy when it is needed for publishing or beneficial to the student. This can be done several ways.
     o You correct the problems, then write or type the clean copy.
     o You correct the problems on the draft, and then have the student copy the writing in its correct form. (This is helpful in short pieces but may be discouraging in longer ones.)
     o Students enter the text into the computer and make their own revisions and corrections. (This is the most desirable if the student has the abilities and the program has the resources.)

Writing Topics

As a class, brainstorm a list of topics that would be of interest for students to write about. Some examples may include sports, scary things, vacation places, current events, favorite things to do, or hobbies. This class list can be posted in the classroom to serve as an idea generator when students are expected to write in journals or any other writing activity. When the student says, "I don't know what to write about," you can direct that student to the list.

Semantic Mapping

This strategy will help students to organize their thoughts before they begin writing. Place the main topic in the center of the paper. Place subcategories around the main topic and then add details pertaining to the subcategories. The character web presented in the "Reading Comprehension" section may be used for this as well.

Journals

According to Rasinski and Padak (2000), journals are collections of personal writing about or around a topic or general theme. Entries should be made on a regular basis—daily or frequently—and are usually kept together in a notebook or folder. The important thing is to write; this is the only way for learners to improve their writing or demonstrate to themselves that they indeed can write.

1. Give learners strategies to use to get the words down when they do not know how to spell; for instance, try one of the following:
   - Write down the first letter of the word and draw a line.
   - Write the word as best you can and underline it to remind yourself that it is possibly misspelled.

2. Model writing in your journal and be willing to share your writing. (Some learners' entries may be too personal to share with others.)

3. Journals are not writing assignments to be corrected or graded but should be used for communicating and writing practice.

Personal Journals or Diaries

In personal journals or diaries, learners are given the opportunity to reflect their own experiences. This can include writing or drawings. Entries in personal journals can be good first drafts for teaching the writing process.

Dialogue Journals

Dialogue journals are kept by two people (teacher and learner, or child and parent, etc.) in which a written conversation over a variety of topics takes place. Learners write informally about a topic of interest, a concern, a book they are reading, or a topic they are studying.

Reader-Response Journals

In reader-response journals, learners are asked to respond to some experience, and the journal can take a variety of forms.

- Noting new vocabulary words
- Writing about the character they identified with
- Making predictions about what might happen next
- Writing about the part they like
- Writing about how the reading made them feel
- Writing about what they would have done in the particular situation described
- Writing about how they could use what they just read about

Entries can be open ended or directed.

- What advice would you give the character?
- What do you think will happen if this story continued?
- How is the character like someone you know?

Double-Entry Journals

For a double-entry journal, learners divide their journal pages into two parts. In the left-hand column, they write quotes or notes from their reading. In the right-hand column, learners write their response or reaction to the information they have written in the first column.

Learning Logs

Learning logs are journals in which students reflect on learning experiences they take part in. They can respond to questions they have about the experience or content, reflect on how well they understand the presentation, connect the material to their own lives, or comment on their interest in the content.

Pen Pals

Arrange opportunities with other teachers to share writing between classrooms. The student may write notes or letters to a student in another classroom in the same school or different schools.

Show, Don't Just Tell

Teach students to create a picture or scene using words. Have students close their eyes and ask them to think of a scene or picture with which they are familiar. Have students describe the image orally and then in writing. The student should describe what the scene feels, tastes, looks, and sounds like. Encourage students to think about and use all of their senses to assist in writing descriptively.

Have students choose a photograph, magazine picture, postcard, or illustration from a story. Ask the students to write a descriptive paragraph about the selected picture. When students have finished writing, display all of the pictures around the classroom. Randomly pass out the paragraphs to all students. Have students read their given paragraph, and then try to match the paragraph with the picture that was described. If you have a student who is unable to write, ask the student to dictate the description to you or a peer.

■ WRITTEN MECHANICS STRATEGIES

Students who struggle academically are often very weak in the mechanics of language. They struggle to seek and find their own errors and to self-correct their written work. Try some of these strategies with students who struggle with the mechanics of writing.

Provide frequent reminders. Students need to be reminded frequently to check their work for capitalization and punctuation errors. You may want to post a checklist in the classroom to which students may refer when proofing their final papers.

Use questioning techniques to help students find their own errors.

Teacher   "What two things do all sentences need?"

Student   "A capital letter at the beginning and a punctuation mark at the end."

Teacher   Does your sentence have both of those things?"

Frequently model how to edit and find mechanical errors. Provide students with examples of work with mechanical errors. As a class, correct the errors by walking through the passage step by step. Be sure to explain why the specific examples are erroneous.

Let students edit each other's work. This works well, as students are often more observant with other's work than with their own.

Dictate to students. Provide one or two sentences orally for the students to write. Ask each student to add the correct punctuation and capital letters. When students have finished with their corrections, write the sentence correctly on the overhead or board and ask the students to check their work. Ask the students, "Do your sentences look like mine?"

Provide short written samples for students to correct. The sentences may also be written on the board or overhead for the students to copy. The written sentences should not contain any capital letters or punctuation. Have the student copy the sentences into a notebook or journal and add the correct punctuation. Then have the students take turns making the corrections on the model and explaining why each correction was made. Students may correct their own work samples. One or two sentences daily are sufficient.

Have the students dictate a few sentences. Copy exactly what the students say onto a chart. Be sure that all students are watching as you are writing what is being said. As you record the student sentences verbatim, omit the capital letters and punctuation in the sentences. Have students identify the errors in the sentences. Always require students to explain the reason for the correction. It is important to continually repeat the rules of written mechanics, as it will help students to become more familiar with the rules and transfer it to their own writing.

Create proofreading checklists to help students review daily written assignments. Create individual proofreading checklist for students to use to help them check their own work. The checklist should include appropriate written language goals for your grade level. The students may keep the checklist at their desks or clip it to a final copy or paper to show that they have proofread their assignment.

	Sample #1
Capital Letters	❑ **Beginning of sentences** ❑ **Names** ❑ **Specific places** ❑ **Title of the story** ❑ **Dates**
Punctuation	❑ **.** ❑ **?** ❑ **!**
Spelling	❑ **Dictionary** ❑ **Ask a friend** ❑ **Ask the teacher** ❑ **In my notes**

Sample #2	Sample #3
❑ **Spelling**	*SPACE*
❑ **Punctuation**	❑ **S** pelling
❑ **Capital Letters**	❑ **P** unctuation
❑ **Paragraphs**	❑ **A** ppearance
____ indented	❑ **C** apitalization
____ topic sentence	❑ **E** rror Analysis
____ details	The word **SPACE** is used as an acronym to help students remember the five items in the proofreading list.
❑ **Margins**	
❑ **Overall Appearance**	
❑ **Name, Date, Class Period**	

From Hammeken, Peggy A. (2003). *Inclusion: An Essential Guide for the Paraprofessional: A Practical Reference Tool for All Paraprofessionals Working in Inclusive Settings* (2nd Ed.). Thousand Oaks: Corwin. Reprinted with permission.

Spelling Strategies

Students are poor spellers for many reasons. Some students are inattentive to visual details, while others struggle to recall the combination of letters. A number of students may be visually unaware of word patterns or may reverse letters such as the letter *b* for *d*. A few students are simply careless in their writing and spelling resulting in numerous errors. Here are some suggestions that may help students with spelling.

Teach high-frequency words. High-frequency words should be top priority in your spelling instruction. It is said that about half of the English language is composed of the 100 most frequently used words. One thousand words account for over 90% of words frequently used in everyday writing.

Have the students write the words in the air using large movements. Ask the students to say the letters out loud as they write the word in the air.

Write words using glitter and glue or starch on a piece of cardboard. Students may sprinkle glitter, sand, salt, or any powdery material over the top of the glue or starch. Once it dries, it creates a textured, 3-D spelling word that can be used for tactile practice of tracing the words.

Provide a tray of sand or salt. Have student write the spelling word with their finger in the sand or salt while spelling out loud.

"Finger-paint" spelling words. Squirt shaving cream on the desktop for students to practice writing words. You may also spread a small amount of pudding, frosting, or whipped cream on a paper plate. Once the word is written, the student can erase it by smoothing over the "cream" and then proceed to write the next word.

Pair students. Students may use their fingers to trace their spelling words on their partner's back, or they can orally spell the words back and forth between partners. Older students can take turns quizzing one another.

Use individual chalkboards or whiteboards. This activity may be used as a whole-group activity. Supply the students with colored chalk for chalkboards or colored pens for whiteboards. Once the spelling words are written, count to three and ask the students to hold up the boards so you are able to make a quick check of individual spelling boards. If using chalk, students may store their chalk in a sock. The students will have their chalk and "eraser" in one place.

Use a clean paintbrush and water. Students may practice writing words on a chalkboard or desktop.

Use manipulative letters. Provide students with magnetic letters, alphabet cookies, sponge letters, rubber stamps, or stencils to use for individual practice of the words.

Play games. Create various games that incorporate the spelling words. Games such as Scrabble, Wheel of Fortune, and Boggle will help with spelling. Students may create crossword puzzles, word finds, and play games such as hangman. Small groups of students may quiz one another orally or have mini-spelling bees.

Make use of technology. Computer spelling programs are often enjoyed by students. Weekly spelling lists can be inserted into the program. There are many Web sites that offer the option to make words finds and crossword puzzles using the weekly lists.

Use configuration clues. Print a word, and then outline the shape in a different color. This will help students to recognize the use of tall letters and letters that go below the bottom line. There are Web sites that allow the development of "word shapes" for spelling lists as well.

Use memory aids with spelling. Twelve memory aids help with spelling. Ask students to create their own. Some common examples include the following.

The princi*pal* is a *pal.*	I will have *two* desserts, please.
Ron studied the envi*ron*ment.	No one be*lie*ves a *lie.*
I before E, except after C.	A fri*end* is a fri*end* to the *end.*
Q is always followed by u.	*Here* is in the words w*here* and t*here.*

Have students practice only the words that are misspelled on the pretest.
It is more efficient to focus only on the misspelled words for spelling practice. For some students, the weekly list may need to be modified if the student misses the majority of words on the pretest.

Handwriting Strategies

Some students have trouble writing neatly on or within the given lines of a piece of paper. Letters may be formed incorrectly, and their written work may look disorganized and sloppy. Many students write too quickly, causing their handwriting to be unreadable. Others, however, write very slowly to produce their best work, which may take too much time to complete an assignment; therefore, the work is incomplete. It is often found that the cause of incorrect handwriting is that the student has never learned proper letter formation strokes. The student may have been inattentive or not ready to learn when beginning handwriting was taught. Thus, the student has created his or her own unique way of letter formation. Unfortunately, once letters are learned incorrectly, it is very difficult to break these habits. Often when students have found their own way of writing, it will become permanent. This emphasizes the importance of consistent and correct teaching in the early primary school years. If you have a student struggling with handwriting difficulties, try some of the following suggestions.

Carefully teach and model new letters for the students. Show the strokes as you talk through the steps of letter formation.

Consistently require students to correct mistaken letters in all written work. Bring students' attention to letter reversals and incorrectly formed letters in all assignments. Assist students in correcting their mistakes.

Demonstrate letters using large movements in the air. Talk through the strokes and formation of the letters as you practice writing the letters in the air. Have students write the letters in the air also. Watch each student to ensure that each is making the correct strokes.

Be flexible with each student's letter formation style. Many school districts require a certain style of handwriting to be taught (e.g., D'Nealian, Zaner Bloser). There are some students who will struggle with conforming to the specificity of a particular style. Be flexible and make it a priority for that child's handwriting to be legible—not necessarily perfectly conforming to the "style" that is to be taught.

Always observe while students are practicing. Walk around the room and identify students in need of one-on-one, small group assistance and students who need immediate reteaching. The continual monitoring is very important as once a student learns and practices an incorrect letter formation, it is almost impossible to break the student's habit.

Use visualization and descriptive words whenever possible. When teaching the letter formation, use the "person visualization" to help children understand where letters are supposed to start and finish on the line. Use the visualization below. Have students think of a person standing on their writing paper. The top line is called the "Headline," middle line is called the "Beltline," and the bottom line is called the "Footline." When teaching the formation of a letter (for example the letter *l*), remind students to start at the headline and go all the way down to the footline.

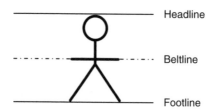

Provide students with special materials.

- Pencil Grips: Placing a grip on the pencil may help the student to hold the pencil more easily. Older students may use tape or a rubber band.
- Pencil Types: Thick beginner pencils may help some students. As the student becomes older, experiment with using felt-tip pens, mechanical pencils, and ballpoint pens.
- Paper: Use a paper that is comfortable for the student. Some students will need to use wide-ruled paper. Alternating green and white lines will help some students with correct formation of letters. Paper with raised lines is useful for students who have difficulty staying within the lines when writing. Graph paper will help students who have spatial problems.

Math Strategies

Often, students who typically struggle with academics have exhibited learning strengths in spatial awareness, logical thinking, reasoning, and/or visualization. They have the ability to excel in a balanced mathematics curriculum that emphasizes patterns, geometry, measurement, probability, and logic. These students need hands-on activities and may benefit from using manipulatives (e.g., pattern blocks, base-ten blocks, interlocking cubes, cubes, or tiles), graphing activities, searching for patterns, and using other nontextbook, nonworksheet-type strategies. It is important that the emphasis of mathematics is not placed on assigning students problem after problem or page after page of tedious computation. The emphasis of math should be placed on providing adequate and appropriate support to students to assist them in understanding those concepts.

Evaluate the students' math skills in alternate ways. If using the traditional paper-and-pencil test, allow additional testing time for students that need it. Consider alternative forms of testing such as a take-home test, computer-assisted assessments, math portfolios, or a project, or give credit if the students are able to demonstrate knowledge of the process.

Provide cubes, buttons, counter, or other concrete objects. Allow students to utilize materials that will assist them with the problem-solving process. Manipulative objects may include any items that can be counted or will convey a quantity. As the students understand the process, the students will be able to move from the concrete to the conceptual level.

Number squares (or a hundreds chart) may be used to help student see patterns. They are helpful for students who have difficulty with number concepts. Number squares may be used to show patterns or to teach even and odd numbers, addition, subtraction, multiplication, and division. The following number square is a visual picture of counting by fives or multiples of five. A hundreds chart and multiplication charts should be readily available and easily accessible for students as well. The following charts are available to be photocopied for student use.

NUMBER SQUARE/ 5'S AND 10'S

1	2	3	4		6	7	8	9	
11	12	13	14		16	17	18	19	
21	22	23	24		26	27	28	29	
31	32	33	34		36	37	38	39	
41	42	43	44		46	47	48	49	
51	52	53	54		56	57	58	59	
61	62	63	64		66	67	68	69	
71	72	73	74		76	77	78	79	
81	82	83	84		86	87	88	89	
91	92	93	94		96	97	98	99	

NUMBER SQUARES/HUNDREDS CHART

1	2	3	4	5	6	7	8	9	10
11	12	13	14	15	16	17	18	19	20
21	22	23	24	25	26	27	28	29	30
31	32	33	34	35	36	37	38	39	40
41	42	43	44	45	46	47	48	49	50
51	52	53	54	55	56	57	58	59	60
61	62	63	64	65	66	67	68	69	70
71	72	73	74	75	76	77	78	79	80
81	82	83	84	85	86	87	88	89	90
91	92	93	94	95	96	97	98	99	100

Provide Touch Math strategies. Touch Math is available from Innovative Learning. It may be used as a complete program or as a supplement to regular mathematics instruction. The program strategically places "touch points" on numbers one through nine. Students memorize the points. The program will help students add (counting forward) and subtract (counting backward). It may also be used for multiplication.

Permit and encourage the use of calculators. If students are struggling with computational aspects, allow them to use calculators once the student has demonstrated that the concept is understood. The number square concept presented earlier is an alternative to calculator use if students have difficultly with basic math-fact computation.

Provide students with various paper options. When working on problems that require the students to demonstrate their work, allow them to record their work on regular notebook paper with two or three lines of space between problems. It may be helpful to provide graph paper for math computation problems. (Write one number in each section of the graph paper to help keep track of the place-value columns.) Or encourage students to use regular notebook paper turned sideways so the lines run vertically instead of horizontally across the page. This will help students keep their columns aligned properly.

Graph Paper Sample

1.		4	3	7
	+	2	2	2
		6	5	9

Lined Paper Turned Sideways

1.		4	7	2
			2	2
		4	9	4

Assign an appropriate number of problems. In an attempt to determine whether or not students grasp a specific mathematical concept or to provide practice on the concept, there is little value in assigning an entire page of math calculations if the struggling students are able to demonstrate mastery by completing 40% to 50 % of the calculations.

Avoid the stress of timed tests of basic facts. Many students struggle with the memorization of basic addition, subtraction, multiplication, and division facts. Often, when given time to think, the student is well aware of the basic facts; however, the essence of the "timed test" contributes to anxiety causing the student to perform poorly on the timed test. Struggling students may be expected to complete the same test; however, do not require it to be completed in a specific amount of time. Also, give credit to the student who responds orally and the student who needs to rely on manipulatives. Students are learning when they understand the process of how to arrive at the answer of a mathematical problem. The students should not be penalized if it takes a longer period of time to complete the process.

Reduce the amount of copying. Provide students who struggle with photocopied pages of assignments. Allow another person (aide, parent, or volunteer) to help by copying the problems onto paper for the student.

Highlight processing signs. Highlighting math symbols will draw attention to the mathematical operation necessary for successful completion of the problem. Many students are not attentive to operation signs on a page, especially if they change frequently (e.g., between addition and subtraction).

Color or highlight the *ones* column. Draw attention to where the student is supposed to begin working on the problem.

Provide students with only one worksheet at a time. Avoid overwhelming the student with too many pages at one time.

Visually list all the steps for each process. Write the steps for the different mathematical processes and have them posted throughout the room for students to refer when needed. Students may also create small books containing the steps in the process to keep in their math folders and use at home. Whenever possible, include a mnemonic memory device to help.

Example Mnemonic for Order of Operations

Please Excuse My Dear Aunt Sally—PEMDAS

P = Parenthesis

E = Exponents

M = Multiplication

D = Division

A = Addition

S = Subtraction

Use whiteboards and overhead projectors for teaching mathematical concepts. Utilize overhead transparent manipulatives such as calculators, pattern blocks, and cubes in daily teaching. Students often grasp materials when they can visually see as well as hear how to work through a specific process.

Keep the copying of math problems from the board or overhead to a minimum. Struggling students may have difficulty copying assignments from the board or overhead. Keep in mind that math is about number relationships and **not** about accurate copying.

Transition Strategies

Transition and noninstructional times during the day are often challenging times for students. Here are some ways to help avoid behavior difficulties during unstructured times.

Inform students of any upcoming changes in the daily schedule. Try to avoid surprises in the routine. If there is an assembly, guest speaker, substitute teacher, or other changes in routine, if possible, inform students in advance.

Discuss what will happen and teach the specific behaviors that are expected and required for each new situation. Use techniques such as role-playing and practicing of specific behaviors before introducing a new situation to the students.

Use flashing lights, a ringing bell, a low whistle, or some sort of cue to inform students that an activity will soon be ending. Be consistent with the cues used during transition times so that students are familiar with them and always know what it means when you utilize the cue. A two-minute warning is often appropriate, as it forewarns the students of the upcoming conclusion of the project or activity.

Allow a short rest time, exercise, or some sort of "down time" between structured activities. This will help students to get some of their "wiggles" and excess energy out before moving on to the next activity.

Be prepared to physically help a student through a transition time. This is very helpful for the student who struggles with transition times. Close proximity to the student is often beneficial and serves as a reminder to help the student remain "in control."

Provide whole-class incentives when smooth transitions occur. There are a variety of ways to do this. The entire class may be rewarded with a point when the transition is smooth. A goal may be set, and once the class meets the goal, the entire class is rewarded. Rewards may include extra free time, a video, outside time, or whatever reward the class would like to work towards.

Attention Strategies

Getting It

Provide a signal to get students' attention. Turn off or flash the lights, ring a bell, clap, or raise your hand to signal to students that you need their attention.

Use different tones and volume of your voice. Use loud, soft, and whispering voices. Try using a consistent chant or action to get attention such as, "Clap once" (children clap once) and "clap twice" (children clap twice). Children should know that voices should be off after clapping twice. Once there has been silence, you can continue in a normal voice to give directions.

Use eye contact. Always ensure that you have eye contact with your students before providing instruction. Students must learn that if they are in a position where they are unable to maintain eye contact, they should move to a position where they are able to see you. Students should be instructed to turn their chairs or bodies towards you during instruction time.

Always show excitement and enthusiasm about the lessons and activities that are being taught. If students see that you are excited about the upcoming lessons and activities, they will tend to become interested and excited as well.

Do what it takes to get attention, even if it means being silly. Sometimes using props or dressing in costume will help to get the students' attention and interest about the upcoming lesson.

Be mysterious. Inside a box or bag, place an item that is related to the upcoming lesson. Show students the box or bag and encourage them to guess or predict what they think is inside the box or bag. This will keep their excitement and interest about the upcoming lesson.

Maintaining It

Use visualization. Write important, key information on the board, on transparencies, or on the overhead.

Add color to presentation. Use colored chalk or pens to highlight the important information and key points on the chalkboard or overhead. Write individual steps to mathematical problems, vocabulary, key words, spelling words, phonics rules, and so forth in different colors.

Draw the students' attention to important information. Point out important information to students both visually and verbally. Verbal clues such as "remember this" or "this is important" will help direct attention. Highlight or frame information with a colored square on transparencies or with your hands when using the board.

Use your finger, pointing stick, knitting needle, or conductor's baton to point out specific information. This will help to focus the students' attention on the important information. The overhead projector allows you to write the important information in color and allows you to face the students while doing so. The overhead projector improves classroom management by helping to reduce behavior problems. Students enjoy participating in activities that use the overhead projector.

Use a flashlight or a lighted pointer. It is very easy to gain students' attention when the lights are turned off and a flashlight or lighted pointer is used to highlight important information.

Utilize hand-on materials and activities whenever possible. Actively involve students in the learning process whenever appropriate.

Use a pleasant but firm voice. Be sure that you can be clearly heard by all students. Tape record and analyze your lectures. Do you speak clearly, too quickly, too slowly?

Keep the lesson easily understandable. Teach lessons at a quick pace but be sure to frequently check for understanding. Monitor and adjust the lessons as needed.

Be prepared. Teaching a lesson takes preparation on your part. When you are prepared and all materials are at hand, the down time during the lesson is decreased. Students are less likely to be disruptive when they are on task.

Help the students to record important information. For some students, note taking is very difficult. Students can practice by taking brief notes during all class lectures. Point out the most important information so the student writes it down. Allow time at the end of the class for students to compare notes and write additional information that they may have missed.

Call on students with equity. Teachers tend to unintentionally ignore or refrain from calling on certain students in the classroom. Most often, teachers are unaware that certain students are overlooked. Some teachers tend to call on females more frequently than males or vice versa. Some teachers are more apt to call on the students who usually provide the correct information. At times, teachers purposefully call on students who they think are unsure of the answer or call on students who have not been paying attention. Students quickly learn their teachers' habits and can often predict their chances of being called on. Students who perceive that they will be required to contribute and speak in front of their peers will remain more attentive.

Try some of these suggestions to assist with greater equity.

- Write each student's name on an index card. When a student response is needed, pull a name from the deck of cards and call on that student. Replace the card in the deck and shuffle the cards. The possibility exists that the student will be called upon again.
- Write each student's name on a Popsicle stick and place the sticks in a cup. During a group activity, select a Popsicle stick. Place the stick back into the cup, making it possible for that student to be called on again.
- Ask students to write their name at the top of an index card and to make a tally mark on the card each time they are called upon during class. Explain to the students that you are trying to be more consistent and want to be sure that all students have an opportunity to participate during class. At the end of the predetermined time, collect the cards to evaluate your pattern of student selection.

Wait, wait, and wait. When directing questions to individual students, allow sufficient wait time so the students are able to process the question, gather their thoughts, and formulate an answer to the question. While waiting for a student to answer, slowly count to five before rephrasing the question or calling on another student.

Allow for special circumstance. Be sensitive to students who are often viewed by peers as struggling or poor students. Help the student feel more comfortable responding to and answering questions during class. Tell students to raise their hand with a closed fist or first finger pointing up when they *think* they know the answer *but are not sure*. If the students are *quite certain* of the answer, they can raise an open hand and signal you to call on them on those occasions.

■ WHOLE-GROUP RESPONSE

Periodically check for understanding of concepts by using whole-group response methods. Whole-group responses help students to be actively involved in the learning process.

Use individual whiteboards or chalkboards. Provide small chalkboards or whiteboards to students. As a question is directed to the class, students write their individual response on the board. Allow sufficient time for the students to respond in writing. Once the students have written their responses, count to three and ask the students to display their answers by holding their board under their chin. This allows the teacher to quickly view the answers and determine which students understand the concepts and which students need remediation.

Have students answer in unison. Hold up an open hand and ask the class a question. Explain to students that when your hand is raised and open, it means students are to be listening and not speaking. After asking the question, allow time for the students to process the question and formulate their answers. On the count of three, close your hand to a fist signaling the students to call out the answer in unison.

Use the point or tap method. This method works well for drilling new vocabulary or spelling words. The location of the pointer indicates how the student is to respond. If your finger, the pointer, the chalk, or the pen is pointing to the left side of the word, the student should read the word silently. As the pointer is moved to the right side of the word, students should say the word out loud, in unison. Be sure to allow time for the students to process the word before asking for a unison response.

Use yes or no whole-class responses. The most effective way to use yes or no whole-class response is through hand signals and colored cards. When hand signals or cards are used, the students should indicate their response close to their chin or their body so that other students are unable to see their response. Some types of yes or no, whole-class responses my include the following:

- Thumbs up or thumbs down
- Open hand closed hand
- Red card or green card
- Happy face or sad face
- Lead end or eraser end of a pencil

■ KEEPING STUDENTS ON TASK

Continually check for understanding. Before asking students to work independently, be sure that all directions are clear and understood by the students.

Give a manageable amount of work. Be sure the amount of work given to a student is not too demanding or overwhelming. This may mean that the assignments need to be modified and/or shortened for some students.

Model and reinforce on-task behavior. Always define the on-task behavior during reinforcement. ("I like the way Johnny is sitting quietly at his desk and working on his assignment.")

Seat students who model appropriate, on-task behavior in the proximity of the student who struggles to remain on task. Often, students who have difficulty staying on task benefit from good role modeling. Good role models also help to reduce the chance of other students' encouraging inappropriate behaviors.

Set a time limit. This works well for students who enjoy the challenge of a "beat the clock" system for getting work done. This is neither effective nor appropriate for all students.

Provide a quiet study space. A study carrel works well for the student who is easily distracted by objects, noises, movement, and events. Try providing the student with a headset (with or without music playing) in order to decrease the classroom noises that may distract the student.

Use contracts, behavior charts, or other behavior modification systems. This works well to encourage on-task behavior.

Use response costs and naturally occurring consequences. This works well for off-task behavior. If students are off task during class time, they can "owe you time" at the end of the day, before school, or for part of recess time. The student must repay the amount of time he or she was not on task during work time.

Use signals or colored signs indicating, "I need help!" Some teachers use a signal (thumbs up or head on desk) or a colored sign that students may place on their desks to alert any adult scanning the room that he or she needs help.

■ BEHAVIORAL INTERVENTIONS

Behavioral problems often occur during the unstructured times of the day. Creating well-organized lessons and beginning class instruction promptly are generally good deterrents to behavior problems. During transition times, such as at the start of the class period, after recess, after physical education, and other times, provide the students with a brief assignment to work on when they enter the room. The assignment should be something that is not graded and that can be completed without assistance such as free-choice reading, journal writing, or spelling practice. The activity ensures that the students have something to work on until you are ready to bring out the next activity. Here are some ways to avoid significant behavioral outbreaks.

Explain your expectations and requirements. Make sure the student understands what you are asking of him. Ask the student to repeat the information back to you to check for understanding.

Directly teach students what is acceptable and unacceptable. This needs to be taught for all areas: classroom, hallway, bathroom, lunchroom, computer room, recess, and other appropriate areas. Provide reinforcement for acceptable behavior as well as consequences for unacceptable behavior.

Provide structure, routine, predictability, and consistency. This is true in the classroom as well as in other areas of the school.

Provide clear and fair consequences for all students. "Fair" does not mean providing the same to everyone; it means meeting the needs of all individuals.

Follow through each and every time. If a student does not follow a specific rule, provide consequences each time. Students need to know that you are serious.

Use proactive tactics rather than reactive. Utilizing proactive reinforcement will minimize the need for reactive consequences.

Keep a structured classroom. Students must know exactly what is expected of them in your classroom. If you are not organized, it will be hard for a student to be organized. If your classroom lacks structure, it will be difficult for students to know what is expected of them.

Positive Reinforcement

Positive reinforcement is the best, least restrictive, behavioral management strategy that can be used in the classroom. Positive reinforcement helps to build self-esteem and respect. When you catch students doing what you want them to do, it is important to recognize and consistently praise each specific incident.

- "Thank you, Sally, for raising your hand and waiting to be called on."
- "Joseph, I like the way that you are sitting quietly and waiting for instructions."
- "I like the way that the blue group is using their 'six-inch' voices while they are talking."
- "First graders, it makes me so happy when you are all settled down and waiting to begin our lesson! Thank you!"

Examples of positive reinforcement in the classroom

- Acknowledging students' appropriate behavior. Acknowledging and praising students is a proactive strategy. This should occur in all settings and at all times.
- Reward students with classroom jobs and responsibilities.
- Use major incentives and rewards only when necessary.

Some additional suggestions for positive reinforcement

- Playing a game with a friend
- Earning "free time"
- Eating breakfast or lunch with the teacher
- Reading or looking at a magazine
- Using the computer alone or with a friend
- Listening to music with a tape recorder, CD player, or MP3 player and earphones
- Working with clay, special pens and paper, or whiteboards
- Skipping an assignment of the student's choice
- Earn a certificate or sticker
- Have extra art time
- Hold class outdoors
- Make deliveries to the office
- Be a helper in another classroom
- Read to a younger class
- Get extra recess time

Classroom Incentives

Classroom incentives are motivators to use for entire classes. The following two suggested incentives can be adapted to meet the needs of any classroom.

Students earn tickets or play money. The tickets or play money may be used towards a weekly, biweekly, or monthly auction or raffle. Students can use their accumulated tickets, money, or points to buy assorted toys, items, or privileges.

The teacher places marbles, beans, or chips in a jar. When students are caught doing something well or behaving appropriately, the teacher will put a marble, bean, or chip in a jar. When the jar is full, the class earns a special party (popcorn, pizza, ice cream), activity (video), or a field trip. Students should help to determine the reward activity.

Assertive Discipline

Students must know what will happen when they are following and not following the rules. One way to do this is to use warnings coupled with incremental consequences when students do not follow the rules. It is much more preferable to provide positive rewards whenever possible. However, students must know from the beginning what the rules and expectations are and what the consequences will be if the rules or expectations are not followed. Various classroom management systems include the following.

Color-Coded Cards

This is a system for monitoring behavior of the entire classroom. There are many variations of this system; thus, it can be changed to meet the different needs of the different classrooms. It may involve using a pocket chart with an individual envelope or compartment for each student identified by that student's name. All students start the day with a green card in the envelopes meaning that every one is ready to go. When there is a rule infraction after a warning, the color of the individual's card is changed to yellow. This is a warning indicating that the student must become aware of what is occurring and needs to slow down. With the next rule infraction, the yellow card is changed to the final red or stop card. This severe consequence may include loss of recess, time away from the class, or a call to a parent. The consequences need to be set up in advance and clearly explained to all students prior to initiating this system.

With this system, students begin each day with a clean slate. For some classes, especially younger ones, it may be wise to start the morning and afternoon with a clean slate. For maximum effectiveness, allow your class to define the consequences associated with the change of each colored card. If you don't want the chart posted for all to see, it is also possible that each student starts the day with a green card at his or her desk. If the card needs to be changed, the teacher can individually and privately go to the student's desk and change the card quietly with few others noticing. The card may remain in the student's desk or facedown on top of the desk so other students are unaware of the color change.

Another variation of this system is to link each classroom rule to a specific color. When a student breaks a specific rule, the teacher places the color card corresponding to the rule broken into the student's pocket. With this system, the student is clearly aware of the rule that was not followed. The same progressive consequences that were explained above also follow the change of each card.

Numbered Cards

If a parent-teacher communication monitoring system would be effective, it can easily be implemented. Prior to starting any system, be sure that the parents are aware of the guidelines. For this behavior system, you will need to make various cards with a number or a number and comment listed (see below). At the end of the day, the student is handed a card to take home.

5 = Very well behaved. Great day!

4 = Good day

3 = So-so day

2 = We had some trouble today.

1 = We had a very difficult day today.

Students are responsible for making sure a parent sees the notice and then signs it. The student must sign and return the card to school the next school day.

Obviously, not all students will need this type of behavior monitoring, but it has been known to work very well for those who need it and for those who have parents who will support it.

Token Economy and Response Costs

Some teachers use a system of rewards and fines (response cost). For example, using plastic-colored links, you could assign a monetary or number value to four colors of the links:

Yellow = a penny or one point

Red = a nickel or two points

Green = a dime or three points

Blue = a quarter or four points

Specific behaviors are attached to the different points or monetary values, as are fines for rule infractions. The teacher "pays" a color link for good behavior. This is the positive reinforcement "token economy" part of the system. When rule infractions occur, the students pay a fine to the teacher for the specific offense. This is the "response cost" part of the system. It is important to discuss the rule infractions and "fines" that go along with each.

This system can be used with an individual student or the entire class. The whole class can earn points, and the teacher awards all students a certain value for the links; or individuals can earn points for on-task behavior, not blurting out answers, or whatever target behavior the student is working on.

This token economy and response cost system can be adapted and adjusted to meet the needs of any teacher in any classroom. It is quite effective and not difficult to manage. Examples of rewards for individual students may include pencils, pens, paper, crayons, candy, or any small items. Class rewards may include a video, additional free time, or whatever is mutually decided on by both the teacher and the class.

Time-Out and Time Away

Time-out and time away are appropriate methods to help students to calm down and regain control if the stimulation in the classroom is causing the student to become anxious or out of control. Use time-out and time away as needed in your classroom. It is important not to view time-out as negative and intrusive. It can be very effective when handled appropriately.

Allow the student to remain in the classroom but away from distractions. If a student needs some time away, a beanbag in the corner of the room or an empty desk away from the other student desks may provide a quiet area for the student.

Send the student to another teacher's classroom. Partner up with another teacher (preferably from a different grade level). If a student needs time away, the students can go to the receiving classroom with an independent assignment to work on for a specified amount of time.

Allow the student to go to the counselor's office for a few minutes. Some students may need someone to talk with. A prearranged location with a social worker or counselor may be appropriate for some students.

Tips for Time-Out and Time Away

Remain calm and positive while you are directing the student to time out. For example, "Jesse, I would like for you to sit quietly without making noises. If you can't do that, then go back to your desk. You can join our activity again when you feel you will be able to sit quietly."

Try a "think-about-it" chair for a specified amount of time. Instruct the student to think about the inappropriate behavior and what could be done differently. A good rule of thumb is one minute of time per year of age. A six-year-old may have about a six-minute time-out.

Decide what consequences will be used if the behavior continues after time away. The majority of students with behavior difficulties will have an alternate plan in place. If the behavior continues, the alternate behavior plan should be implemented. The alternate plan may include calling the special education teacher, a counselor, a social worker, or the principal.

Ask the student to call a parent at home or in the workplace. For some students, a telephone call to the parent often helps.

Allow the student to take a "voluntary" time-out if needed. As students grow and become more aware of their senses, they often can predict when their emotions are escalating to a danger point. In this situation, you may want to create a special pass for the student. The student may use this pass and take a voluntary time-out in the area previously designated. You may want to document the voluntary time-outs to see if they occur at a specific time during the day, during a specific class, or during a specific activity.

Do not overuse time-outs. Be sure that the student is always aware of the behavior that caused him or her to receive the time-out.

■ BEHAVIOR MANAGEMENT STRATEGIES

Proximity Control

While circulating in the classroom, try to be near the students with the attention and behavioral problems. Sometimes a hand on the shoulder or establishing eye contact as a quick reminder is effective. It is often helpful to seat children with behavioral or attention difficulties near the teacher or next to a well-focused student. Avoid seating the students near learning centers, the door, windows, or other distracters. Proximity control seems quite simple, and it often has a positive effect on students who need constant reminders to return to task.

Preventative Cueing

This technique helps to prevent disruptive behavior. When the behavior is prevented, it helps the students, as there is no confrontation; therefore, the students are not embarrassed in front of their peers. Before beginning this technique, arrange with the student privately a specific hand signal or word signal to use that will help remind the student to calm down, pay attention, stop talking, or change whatever other behavior the student is struggling with. Here are examples of some cueing reminders.

Use a traffic light or stop sign signal. The red light will help to remind students to slow down or stop the behavior. You may also assign instruction to each of the three colors. The red may mean that the students are to be in their seats working; yellow indicates that students may get out of their seats only to ask questions, turn in papers, and so on; and the green light means that students may freely move about the classroom.

Establish eye contact. Once you have eye contact, touch your eye if you want the student to visually focus on you, or you may tug on your earlobe if you would like the student to listen.

Use the "thumbs up" sign. You could use this sign or any other that is agreed upon between you and the student. When the students see that you are using this sign, they can get up and move to another part of the room in order to aid in concentration.

Self-Monitoring

Self-monitoring is one of the least intrusive and least restrictive methods of monitoring one's behavior. With self-monitoring, a target behavior for the student is chosen for the student to record. An example would be thumb sucking. Every time the teacher or the student "catches" himself or herself sucking his or her thumb, the student records a tally mark on a slip of paper. At the end of the day, the tally marks are totaled. The teacher and student should have a predetermined reward and response cost system in place. If the student reaches the goal, the reward will be given. If the student does not reach the daily goal, the response cost is issued. Recording one's own behavior is an effective way to increase behaviors such as academic productivity and on-task behavior or to decrease inappropriate behaviors such as thumb sucking, talking, or making inappropriate noises.

Planned Ignoring

Planned ignoring is a method used to decrease inappropriate, attention-seeking behaviors. With planned ignoring, the teacher purposefully ignores the behavior, as often the behavior occurs in order to receive the teacher's attention. Obviously, the behavior can only be ignored if it is one that is not destructive to the student or to others. When attempting this strategy, teachers should be aware that the behavior frequently will increase for a short time, as the student will be "testing" to see if he or she can "make" the teacher pay attention to him or her. Hang in there! It will get better! Be strong. If the behavior is affecting the education of the other students and it is not improving, stop this strategy and attempt another one.

Behavior Contracts

Behavior contracts are agreements between a student and the teacher. A contract must specifically state what behavior is expected and what the reinforcement or reward will be when the behavior or task is completed. Behavior contracts are effective with students. The effectiveness, however, can be short-lived and the rewards system may need to be changed frequently. Parental involvement and support is imperative. There are sample behavior contracts on the following pages that may be reproduced.

Contract

I, _____, agree to _____

_____

_____

_____

_____.

My hard work will earn _____

_____

_____

_____

_____.

We will meet again to discuss this contract on _____

_____, _____.

Student's Signature   Date

_____   _____

Teacher's Signature   Date

_____   _____

Contract

I, _____, agree to _____

_____

_____

_____

_____.

on or before _____.

If I meet this goal, I will earn _____

_____

_____

_____.

Student's Signature   Date

_____   _____

Teacher's Signature   Date

_____   _____

Additional Signature (if needed)   Date

_____   _____

5

Transitions for Students With Disabilities

■ EDUCATIONAL TRANSITIONS

According to Merriam-Webster's Online Dictionary (2008), the word *transition* means, "a passage from one state, stage, subject, or place to another." Everyone experiences transitions at different times throughout their days, weeks, years, and lives. Some transitions are much less invasive, while others, by their very nature, require much more planning and attention to work through. Transition means change and change can be difficult for many, but it can be considerably more challenging for children with disabilities and their families.

Careful planning for a significant transition is vital to the success of the change. In fact, planning for a child with a disability to transition from school life to adulthood is required by law to begin once a student reaches at least 16 years of age. Careful consideration and development of a transition plan by the child's IEP team is mandated through IDEA. Partial intent of this section is to discuss the planning that occurs to help a student make a successful transition into life after high school. It is of equal importance, however, to discuss the many educational transitions that this same student may have experienced at other times through his or her schooling. Let's consider the preschool to kindergarten transition or the transition from elementary to middle school. It is certain that each of these passages were met with challenges; however, these transitions may not have been planned as carefully and purposefully as they could and should have.

This section intends to introduce the concept of thorough and smooth educational transitions, as they occur from year to year, grade level to grade level throughout a child's educational years. The ultimate goal for children with disabilities is to ensure that each educational passage distinctively and individually considers the child's welfare, safety, happiness, and dignity not only during the transition from high school to adulthood but also with all educational transition experiences. It is especially true that educational transition for students with special needs requires advanced planning if transitions are to progress smoothly for the student and educational team members (La Paro, Pianta, & Cox, 2000). Hence, the introduction of the "Transition Portfolio."

■ WHAT IS A TRANSITION PORTFOLIO?

Demchak and Greenfield (2003) describe a delightful little girl who has been in the same preschool class for three years. "Susie," despite multiple disabilities, loves her experiences in preschool, especially music, art, snack time, and friends. Her preschool educational team has worked diligently over the past three years to discover strategies and adaptations that are effective for Susie. Susie has made great progress while in preschool, and her parents and preschool teachers are concerned about the transition from preschool to kindergarten as Susie embarks on a new journey in a new setting.

Unfortunately, as discussed by Cox (1999), educational transitions (e.g., from preschool to kindergarten) are often planned for quickly with only the most general of information being transferred. Typical information provided for the "new" teacher is a cumulative file consisting of information that offers little to no help regarding the students' accomplishments and progress made in everyday activities (Keefe, 1995). Receiving teachers of students with IEP's sometimes are unaware that the child has an IEP, which makes it likely they are uninformed of the specific goals and objectives or adaptations and modifications that go along with the plan.

To ensure that Susie's transition proceeded as smoothly as possible, her preschool teacher developed a transition portfolio. Demchak and Greenfield (2003) specifically describe a transition portfolio as "a strategy that documents critical information about a student." They also indicate that a portfolio is student specific and contains basic student information (e.g., age, address, parent names), as well as information seen as imperative in the planning of a smooth transition. Such information may include:

- Personal information
- Medical information
- Educational programming suggestions
- Ideas for adaptations and supports
- Recommendations for physical impairments
- Expressive and receptive communication strategies
- Reinforcement strategies and positive behavior support plans
- Problem-solving techniques and team notes

General educators are essential members of the team when passing students with special needs onto a new teacher into a new classroom or receiving a student with special needs into a classroom. The more information that is provided to the child's new teacher or the more information received prior to the child entering a classroom, the more thorough and smooth the transition will be for the child. It is also imperative that the receiving teacher is aware of the contents of the current

IEP. It is the responsibility of the classroom teacher to follow what is stated in the IEP and work toward meeting the goals and objectives and providing the accommodations and modifications that are granted in the IEP.

The contents of the transition portfolio will be determined by the team as they decide what information will be beneficial for the receiving team. As described by Demchak and Greenfield (2003), the transition portfolio for a student with mild disabilities will be basically straightforward and easy to implement. A student with multiple disabilities, however, and a long history of experiences will have a more complex and lengthy portfolio to put into place.

The purpose of the first part of this section was to provide an understanding of the need for transition portfolios and a conceptual basis on what a transition portfolio is. For further, more specific information regarding transition portfolios, consult Demchak and Greenfield's (2003) excellent resource *Transition Portfolios for Students With Disabilities* to assist you in further developing a useful and comprehensive transition portfolio for students with special needs.

■ SECONDARY TRANSITION NEEDS FROM HIGH SCHOOL TO ADULTHOOD

The second purpose of this section is to provide a specific description of a student's IEP-based transition plan. According to Pierangelo and Guiliani (2007), IDEA requires that each student's IEP facilitates the student's transition from school to postschool activities. The law requires this plan to be developed on or before a child turns 16 years of age and should address the specific areas of postsecondary education, vocational education, integrated employment, continuing and adult education, adult services, independent living, and community participation.

Purpose of Transition Planning

The purpose of transition planning at age 16 or earlier is to ensure that the student's educational plan is written in a step-by-step manner to help support a successful transition after high school. Pierangelo and Guiliani (2007) suggest that such plans should do the following.

- Provide instruction and courses of study that are of interest and meaningful to the student's future and will motivate the student to continue working toward completion of his or her education
- Provide the student access to the knowledge and skills needed in adult life (career development and job skills)
- Provide contacts with outside agencies that will also assist in the smooth transition

Postsecondary Transition Plan

The plan is developed considering the individual student's needs, preferences, and interests as well as his or her goals for postsecondary life. The IEP must include transition services and activities in each of the following areas, appropriate to the needs of the individual student.

Instruction

The IEP must address any further instruction or classes that the student may need to prepare the student for adult living. Such instruction could include specific general education or special education classes or specific skills such as using public transportation, balancing a checkbook, and completing job applications.

Related Services

The IEP must address any related services (counseling services, job coach, social worker) that the students may need to support them in attaining postsecondary education goals.

Employment and Other Adult Living Objectives

The IEP must address what activities or services the students will need in order to prepare them for employment as well as other living objectives such as practicing interviewing skills, completing job or college applications, and participating in work experience programs.

Community Experiences

The IEP must address a student's need to participate in community-based experience or learn to access community resources (e.g., public library, post office, community recreational activities).

Activities of Daily Living

If appropriate to student needs, the IEP must address the services or activities of daily living (e.g., dressing, hygiene, taking medication, grooming self).

Functional Vocational Assessment

The IEP must address the need for functional vocational assessments to determine a student's strengths, abilities, and needs in an actual or simulated work setting or experience.

The transition plan is the responsibility of the IEP team. The student and his or her parents will provide unparalleled input into this plan. When developing the plan, it is important to keep the focus on how the student's educational program can be planned to help the student make a successful transition to his or her goals for life after secondary school.

Medication Resources

Disclaimer: The information presented in this section on medications has been gathered from a variety of resources in order to provide the most accurate and current information at the time of printing. This resource is intended as a general reference *only* and is not intended to replace the opinion and/or advice of medical personnel.

■ GENERAL INFORMATION ABOUT MEDICATION

Each child and adolescent is different, and no two children or people have exactly the same combination of medical and psychological diagnoses. When you are working with a child who is prescribed medication, it is a good idea to talk with the parents regarding the medication and purpose for medicating. It is important to administer the medication exactly as the doctor instructs. If a dosage of medication is forgotten while a child is in school, there may be special steps that will need to be followed regarding the missed dosage. School staff is not allowed, without parental permission, to change the way of administering the medication. Many times a medication is required to be taken with food, but lunchtime or snack time may change. If this is the case, be sure to notify the parent so that appropriate adjustments can be made.

Judging by the child's behavior in your classroom, if it appears that a medication is no longer being effective, this could mean that it is not being taken regularly. The student may be "cheeking," hiding the medicine or forgetting to take it. Please inform the child's parents if you are noticing changes. Taking medication is a private matter and must be handled discreetly and confidentially. It is important to be sensitive to the student's feeling about taking the medicine.

Each medicine has a generic or chemical name. Just like laundry soap, some medicines are sold by more than one company under different brand names. The same medicine may be available under a generic name and several brand names. It is important to know if the medication is a generic name or a brand name.

Antianxiety Medication: Benzodiazepines

Often called sedatives or tranquilizers, antianxiety medications are used to treat anxiety or sleep problems.

Brand Name	Generic Name
Ativan	lorazepam
Dalmane	flurazepam
Klonopin	clonazepam
Librium	chlordiazepoxide
Valium	diazepam
Xanax	alprazolam

Anticonvulsants

Anticonvulsants are usually used to treat seizures (convulsions). They are sometimes used to treat behavioral problems even if the student does not have seizures.

Brand Name	Generic Name
Depakene/Depakote	valproate/valproic acid
Klonopin	clonazepam
Tegretol	carbamazepine

Antidepressants

Antidepressants are used to treat depression, enuresis (bed wetting), attention deficit hyperactivity disorder (ADHD), school phobia, separation anxiety, panic disorder, obsessive-compulsive disorder (OCD), some sleep disorders, and trichotillomaniea (compulsive pulling out of one's hair).

Brand Name	Generic Name
Anafranil	clomipramine
Effexor XR	venlafaxine
Elavil, Endep	amitriptyline
Norpramin/Petofrane	desipramine
Pamelor/Aventryl	nortiptyline
Tofranil	Impramin
Wellbutrin	bupropion

Antihistamines

Antihistamines were developed to treat allergies. They are often used in children. They may be used to treat anxiety, insomnia, or the side effects of certain other medicines.

Brand Name	Generic Name
Atarax or Vistaril*	hydroxyzine*
Benadryl*	diphenhydramine*
Periactin*	cyproheptadine*
Allegra	fexofenadine
Claritin	loratadine
Clarinex	desloratadine
Zyrtec	cetrizine

*May cause drowsiness.

Antihypertensives

Catapres and Tenex are being used to treat symptoms of Tourette disorder, chronic tics, and attention deficit hyperactivity disorder (ADHD). They are occasionally used to treat aggression, posttraumatic stress disorder, anxiety, panic disorder, and bipolar (manic-depressive) disorder in children and adolescents.

Brand Name	Generic Name
Catapres	clonodine
Tenex	guanfacine

Buspar

Buspar is an antianxiety medication that decreases nervousness, fears, and excessive worrying. This is used for a short time when symptoms are very uncomfortable or frightening, or when it is hard to do important things such as go to school. Buspar does not begin to help immediately. The full effect may not appear for three to four weeks.

Brand Name	Generic Name
Buspar	buspirone

Beta-Blockers

Beta-blockers have been used primarily to treat high blood pressure and irregular heartbeat. Recently, however, these medications shave also been used to treat emotional and behavior problems.

Brand Name	Generic Name
Corgard	nadolol
Inderal	propranolol
Tenormin	atenolol
Visken	pindolol

Desyrel and Serzone

Desyrel and Serzone are being used to treat emotional and behavior problems, including depression, insomnia, and disruptive behavior disorders in children and adolescents.

Brand Name	Generic Name
Desyrel	trazodone
Serzone	nefazodone

Lithium

Lithium has been used to treat bipolar (manic-depressive) disorder, certain types of depression, severe mood swing, and very serious aggression.

Neuroleptics

Neuroleptics are used to treat psychoses such as schizophrenia, mania, or very severe depression. They may also be used for behavior problems after a head injury.

Brand Name	Generic Name
Clozaril	clozapine
Haldol	haloperidol
Loxitane	loxapine
Mellaril	thioridazine
Moban	molindone

Brand Name	Generic Name
Navane	thiothixene
Orap	pimozide
Prolixin	fluphenazine
Risperdal	risperidone
Stelazine	trifluoperazine
Thorazine	chlorpromazine
Trilafon	perphenazine
Zyprexa	olanapine

Nonstimulants

Strattera is a selective norepinephrine reuptake inhibitor used to treat ADHD.

Brand Name	Generic Name
Strattera	atomoxetine

Selective Serotonin Reuptake Inhibitors (SSRIs)

SSRIs have been used to treat emotional and behavior problems, including depression, panic disorder, obsessive-compulsive disorder (OCD), bulimia, and posttraumatic stress disorder.

Brand Name	Generic Name
Celexa	citalopram
Luvox	flumoxamine
Paxil	paroxetine
Prozac	fluoxetine
Zoloft	sertraline

Stimulants

Stimulants have been used to improve attention span, decrease distractibility, increase ability to finish things, improve ability to follow directions, decrease hyperactivity, and improve ability to think before acting (decrease impulsivity).

Brand Name	Generic Name
Adderall	amphetamine
Concerta	methylphenidate
Cylert	pemoline
Desoxyn Gadumet	methamphetamine
Dexedrine	dextroamphetamine
Ritalin	methylphenidate
Vyvanse	lisdexamfetamine

References

American Academy of Child & Adolescent Psychiatry. (2004a). *Conduct disorder.* Retrieved June 29, 2008, from http://www.aacap.org/cs/root/publication_store/your_child_conduct_disorders

American Academy of Child & Adolescent Psychiatry. (2004b). *Oppositional defiant disorder.* Retrieved June 29, 2008, from http://www.aacap.org/cs/odd.resourcecenter

American Academy of Family Physicians. (2006). *Diabetes: What the diagnosis means.* Retrieved June 14, 2008, from http://familydoctor.org/online/fadocen/home/common/diabetes/basics/350.html

American Lung Association. (2007). *Asthma—Help with treatment decisions.* Retrieved June 14, 2008, from http://lungusa.org/site/pp.asp?c=dvLuk900E&b=38472

American Psychiatric Association. (1994). *Diagnostic and statistical manual of mental Disorders.* Washington, DC: American Psychiatric Association.

American Society for Deaf Children. (2006). *IDEA and deaf children.* Retrieved June 15, 2008, from http://www.deafchildren.org/resources.aspx

American Speech-Language-Hearing Association. (2007). *Speech and language disorders and diseases.* Retrieved June 15, 2008, from http://www.asha.org/public/speech/disorders/

Appleboom, T. M. (1985). A history of vision screening. *Journal of School Health,* 55(4), 138–141.

Autism Speaks. (2008). *What is autism? An overview.* Retrieved on July 12, 2008, from www.autismspeaks.org/whatisit/index.php?WT,syl=Top.Nav

Baumel, J. (2008a). *What is section 504?* Retrieved July 4, 2008, from http://www.great schools.net/cgi-bin/showarticle/987

Baumel, J. (2008b). General Education Accommodations. Retrieved July 4, 2008, from www.schwablearning.org/Articles. Asp?r=77&d=5

Bender, N. W., & Shores, C. (2007). Response to intervention—A practical guide for every teacher. Thousand Oaks, CA: Corwin.

Bergen, J. R., & Kratchowill, T. R. (1990). *Behavior consultation.* Columbus, OH: Merrill.

Bondy, A., & Frost, L. (2002). *Pyramid approach to education.* Newark, DE: Pyramid Education Products.

British Columbia Ministry of Education. (2001). *Special education services: A manual of policies, procedures, and guidelines.* Retrieved June 22, 2008, from www.bced.gov.bc.ca/specialed/ppandg/planning_5.htm

Childhood Anxiety Network. (2001). *Social phobia.* Retrieved June 13, 2008, from http://www.Childanxiety.net/Social_Phobia.htm

Children and Adults with Attention Deficit/Hyperactivity Disorder. (n.d.). *Understanding AD/HD.* Retrieved June 27, 2008, from http://www.chadd.org/Content/CHADD/Understanding/Evaluation/default.htm

Clark, W., Fuerstenberg, R., Gabler, C., Goethel, J., & Milne, E. (1994). Put it in print: How to produce a book of writings by adult literacy students. Eau Claire, WI: Chippewa Valley Publishing.

Cox, M. (1999). Making the transition. *Early Developments, 3(1),* 4–6.

Cunningham, P., & Allington, R. (2006). *Classrooms that work: They can all read and write* (4th ed.). Columbus, OH: Allyn & Bacon.

Cystic Fibrosis Foundation. (2007). *What you need to know. What is Cystic Fibrosis?* Retrieved June 14, 2008, from http://www.cff.org/AboutCF/

D'Arcangelo, M. (2002). The challenge of content-area reading: A conversation with Donna Ogle. *Educational Leadership, 60(3),* 12–15.

Demchak, M., & Greenfield, R. G. (2003). *Transition portfolios for students with disabilities.* Thousand Oaks, CA: Corwin.

Department of Health and Human Services Center for Disease Control and Prevention. (2006). *Chronic fatigue syndrome: Basic facts.* Retrieved June 17, 2008, from http://www.cdc.gov/cfs/cfsbasicfacts.htm

Department of Health and Human Services Center for Disease Control and Prevention. (2008). *Fetal alcohol spectrum disorder.* Retrieved June 14, 2008, from http://www.cdc.gov.ncbddd/fas/

Epilepsy Foundation of America. (n.d.). *What is epilepsy?* Retrieved June 17, 2008, from http:www.epilepsyfoundation.org/about/faq/

Fragile X Research Foundation. (2008). *What are the common symptoms?* Retrieved June 17, 2008, from http://www.fraxa.org/aboutfx.aspx

Gutstein, S. E., & Sheely, R. K. (2002). *Relationship development intervention activities with young children: Social and emotional development activities for Asperger Syndrome, Autism, PDD, and NLD.* England: Jessica Kingsley Publishers.

Individuals with Disabilities Education Act of 2004 (IDEA). (2004). 20 U.S.C. § 1400–1485 (2004).

International Dyslexia Association. (2008). *Just the facts: Definition of dyslexia.* Retrieved June 21, 2008, from http://www.interdys.org

International Rett Syndrome Foundation. (2008). *About Rett Syndrome.* Retrieved June 23, 2008, from http://www.rettsyndrome.org

Joseph, B., & Pearl, E. (2008). *Asthma.* Retrieved July 7, 2008, from www.kidshealth.org/kid/asthma_basics/what/asthma,html

Juvenile Bipolar Research Foundation. (n.d.). *About juvenile-onset bipolar disorder.* Retrieved July 1, 2008, from http://www.bpchildresearch.org/juv_bipolar/index.html

Keefe, C. Y. (1995). Portfolios: Mirrors of learning. *TEACHING Exceptional Children, 27*(2), 66–67.

Kidshealth. (2005). *Muscular Dystrophy.* Retrieved July 1, 2008, from http://kidshealth.org/parent/medical/bones/muscular_dystrophy.html

La Paro, K. M., Pianta, Robert, M., & Cox, M. (2001). Transition practices: Findings from a national survey of kindergarten teachers. *Early Childhood Education Journal, 55*(4),199–206.

Laverick, C. (2002). B-D-A strategy: Reinventing the wheel can be a good thing. *Journal of Adolescent & Adult Literacy, 46,* 144–147.

LD OnLine. (2008). *What is a learning disability?* Retrieved June 29, 2008, from http://www.ldonline.org/ldbasics/whatisld

Merkley, D. J. (1996). Modified Anticipation Guide. *Reading Teacher, 50,* 365–368.

National Alliance on Mental Illness. (2008). *Early onset depression.* Retrieved June 14, 2008, from http://www.nami.org/Content/ContentGroups/Helpline1/Facts_About_Childhood_Depression.htm

National Center for Post Traumatic Stress Disorder. (2007). *PTSD information center.* Retrieved July 3, 2008, from http://www.ncptsd.va.gov/ncmain/index.jsp

National Dissemination Center for Children With Disabilities. (2003). *Pervasive developmental disorders, fact sheet 20.* Retrieved June 20, 2008, from http://www.nichcy.org/pubs/factshe/fs20txt.htm

National Dissemination Center for Children With Disabilities. (2004). *Spina Bifida, fact sheet 12.* Retrieved July 2, 2008, from http://www.nichcy.org/pubs/factshe/fs12.pdf

National Dissemination Center for Children With Disabilities. (2006). *Traumatic brain injury, fact sheet 18.* Retrieved June 30, 2008, from http://www.nichcy.org/pubs/factshe/fs18txt.htm

National Down Syndrome Society. (2008). *Information topics.* Retrieved July 3, 2008, from www1.ndss.org/index.php?option=com_content&task=view&id=1949&Item

National Institute of Mental Health. (2008). *Generalized anxiety disorder.* Retrieved June 29, 2008, from http://www.nimh.nih.gov/health/topics/generalized-anxiety-disorder-gad/index.shtml

National Institute of Mental Health. (2008). *Schizophrenia.* Retrieved July 1, 2008, from http://www.nimh.nih.gov/health/topics/schizophrenia/index.shtml

National Organization on Fetal Alcohol Syndrome. (2002). *FASD: What everyone should know.* Retrieved June 14, 2008, from http://www.nofas.org/MediaFiles/PDFs/factsheets/everyone.pdf

National Reading Panel. (2000). *Teaching children to read.* Retrieved July 22, 2008, from http://www.nationalreadingpanel.org/Publications/summary.htm

Nielsen, L. B. (2009). *Brief reference of student disabilities . . . with strategies for the classroom.* (2nd Ed.). Thousand Oaks, CA: Corwin.

No Child Left Behind Act (NCLB). (2001). 20 U.S.C. §§ 6301. (2002).

Nolet, V., & McLaughlin, M. J. (2005). *Accessing the general curriculum: Including students with disabilities in standards-based reform.* Thousand Oaks, CA: Cowin.

Pierangelo, R., & Giuliani, G. (2007). *Understanding, developing, and writing effective IEPs.* Thousand Oaks, CA: Corwin.

Prizant, B. M., Wetherby, A., Rubin, E., Rydell, P. J., & Laurent, A. (2006). *The SCERTS model: A comprehensive educational approach for children with autism spectrum disorders.* Baltimore, MD: Paul Brookes Publishing Company.

Proctor, S. E. (2005). *To see or not to see: Screening the vision of children in school.* Castle Rock, CO: National Association of School Nurses.

Purcell, S. L., & Grant, D. (2002). *Assistive technology solutions for IEP teams.* Verona, WI: Attainment Co.

Rasinski, T. V., & Padak, N. D. (2000). *From phonics to fluency: Effective teaching of decoding and reading fluency in the elementary school.* Columbus, OH: Allyn & Bacon.

Region 10 Education Service Center. (2008). *Dyslexia program awareness for educators and parents.* Retrieved on July 12, 2008, from http://www.region10.org/dyslexia/Documents/DyslexiaBrochure_eng.pdf

Rehabilitation Act of 1973. 29 U.S.C. §§701 (1982).

Save Babies Through Screening Foundations. (2006). *Galactosemia.* Retrieved July 2, 2008, from http://www.savebabies.org/diseasedescriptions/galactosemia.php

Schuett, V. E. (2008). *What is PKU?* (On-line). Retrieved July 2, 2008, from http://www.savebabies.org/diseasedescriptions/pku.php

Separation Anxiety Solution. (2008). *Beat childhood anxiety separation disorder.* Retrieved July 14, 2008, from http://www.separation-anxiety-solution.com

The ARC of the United States, (2001). *Preventing mental retardation: A guide to the causes of mental retardation and strategies for prevention.* Retrieved June 25, 2008, from http://www.thearc.org/NetCommunity/Document.Doc?&id=147

Transition. (2008). In Merriam-Webster Online Dictionary. Retrieved November 5, 2008, from http://www.merriam-webster.com/dictionary/transition

United Cerebral Palsy Organization. (2008). *Education.* Retrieved July 6, 2008, from http://www.ucp.org/ucp_channel.cfm/1/12

Wright, J. (2007). *RTI toolkit: A practical guide for schools.* Port Chester, NY: Dude Publishing.

Index

CORWIN
A SAGE Company

The Corwin logo—a raven striding across an open book—represents the union of courage and learning. Corwin is committed to improving education for all learners by publishing books and other professional development resources for those serving the field of PreK–12 education. By providing practical, hands-on materials, Corwin continues to carry out the promise of its motto: **"Helping Educators Do Their Work Better."**

NOV   2009

Northport-East Northport Public Library

To view your patron record from a computer, click on
the Library's homepage: **www.nenpl.org**

You may:
- request an item be placed on hold
- renew an item that is overdue
- view titles and due dates checked out on your card
- view your own outstanding fines

**185 Larkfield Road
East Northport, NY 11731
631-261-2313**